PRAISE FOR *HOW TO* ON $3,000 A WEEK

"These boys know property. Smart strategies designed to safely build wealth through real estate."

Effie Zahos, Channel 9 Money Editor and Author of
A Real Girl's Guide to Money

"I've had the pleasure of working with Ben and Bryce for years, and I can confidently say they're two of the most genuine and kind-hearted guys in our industry. They've always been driven by one simple yet impactful mission – education. Their latest book is another shining example of their unwavering commitment to helping Australians improve their financial well-being throughout their lives and into retirement."

Nicola McDougall, Chair, Property Investment Professionals of Australia and Author of *The Female Investor*

"Bryce and Ben have forged enviable careers becoming two of Australia's leading property experts and commentators. Their appeal is remarkably simple and refreshing; they rely on facts and focus on delivering practical, smart and well-informed advice. This book is filled with the quality insights and guidance we have come to expect of this duo."

Antonia Mercorella, CEO Real Estate Institute of Qld (REIQ)

"Everyday Australians are fortunate to have Bryce and Ben as their trusted guides. These champions continue to inspire Australians to their right to financial security and making property investing both accessible and understandable. Through their unwavering advocacy, they've shielded countless Aussies from scams and empowered them to take control of their finances."

Jane Slack-Smith, Author of *Your Property Success* and Founder of Your Success Club

"You would have to go a long way to find two people like Ben and Bryce who are so passionate about helping people along their property investment journey. The education they provide through their books and podcast is outstanding!"

Peter Koulizos, Program Director of the Master of Property, The University of Adelaide

"Over the decades, Ben and Bryce educated, guided and inspired us to invest in property and reach our financial freedom and retirement goals. Their abundance mindset, unconditional passion to contribute and ability to navigate through noise to find lasting wisdom make them unique. Read and please re-read *How to Retire on $3,000 a week* and, I can assure you, with every re-read, you will learn something new."

Munzurul Khan, Founder and Chair of Board at KHI Partners,

"Bryce and Ben have been a cornerstone of sound, transparent, and actionable advice in the industry for so many years now. There's no doubt that their level-headed and proven strategies have provided a life-changing success framework for countless Australian investors. We're all very grateful to them for raising the bar, and long may that continue."

Pete Wargent, CEO, Allen Wargent Property Buyers

"Ben and Bryce are genuinely dedicated to empowering Australians to build wealth. They've generously shared knowledge and guidance on enhancing cash flow management, including with their innovative tool, Moorr. Effective cash flow management forms the bedrock of wealth creation – its importance cannot be understated. Additionally, they've empowered thousands of Australians to confidently invest in property. Congratulations to Ben and Bryce for their generous sharing of knowledge, tools, and insight!"

Stuart Wemyss, Host of the Investopoly podcast and Author of
Investopoly: The 8 rules of mastering the game of building wealth

How to Retire on $3,000 a Week

BRYCE HOLDAWAY & BEN KINGSLEY

MAJOR
STREET

BRYCE'S DEDICATION

To Andi – writing a book demands intense focus, early mornings, late nights, and a level of tunnel vision that inevitably places extra weight on the people you love the most. Throughout this project (and countless others!), you've not only kept our family thriving but have been my greatest encourager – cheering me on when the finish line felt miles away. You chose the road less travelled by doing life with me, and that's not lost on me at all. I'm forever grateful for you!

Jack and Samuel – you two are the reason I've thought so hard about making these concepts clear, simple, and (hopefully) something that sparks your own curiosity. My hope is that when the time is right, you'll choose this path not because I said so, but because you see the freedom and fulfilment it can create. Love you, legends.

Mum and Dad – the ovarian lottery was very kind to me. Your love, support, and work ethic shaped the foundation of everything I've done. You led by example, showing me the value of hard work while always encouraging me to learn, explore, and chase opportunities.

BEN'S DEDICATION

My folks – through your hard work and sacrifice, I received an upbringing full of experiences and learning that remain the foundations for most of my core values today. I remain forever grateful for all that you shared and exposed me to.

My beautiful Jane and Boys – your sacrifice in allowing me the time to pursue my passion for helping others through their financial transformation journey towards financial security is not lost on me. You see the effort and dedication required, the weekends, the late nights, where this work comes before our play. Yet you support me one hundred per cent and gracefully allow me to pursue what is really important work for me, and the time it takes away from our own family time. For that sacrifice and understanding, and for believing in me doing this important work, you allow me to fill my bucket, and as a family unit, you complete me and my own 'lifestyle by design' outcomes.

For Jack and Harry, as you grow into young men, I hope my example of following my dreams will inspire you to work hard and follow your own dreams that will impact the world in a positive way.

ACKNOWLEDGEMENTS

To our incredible community of *Property Couch* listeners and Empower Wealth clients, we couldn't do what we do without you. Your ongoing patronage and support have given us a platform to sharpen our thinking, because the more we've learned, the more we've shared – and in doing so, you've pushed us to keep learning, refining, and improving. You've kept us on our game, challenged us to refine our frameworks, and inspired us to simplify complex ideas for maximum impact. This book exists because of the real and virtual conversations we've had with you.

To our Empower Wealth team – your dedication to your craft, the lives you've helped change, and the intellectual horsepower we get to tap into daily are things we never take for granted. Thank you for being part of this movement and for helping us make a real difference in the lives of those we're called to serve.

To The Stig (a.k.a. Ivise Gan) – *The Property Couch* podcast may look like a duo, but those who know understand it's very much a trio. We're all incredibly fortunate to have your heart, your counsel, and access to your brilliant mind and deep well of experience. Your fingerprints are all over the podcast—and now this book too. The illustrations throughout were expertly crafted under your guidance and bring the content to life with clarity and charm. Thank you for being such an integral part of this journey. We wouldn't have it any other way.

To David Robertson – your can-do attitude, subject matter expertise, and technical precision are deeply woven throughout the case studies in this book. The reader is better off because of your insights, and so are we.

To Connor Christie – your sharp eye and dedication to detail ensured the numbers in this book are accurate and reliable. Thanks for helping us make it count – literally.

Michael Pope – we miss you every day, mate. Your wisdom, insight, and influence are woven into the fabric of this book – just as they were in the last two. This time, we didn't get to have those deep conversations with you, and we felt that absence keenly.

RIP Popey – your legacy lives on.

MAJOR STREET

First published in 2025 by Major Street Publishing Pty Ltd
info@majorstreet.com.au | majorstreet.com.au

A catalogue record for this book is available
from the National Library of Australia

Printed book ISBN: 978-1-923186-29-3
Ebook ISBN: 978-1-923186-30-9

Cover design by Tess McCabe
Internal design by Production Works

10 9 8 7 6 5 4 3 2 1

Contents

Preface

The truth will set you free

Imagine you're a barber who's been in business for 30 years, charging $25 per haircut, and you have a loyal clientele of happy customers who trust your work. Then, one day, a new barber shop opens next door with a big A-frame sign on the footpath that reads: 'Haircuts $10'.

What do you do? Do you slash your prices to compete? Do you stick to your rates and hope your customers remain loyal? Or do you think outside the box?

After some deliberation, you decide to fight fire with fire and put up your own A-frame sign that reads: 'Haircuts $25 – we fix $10 haircuts!'

Now, this bold approach is more than just a business tactic, it's the metaphor for why we started our top-rated podcast, *The Property Couch*, and wrote this book. Because frankly, we got tired of fixing $10 haircuts.

In our case, the $10 haircuts were the costly mistakes people made with their money before they even thought about investing – unconsciously overspending, chasing temporary highs, or falling for schemes that sounded too good to be true. And when it came to property investing, the stakes were significantly higher, making the losses even more painful to witness. Unlike a bad haircut, which you can fix in a couple of weeks, poor financial decisions can take years to undo – or worse, they can completely derail your journey to financial freedom.

WE FIX $10 HAIRCUTS

Here's the uncomfortable truth: people do dumb things with money. We ignore the fundamentals, follow the herd, or fall prey to the latest financial shiny object. Despite all the resources available, the same patterns keep repeating themselves time and time again – client after client. It's not so much that history repeats itself but that *people* repeat history.

That's why we're here: to help you avoid those pitfalls. This book isn't just a guide, it's your chance to get ahead of the game. We're done fixing $10 haircuts. We want to equip you with the right strategies, frameworks, and knowledge to make smarter decisions upfront and minimise costly mistakes, so you can focus on building wealth the right way.

Picture this: you're waking up on a sunny morning, no alarm clock blaring, no emails screaming for your attention, and the day is entirely yours to design. This isn't just a dream – it's the reality of financial freedom for many, and it's closer than you think.

Imagine a life where money is no longer a concern. A life where you're not constantly checking your bank balance and worrying, where you have the freedom to spend quality time with family, travel, pursue your passions, and live on your terms.

Now, imagine if that vision includes $3,000 a week – for life! That's $156,000 per year in passive income – enough to fund the life you've always dreamed of, with just 10 hours per year spent managing each property in your portfolio. It sounds good, right?

Unfortunately, for many people, this dream remains just that – a dream! The truth is that most Australians are not prepared for retirement. According to research by demographer Mark McCrindle on Episode 507 of the podcast, 'I Won't Have Enough to Live Comfortably: The 3 Greatest Generational Fears of All Time!', this isn't just a challenge for Baby Boomers and Generation X – it's also the number one concern for Millennials and Generation Z. As he states, 'not having enough in retirement' is a universal worry across all generations. Without a strategic plan, the future can feel overwhelming: limited savings, inadequate investments, and the reality of working longer just to maintain a modest standard of living.

But here's the good news: it's not impossible. With the right guidance, it's absolutely achievable.

We know that property investing can feel daunting, especially for beginners. The complexities, risks, and misinformation out there can be overwhelming. Add the rise of finfluencers – financial influencers promising riches on social media platforms like Instagram, TikTok, and YouTube – and the noise becomes deafening. Many 'gurus' trade on complexity to confuse people, casting a stain on the financial and property services industry.

We're here to remove that stain. Our goal is to simplify property investing, breaking it down into actionable steps that anyone can follow. Think of this book as a conversation at your kitchen table – a casual chat over coffee – where we share what's worked for us and our clients, and what can work for you too.

As successful property investors ourselves, enjoying $3,000+ per week passive income from our portfolios, we know the challenges, the risks, the right moves – and when to make them – and the overall rewards of this journey. We're not here to boast about our success but to act as your guides, offering the same proven frameworks we've used to help tens of thousands of Australians.

So, this book is your starting point. You don't need to be a financial expert to succeed in property investing, but you do need the right guidance.

We're not just handing you a playbook; we're giving you an 'insider's guide' because, frankly, property is an insider's game, and we're lifting the veil for you. By adopting this guide, you'll learn the real, unvarnished truths, which free you to make smarter choices and take control of your financial future.

Finally, this is YOUR journey, and we're honoured to play a part in it. Property investing isn't about chasing quick wins or following the crowd – it's about creating your life by design, not by chance. So, as you turn the pages, remember: the first step starts with you, and we'll be with you every step of the way.

As Ben signs off every week on our podcast: **Knowledge is empowering, but only if you act on it.**

Let's begin…

PART I
The Foundations

You wouldn't climb Mount Everest without a plan, a map, and the right gear. And you certainly wouldn't start at the summit. Property investing is no different.

If the ultimate goal is reaching the financial peak – $3,000 per week in passive income – then we need to start at base camp, where we find the foundations, the bedrock principles, that support everything else. Before we dive into strategy, tactics, or execution, we need to get your mindset, understanding, and approach locked in, because sadly, most people never make it past the first stage. They get caught in the fog of uncertainty, distracted by quick wins, or overwhelmed by complexity. They take the wrong path, get lost, or turn back before making real progress.

That's why this first part of the ascent is critical. We'll lay out the core principles of wealth-building, explain why property is the best vehicle to get you there and, most importantly, help you define what financial success actually looks like for you. We're not here to sell you a dream. We're here to show you how to build one.

We've divided this book into the following four parts – each one is a key stage in your climb toward financial freedom:

1. **The foundations:** Understanding wealth, goal setting, and why property is the ultimate vehicle.
2. **The Property Investment Formula:** The proven, step-by-step framework for mastering property investing and building a high-performing portfolio.
3. **Taking action:** The final ascent, where we show you exactly how to turn property into passive income for life and retire on $3,000 per week.
4. **What action looks like:** Case studies of people who decided to act and have built a small but mighty portfolio and completely changed their financial future.

Think of this as the map we wish we had when we started. It took us years of experience, mistakes, and lessons to refine – but you get the shortcut. So, let's get started. First, we build the base. Then, we climb.

LET THE ASCENT BEGIN

Chapter 1
The goal

True wealth is more than money

Property investing isn't just about accumulating wealth; it's about securing a life of personal sovereignty – the freedom to do what you want, when you want, for as long as you want, and with the people who matter most to you.

We call this 'lifestyle by design – not by chance'. For us, personal sovereignty – or, as we refer to it, 'financial peace' – means having the financial independence to shape your life on your terms, free from the constraints of financial insecurity or the pressures of societal expectations. It's not about chasing numbers for the sake of it; it's about crafting a life that feels authentically fulfilling, where you have both time and financial peace.

So, here's a question worth pondering: have you thought about how much is enough? In our experience, people without a clear vision of personal financial peace can easily get caught in the race for more. They chase temporary highs, compare themselves to others, and measure success by someone else's standards. But what's the point of sacrificing your health, relationships, or peace of mind just to climb someone else's ladder? In his book, *Never Enough: From Barista to Billionaire*, Andrew Wilkinson echoes this sentiment, explaining that the relentless chase for 'more' – more money, more success, more recognition, or more material possessions – often leads to dissatisfaction and unhappiness. The pursuit of 'enough' can become a never-ending cycle, with each new milestone shifting the goalposts further away.

True financial peace isn't about amassing wealth but creating freedom. Freedom to buy back your time, to prioritise what matters most, and to live with intention. It's not about working harder to earn more money – it's about making your money work harder for you.

And real wealth is so much more than what's in your bank account. In his best-selling book, *The Wealth Money Can't Buy*, Robin Sharma identifies eight forms of wealth that he believes are essential for a more fulfilling life:

1. Growth
2. Wellness
3. Family
4. Craft
5. Money
6. Community
7. Adventure
8. Service

When you achieve financial peace, you create the space to invest in all these areas of your life. These are the treasures that bring you lasting happiness and meaning – far beyond what any salary or property portfolio can deliver.

However, one of the biggest roadblocks to this freedom is comparison. Too often, people measure their progress by looking at others – whether it's their lifestyle, investments, or social media highlights. Here's the truth: *we're all playing totally different games.*

Each person has a unique set of goals, aspirations, and circumstances. Trying to follow someone else's investment journey is like using their GPS route instead of your own. Their starting point, destination, and stopovers are different from yours, so thoughtlessly following their path will only get you lost. True freedom and peace come when you focus on what matters to *you*, aligning your investments and decisions with your values and priorities.

Research consistently shows that material possessions bring only fleeting happiness. What truly sustains us are experiences, relationships, and opportunities to live with purpose. This is why we advocate for personal sovereignty – not as a path to accumulate 'stuff' but as a means to reclaim your time and energy for what really matters.

When your financial independence allows you to focus on your passions, spend time with loved ones, and savour life's experiences, you'll find yourself living a life that feels truly rich.

As you move through these pages, remember that property investing is a tool, not the end goal. This tool can help you create YOUR 'lifestyle by design – not by chance'. It's about achieving freedom – the kind that lets you live authentically and purposefully on your terms.

True wealth isn't about the things you own but the life you create. Following the path outlined in this book will give you the clarity, tools, and confidence to shape a future that prioritises what matters most.

Why $3,000 per week?

In 2015, we released our first best-selling book, *The Armchair Guide to Property Investing: How to retire on $2,000 per week*, with a clear mission: to share our insights, frameworks, and passion for property investment with everyday Australians. That same year, we launched *The Property Couch* podcast, where these ideas and others came to life. Week after week, we explored real-world scenarios, welcomed experts, and watched listeners apply these principles to transform their lives.

Those who read that book will find the principles refreshed, refined, and updated here for today's realities. Your questions, challenges, and overall successes have helped us refine our frameworks, ensuring they're as actionable and relevant as ever. And for those joining us for the first time, welcome to the journey! This book integrates nearly a decade of podcasting insights and 50+ years of combined personal hands-on experience, plus the hundreds of years of combined experience of our team through our multi-award-winning business, Empower Wealth.

When we wrote *The Armchair Guide to Property Investing* in 2015, we set an ambitious yet achievable target: to build a property portfolio capable of generating $2,000 per week in retirement income. This wasn't just a random number; it was inspired by an article Bryce wrote for *Money Magazine*, commissioned by then-editor Effie Zahos, which outlined how everyday Australians could secure a comfortable retirement through property investment. The response was incredible, and the article became the second-highest-selling cover in the magazine's history. We were on to something, and that book has gone on to sell more than 30,000 copies, proving there was an appetite for this vision.

Back in 2015, $2,000 per week was an appropriate and motivating benchmark that reflected the financial realities of the time. For many readers, it became the cornerstone of their journey toward a lifestyle by design – a goal so compelling that many Australians who come into our business still seek guidance on how to reach this exact North Star figure. But times have changed. In this book, we've updated the benchmark to $3,000 per week – not only to future-proof the aspiration of a fulfilling retirement but also to ensure the goal remains relevant and attainable for years to come. This new target provides a foundation that adapts to changing times and rising expectations, keeping financial freedom within reach.

What has changed?

While much of our original content remains evergreen, the world has moved forward, and so have we. This book reflects the realities of today's market, addressing key shifts that impact property investors. Here's what we'll cover:

1. **Enduring principles:** We've thoughtfully crafted this book to be even more evergreen. Whether you're reading this in 2025, 2037, or decades from now, the core principles here are timeless. We've designed this book to endure, ensuring that no matter when you pick it up, you'll have the tools to create a life of financial freedom perfectly suited to your era.

2. **A bigger goal:** We've raised the benchmark to $3,000 per week to reflect both the realities of indexation and the future-focused goals we believe in. This new income target broadly represents the same purchasing power as $2,000 did when we wrote our previous book, adjusted for the general increases in cost of living (inflation) over the past decade.

3. **Rising property prices:** Looking back at the numbers from 2015 brings a sense of nostalgia – it reminds us how much the market has changed and how far we've come. Real estate prices, as we anticipated, have risen significantly since then. Yet, those who acted on our advice back then are now well on their way to securing a very comfortable retirement.

The good news? For those starting today, the same opportunity exists. To ensure this guide remains future-proof, we've updated projections and frameworks to reflect current market conditions while maintaining our long-term, timeless approach.

4. **Tax updates:** Since our first book, personal tax, stamp duty, and land tax rates have shifted, impacting property investment strategies. We've included the latest tax information to help you navigate these changes so you can focus on growing your portfolio without unnecessary surprises. However, since legislation can change, getting professional advice to keep your strategy on track is always a good idea.

So, why focus on $3,000 per week instead of, say, $1 million in total wealth? It's simple: we've observed that most Australians think about their finances, especially incomes, in weekly terms. A weekly target offers clarity, helping to visualise how your investments translate into a lifestyle that aligns with your goals. Whether it's covering daily expenses, travelling, or supporting your family, this approach provides a clear, meaningful target.

Sadly, most Australians retire with far less than they need. According to the Australian Institute of Health and Welfare (AIHW), as of March 2023, approximately 63% of Australians aged 65 and over received income support payments, with the vast majority (92%) of these recipients receiving the Age Pension. Relying solely on the pension falls far short of achieving any meaningful level of financial peace. The table opposite draws from the ASFA Retirement Standard comparison, which highlights the lifestyle you can expect on the Age Pension compared to a modest or comfortable retirement.

The goal

Comfortable retirement	Modest retirement	Age Pension
One annual holiday in Australia	One or two short breaks in Australia near where you live each year	Even shorter breaks or day trips in your own city
Regularly eat out at restaurants. Good range and quality of food	Infrequently eat out at restaurants that have cheap food. Cheaper and less food than a 'comfortable' lifestyle standard	Only club special meals or inexpensive takeaway
Owning a reasonable car	Owning an older, less reliable car	No car or, if you have a car, it will be a struggle to afford repairs
Afford bottled wine	Afford cask wine	Home brew beer or no alcohol at all
Good clothes	Reasonable clothes	Basic clothes
Afford regular hair cuts at a good hairdresser	Afford regular hair cuts only at a basic salon or pensioner special day	Less frequent hair cuts or getting a friend to cut your hair
Take part in a range of regular leisure activities	Take part in one paid leisure activity infrequently. Some trips to the cinema	Only taking part in no cost or very low cost leisure activities. Rare trips to the cinema
A range of electronic equipment	Not much scope to run air conditioner	Less heating in winter
Replace kitchen and bathroom over 20 years	No budget for home improvements. Can do repairs, but can't replace kitchen or bathroom	No budget to fix home problems like a leaky roof
Private health insurance	Private health insurance	No private health insurance

I'm sure you'll agree, the Age Pension is not appealing when reflected in this way. The good news is that our approach to property investing offers a proactive alternative, empowering you to create a retirement that is beyond 'comfortable', defined by more time, more choice, and more freedom.

Before we go any further, let's pause and reflect on something important. While $3,000 per week is the benchmark we're working towards in this book, the real goal is finding what's meaningful for you. Maybe $1,000 or $2,000 per week is all you need to live your best life. In fact, on Episode 323 of the summer series of our podcast, 'Rising From A Decade Of Addiction', our guest Sam found her financial peace at $575 per week ($30,000 per year). This is real proof that there's no single 'right' or 'better' outcome – only the outcome that gives you true peace and freedom. The only goal that matters is one that brings *you* peace and meaning.

One of the biggest regrets we hear from retirees is that they worked too hard, for too long, chasing a number they didn't actually need. So, take a moment to consider: how much do you *really* need to live comfortably? If it's less than $3,000 per week, why not give yourself permission to enjoy more time, freedom, and balance *today*? Remember, we're all playing different games, so cut your own path to financial peace and happiness. Focus on what number truly matters to *you*.

The beauty of this journey is that it's yours to customise. Set a goal that aligns with your life, your values, and your definition of happiness (more on that shortly). That way, you'll avoid the regret of lost time chasing someone else's number and instead create a life worth living.

Whether you're a returning reader or joining us for the first time, this book is your starting point for a life free from financial stress and full of financial peace.

You're the hero, we're the guide

Now, there's an important question to ponder here. Have you ever noticed how many property investing books feel more like an author's highlight reel than a practical roadmap? They contain pages filled with claims of big wins/returns, flashy toys, opulent stories, and the spoils of someone else's success. It might be inspiring for some – for a moment at least – but eventually, you end up asking: 'How does this actually help *me*?'

We hear you, and we wanted to offer something different from that.

This book isn't about us – it's about you. Rather than a showcase of our achievements, it's a guide to help you create your pathway and journey. Our role here isn't to brag and be the hero of the story but to help you become the hero of yours. We're here to share how we've helped others climb their mountains and show you how to confidently navigate your path to the summit of financial peace.

To illustrate this further, imagine you're choosing a personal trainer between two aspirational options. Trainer A has a physique that would turn heads – sculpted to perfection, a living advertisement for their discipline. But when you look 'under the bonnet', they haven't helped anyone else achieve the same fitness results as they have. On the other hand, Trainer B is fit and healthy – not as chiselled as the first, but still a walking advertisement of the result you're after – but their real superpower is evident: they've guided hundreds of people to transform their lives. They walk the talk themselves, but their focus is equally on empowering others and helping them get what they want. In this analogy, Trainer A is the classic hero focused on what they want, but Trainer B is the guide who is there to help others. When it comes to your property investment journey, you need a guide – someone who's walked the path before you and knows the terrain but whose focus is on helping you achieve your goals.

Think of classic hero-guide pairs from your favourite stories: Luke Skywalker and Yoda from *Star Wars*, Frodo and Gandalf from *The Lord of the Rings*, or Harry and Dumbledore from *Harry Potter*. These heroes didn't set off alone; they had wise guides to provide clarity, perspective, and support, helping them become the heroes of their own stories. That's exactly the relationship we hope to build with you throughout this book.

We're property investors ourselves, and we've walked this path before. We've made mistakes, learned from them, and refined our strategies. But, again, this isn't a book about our wins – it's about the mindset, tools, insights, and behaviours, combined with proven frameworks and action steps, that have helped others build their own success stories.

Our goal? To help another 10,000 households achieve financial peace (becoming multi-millionaires and living a lifestyle by design) within the next 15 years. Not our design – theirs. This purpose gets us up in the morning. We are on track to do that, and this book is your invitation to join this movement.

Through these pages, we want you to imagine us sitting across from you, chatting about what's worked for us, what hasn't, and what can work for you too. By adopting the principles, steps, and strategies we share in this book – the same ones we offer our clients – we aim to equip you with the foundational knowledge, clarity, and confidence to write *your own* success story, achieve financial peace, and create a lifestyle by design that's truly yours.

You're the hero, and it's time to hit the gym floor – Trainer B is here to guide you. Are you in?

YOU'RE THE HERO, WE'RE YOUR GUIDE

Chapter 2

Lifestyle by design

Now that we've set the goal – $3,000 per week and financial peace – it's time to assess where you are today. Knowing your starting point is critical to mapping your way forward.

Enter the seven grades of financial well-being – a roadmap to pinpoint your current stage and highlight the steps to financial peace. And for those aiming even higher, it reveals a path to financial contribution, where wealth becomes a tool for greater impact.

But this isn't just about numbers – it's about the choices, behaviours, and actions that define your financial journey. Each grade builds on the last, progressing from financial survival to financial peace and, for some, a lasting legacy. Now, let's unpack it.

The seven grades of financial well-being

Grade 1: Financial turmoil

This stage is marked by very poor financial decision-making, resulting in severe financial stress and overwhelming debt. Meeting basic needs feels insurmountable, with constant worry about how to stay afloat. It's like being stuck in a financial storm with no shelter in sight. The focus here is survival, and the first step out of turmoil often requires seeking external help, such as financial counselling, to completely reset and regain stability.

Grade 2: Financial survival

In this stage, individuals are living payday to payday, juggling bills and relying on short-term fixes to stay afloat. There's an awareness of financial strain, but clarity and control feel out of reach. It's like treading water – you're keeping your head above the surface but not moving forward, and one unexpected wave could send you down to financial turmoil. The key to progress here is taking responsibility, creating a plan, and seeking guidance towards more stability.

Grade 3: Financial consciousness

Think of this as the moment when you switch off financial passenger mode and start actively steering the wheel. At this level, individuals become aware of their financial habits, tracking income and expenses for the first time. This foundational awareness is like discovering a compass – it doesn't get you to your destination on its own, but it ensures you're no longer lost.

Grade 4: Financial stability

This is the stage when the financial fog begins to lift, and fundamental understandings and habits begin to form. With a rules-based money management system in place like MoneySMARTS (more on that later), individuals gain control over their finances and surplus savings start to flow in. It's like building a solid foundation for a house – each brick of clarity and organisation strengthens the structure. With this newfound stability, short-term goals become achievable, and financial setbacks feel manageable.

Grade 5: Financial control

At this proactive stage, financial management shifts from 'the basics' to 'planned and executed' strategic actions. Investments take centre stage, and individuals work toward long-term wealth-building. It's like planting seeds in a well-tended garden – you're not just growing for today but cultivating a future harvest. Confidence grows as financial independence becomes an obtainable reality.

Grade 6: Financial peace

This is where everything clicks. Grade 6 represents the achievement of financial independence – where your wealth and cashflow cover all life's needs without stress. It's not just about having money; it's about experiencing peace. Money management becomes second nature, and the focus has shifted beyond surviving and building wealth to truly enjoying life. This level is the heart of this book: to guide you toward this place of personal sovereignty – a lifestyle defined by freedom, purpose, and peace of mind.

Grade 7: Financial contribution

Grade 7 is the pinnacle of our financial well-being grades. At this stage, the focus turns outward. With your financial needs met, you can give back through philanthropy, creating legacies, or supporting loved ones and communities. It's like reaching the summit of a mountain and realising your view can inspire and uplift others. Financial contribution transforms your success into a gift for the greater good.

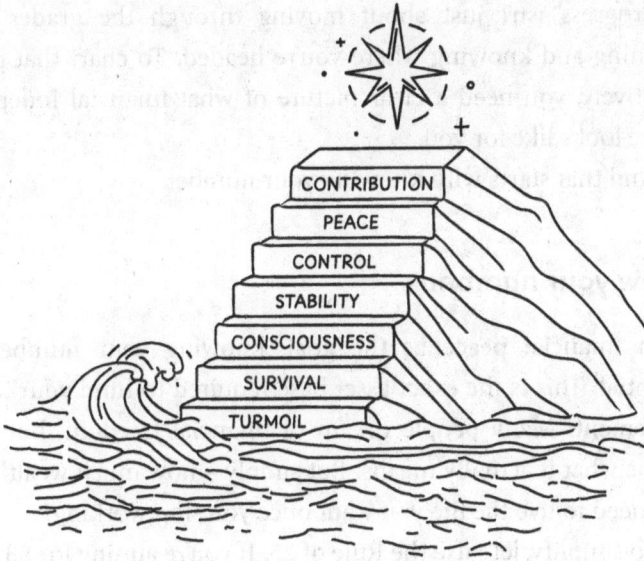

THE SEVEN GRADES OF FINANCIAL WELL-BEING

These seven grades represent a financial growth journey measured by understanding, actions, and results. Ideally, you'll never experience Grade 1 or 2, but recognising these stages and progressing through them allows you to move beyond simply managing money to reclaiming your time, energy, and peace of mind. Each grade aligns with the core principle of creating a lifestyle by design – not by chance.

For most people, the goal is Grade 6 – financial peace – a stage where money serves you rather than controls you, giving you the freedom to shape a life that reflects your values and priorities. For those inspired to go further, Grade 7 offers the opportunity to leave a legacy, impacting others beyond personal wealth and living with greater purpose.

Progress isn't just about moving through the grades but planning and knowing where you're headed. To chart that path effectively, you need a clear picture of what financial independence looks like for you.

And that starts with knowing your number.

Know your number

With financial peace as the goal, knowing your number is essential. This is the exact asset base required to fund your ideal retirement. Many people dream of financial freedom, but few define what it actually means. Put simply – how much wealth do you need to live the life you want once you stop working?

To simplify, let's use the Rule of 25. If you're aiming for $3,000 per week in retirement income – $156,000 annually – you'd multiply $156,000 by 25, giving a target of $3.9 million. This number represents the total value of income-producing assets you need in your portfolio – outside of your family home – to generate your desired retirement income, assuming a 4% return. Your home, while valuable, isn't included because it doesn't provide income.

At first glance, this might seem like a big number, but remember that property investment and capital growth will help you reach this target over time. It's also important to note that the Rule of 25 is just a rule of thumb – a quick-start guide to help you focus on the end result. While it provides a helpful framework, it's not intended to replace a fully tailored solution. Later in this book, we'll explore detailed case studies that offer a more nuanced approach, showing how specific strategies and decisions can adjust this number based on your unique circumstances. For now, this is a great starting point.

OK, let's break it down. Many people are surprised to learn they'll need less than expected in retirement – especially once major expenses such as loan repayments from the property accumulation phase drop off.

To calculate your number, start by breaking down your current household expenses into these four core categories:

1. **Essential bills:** Regular expenses like utilities, groceries, school fees, and insurance.

2. **Discretionary spending:** Non-essentials like dining out, entertainment, and hobbies.

3. **Loan payments:** Mortgages, car loans, or personal debts.

4. **Investment holding costs:** Contributions toward your property investment portfolio, such as interest, property maintenance, or taxes.

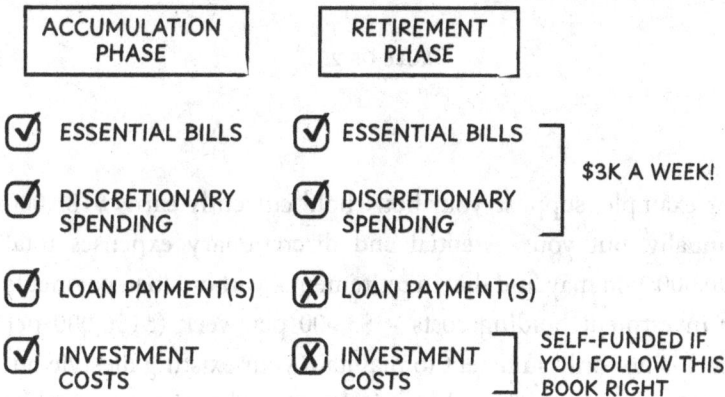

ACCUMULATION PHASE	RETIREMENT PHASE	
☑ ESSENTIAL BILLS	☑ ESSENTIAL BILLS	⎤
☑ DISCRETIONARY SPENDING	☑ DISCRETIONARY SPENDING	⎦ $3K A WEEK!
☑ LOAN PAYMENT(S)	☒ LOAN PAYMENT(S)	
☑ INVESTMENT COSTS	☒ INVESTMENT COSTS	⎤ SELF-FUNDED IF YOU FOLLOW THIS BOOK RIGHT

HOW YOUR EXPENSES CHANGE FROM ACCUMULATION TO RETIREMENT

Once you're in retirement – with your debts paid off, your kids living independently, and no longer needing to invest for the future – your expenses typically reduce to essential bills and discretionary spending. Add up these costs to determine how much annual income you'll need, then multiply that number by 25 to calculate the portfolio size required to generate that income sustainably.

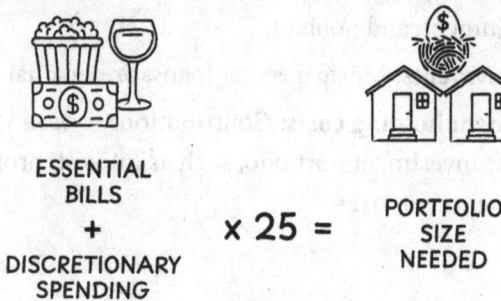

ESSENTIAL
BILLS
+
DISCRETIONARY
SPENDING

x 25 =

PORTFOLIO
SIZE
NEEDED

RULE OF 25

For example, suppose your household currently earns $180,000 annually, but your essential and discretionary expenses total $90,000; you may find that in retirement – without loan payments or investment holding costs – $3,000 per week ($156,000 per year) is not only sufficient to maintain your existing lifestyle but may even allow you to enhance it. What might initially seem like a pay cut compared to your current income is actually a shift to passive income – money working for you rather than the other way around. Let the joy of that thought sink in!

Knowing your number is empowering. It provides clarity, direction, and a target to aim for. With this knowledge, you can reverse-engineer your financial decisions today to ensure they align with your long-term lifestyle goals.

What does money mean to you?

This question comes on the heels of understanding your number – the financial goal that sets the foundation for your journey. But numbers alone won't get you there. This next step is about something equally important: *mindset.*

Many of you may be tempted to skip over this section, eager to dive into the 'doing' of wealth creation. But as William Whitecloud explains in his best-selling book *The Magician's Way: What it really takes to find your treasure*, there's a profound distinction between *action* and *doing* deeply rooted in our mindset. Doing is tied to the belief that you must fix, improve, or change yourself and your circumstances before moving forward. It's your belief system throwing up roadblocks, convincing you that you're not quite ready or capable yet. Action, on the other hand, is about taking direct, obvious steps toward your end goal. It's about trusting your heart and focusing on the outcome as your guiding light in making your decisions.

Whitecloud illustrates this concept through a golf analogy:

'Picture this. You're standing on a pristine golf course, club in hand, ready to take your swing. The sun is shining, the grass is a vibrant green, and the hole is clearly in sight. Your instructor approaches and says, "Forget about your stance, the angle of your club, or even your swing. Don't overthink it. Just focus on one thing – the ball landing in the hole."

'You pause, skeptical. Isn't golf supposed to be about perfecting every detail of your mechanics? But the instructor insists: "Picture the ball sinking into the hole. Feel the joy of the moment it drops in. Let that vision guide you."

'And so you focus. You take a breath, clear your mind, and hold that image of success. Suddenly, the swing feels effortless, and the ball arcs beautifully through the air, landing exactly where you intended.'

But here's the twist: many people aren't truly focused on what they want, even when they think they're aiming for success. Instead, they're consumed by avoiding what they *don't* want. Standing in your shoes, they'd be muttering, 'Don't land in the water, don't land in the water, don't land in the water!'

Sound familiar? By fixating on the hazard, they reinforce their fears, letting their beliefs dictate their actions. Their body, swing, and energy align to avoid failure, but in doing so, they often hit exactly where they *don't* want to go.

This is the trap so many of us fall into, not just in golf but in life, money, and investing. We want financial freedom, but our inner dialogue says, 'Don't run out of money', 'Don't make a bad investment', or 'Don't get stuck in debt'. Instead of moving toward the hole – our goal – we unconsciously focus on avoiding the water hazards of our fears.

The lesson here is simple but profound: when you fix your mind solely on what you want – the ball in the hole, the $3,000 a week in passive income, or the freedom to live life on your terms – you align your thoughts, actions, and sixth sense to make it happen. By contrast, when you dwell on what you're trying to avoid, you give power to your doubts and reinforce the very patterns holding you back.

Here's the challenge: your beliefs about money will often get in your way. They manifest as barriers like:

- **Fear:** Paralysing inaction driven by a fear of failure or losing money.
- **Doubt:** Sure, it worked for them, but it won't work for me.
- **Procrastination:** Waiting too long and missing valuable opportunities.
- **Greed:** Overextending and taking on unnecessary risks.
- **Lack of knowledge:** Not knowing where to start or how to manage money effectively.
- **Noise:** Getting distracted by misinformation, societal pressures, or unqualified advice.

In our experience, these barriers are rooted in deep-seated attitudes towards money formed in childhood. For example, if you grew up in a household where money was scarce or viewed as unattainable, those beliefs might still influence your mindset today.

So, what *does* money mean to you?

For some, it's about security – ensuring their family is cared for. For others, it's freedom – the ability to make choices without financial constraints. On Moorr.com.au, our free 'lifestyle by design' platform, tens of thousands of Australians have shared what money means to them. Here are some of the most common responses:

- **Security:** Knowing the future is financially stable (12,000).
- **Freedom:** The power to choose what to do and when to do it. (11,000)
- **Work-Life Balance:** The flexibility to work on your terms without financial stress (9,767).

- **Time with Family:** The ability to be present for loved ones and create lasting memories (8,388).
- **Comfort:** Enjoying a better standard of living (8,158).
- **Growth:** Pursuing self-development and opportunities (6,844).
- **Adventure:** The ability to explore and take risks (5,027).
- **Purpose:** Funding passions and meaningful goals (3,708).

Can you relate to any of these? Or do you have your own list? Whatever your definition, the key is aligning your values with your financial strategy. This is why mindset matters.

Investing is both an art and a science. This book will guide you through the science – the frameworks, strategies, and practical steps. But the art? That's uniquely yours. It's the reason, sadly, our frameworks deliver success for most but not for everyone. Make no mistake: the science works 100% of the time and doesn't discriminate, but the art is where we have no control – that's entirely up to you and lives in your conscious and subconscious mind.

The art of investing begins with clarity: at the big picture level, what does money mean to you? If we think back to Whitecloud's golf analogy, what is the 'hole' (the financial goal) you're aiming for, and how focused are you on getting there? Are you aiming for it or just hoping to stay out of the rough? What are the beliefs holding you back, and how can you avoid them derailing you? Lean into the process (science), trust your intuition (art), and let this book equip you with the tools to make your vision a reality.

So, what's the 'hole' that you want? Are you focused on it or are you just hoping to avoid the water?

Chapter 3
What is wealth?

What's the difference between rich and wealthy?

People in the developed world say they want to be *rich*, but what they actually crave is *wealth*. There is a big difference. Being *rich* is about how much money you have. It's a number in your bank account. But being *wealthy*? That's about how much *time* you have.

We don't love the term *rich* – to us, it's fleeting, materialistic, superficial, and often just means a high income paired with high expenses. Wealth, on the other hand, means freedom. It's having assets that work for you, not just a bank balance that looks impressive but disappears when you stop working.

Here's a simple way to look at it:

- Someone who has $100,000 in savings but spends $10,000 per month has 10 months of financial runway before they run out of money.

- Someone who spends $10,000 per month but owns assets that generate $12,000 per month in passive income is *infinitely wealthy*. They never need to trade their time for money again.

Therefore, true wealth isn't just about having money but having assets that sustain your lifestyle without you needing to work, and it's measured by the combined value of:

- The appreciating assets you directly hold less the borrowings and holding costs against them. This includes property and direct shareholdings (when they increase in value and/or the companies pay dividends).

- The amount of savings and other investments you have. This includes bank deposits earning interest, term deposits, bonds, superannuation, and managed funds, less holding costs.

- Your ability to *generate* money, whether through earning an income or, ideally, profiting from the assets you control. You are an *appreciating asset* – a fact many overlook but one that is absolutely critical to the bigger picture.

While wealth is easy to measure in theory, many people make mistakes in practice by including assets that depreciate over time – items like cars, boats, or the latest gadgets. These do not contribute to your long-term net worth and only detract from your ability to build real, lasting wealth. Creating financial wealth has several components and variables, but essentially, it's created by:

- **Money management:** You can't build wealth without surplus money. Effectively managing your finances to create and trap this surplus is the foundation of financial success.

- **Asset accumulation:** The ability to acquire appreciating assets, combined with income and savings, that steadily build wealth over time.

- **Skill and time:** The combination of knowledge, strategic execution, and the time available to let your investments grow, whether through your own expertise or a professional team.
- **Performance:** The measure of increase (or decrease) in the value of your assets over a period of time.
- **Protection:** The ability to protect the value of the assets. In good times, this should result in the value of the asset growing, and in tough times, it should limit the downside risk of the asset losing value.

The four types of wealth

True wealth extends far beyond financial measures, encompassing the key dimensions that define a fulfilling and balanced life. Let's explore the four key types of wealth:

1. **Social wealth:** Wealth is rarely built in isolation. Social wealth is the support system that fuels your journey – relationships, networks, and communities that open doors, provide guidance, and enrich your life. As Jim Collins, author of *Good to Great*, says, 'Life is people!'

2. **Physical wealth:** Good health is the cornerstone of all other forms of wealth. Physical wealth encompasses:
   i. **Health:** Vitality, energy, and the ability to live life to the fullest.
   ii. **Emotional well-being:** Resilience, stress management, and happiness.

   Without physical wealth, pursuing social, financial, or time wealth becomes infinitely harder. A healthy person has a thousand goals, but a sick person has only one!

3. **Time wealth:** The freedom to choose how you spend your time is one of the greatest luxuries of true wealth.

4. **Financial wealth:** This is the most familiar form of wealth and the foundation of all others. Financial wealth provides security, opportunity, and the means to achieve other types of wealth.

With these wealth dimensions in mind, let's explore the four primary pathways through which we access or generate financial wealth.

Work

The most common and accessible way to generate money is through work, such as earning income as a PAYG employee or as a self-employed individual generating profits from a business. We refer to this as 'exertions income' – taking a lot of time and effort. For most of us, work accounts for a significant portion of our income. It's the bedrock of wealth creation, but it's also time-intensive, costing around a third of your day. While work provides a stable foundation, relying solely on it can limit your financial potential over time.

Borrowing

Borrowing can be a powerful tool for building wealth when used strategically. By leveraging borrowed funds, you can invest in assets that generate overall higher returns than the cost of the loan itself. This concept underpins many successful wealth strategies, including property investing. However, borrowing also carries risks. The key is to calculate potential returns against downside risks and ensure the asset can generate enough value to justify the leverage. When used wisely, borrowing can accelerate your financial goals, but you must approach it with careful cashflow planning.

Investment returns

Investment returns are one of the most effective ways to generate money. They include passive income streams like rental income, dividends from shares, or capital growth from appreciating assets. The beauty of investment returns is that your money works for you. Unlike income from work, which requires your direct time and effort, investments grow over time – especially when they're stable and sound.

Charity and government support

Charitable donations or government handouts represent another way to access money, though often these sources are less reliable. This could include financial gifts from family, one-off donations, or ongoing government assistance like pensions. While these options may provide temporary relief, they're not designed for long-term financial independence. For retirees, relying on government pensions poses significant risks due to changing policies, inflation, and limited payout amounts. The goal is to create a self-funded future where you control your financial destiny.

More than one path

You don't need to choose just one path! Often, wealth creation involves a set of the following interconnected activities.

Work and earn

Your ability to generate income is the initial cornerstone of wealth creation. This involves:

- **Work:** Whether as a PAYG employee, self-employed individual, or business operator, work is the primary and most accessible pathway to earn money. While foundational, it often requires a significant time investment.
- **Savings accumulation:** Consistent saving helps bridge the gap between immediate needs and long-term opportunities. Building an emergency fund and maintaining disciplined spending habits are key components.
- **Skill development:** Enhancing your expertise through upskilling can increase your earning potential, allowing you to secure higher income opportunities or diversify your income streams.

Invest and grow

Wealth grows when your money works for you. This pillar focuses on creating passive income streams and capital growth through smart investments:

- **Strategic borrowing:** Responsibly leveraging borrowed funds can amplify your earning potential, allowing you to invest in opportunities with returns greater than the cost of borrowing. Balancing risks and rewards is crucial.
- **Investment returns:** This includes income from rental properties, dividends from direct business or shares, or the growth in value of appreciating assets like property or stocks.

IN REALITY ...
HOW THEY CONNECT

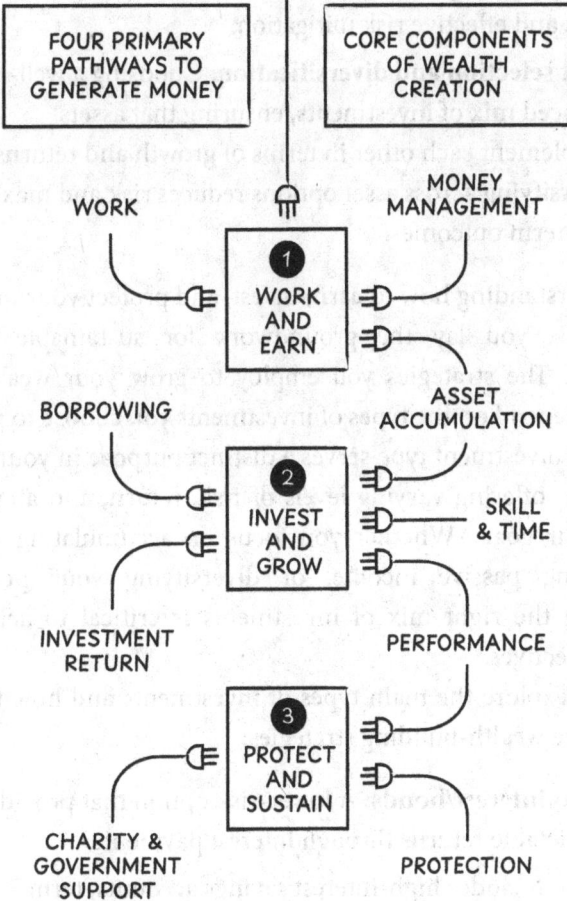

FOUR PRIMARY
PATHWAYS TO
GENERATE MONEY

CORE COMPONENTS
OF WEALTH
CREATION

WORK

MONEY
MANAGEMENT

1
WORK
AND
EARN

BORROWING

ASSET
ACCUMULATION

2
INVEST
AND
GROW

SKILL
& TIME

INVESTMENT
RETURN

PERFORMANCE

3
PROTECT
AND
SUSTAIN

CHARITY &
GOVERNMENT
SUPPORT

PROTECTION

INTERCONNECTED ACTIVITIES OF WEALTH CREATION

Protect and sustain

Building wealth is only half the battle – protecting it ensures your financial stability. This includes:

- **Risk management:** Safeguarding your income and assets through strategies like insurance, maintaining an emergency fund, and effective risk mitigation.
- **Asset selection and diversification:** Choosing a well-balanced mix of investments, ensuring that assets complement each other in terms of growth and returns. Diversifying across asset options reduces risk and maximises long-term outcomes.

By understanding how to earn, invest, and protect your financial resources, you lay the groundwork for sustainable wealth creation. The strategies you employ to grow your wealth will largely depend on the types of investments you choose to pursue.

Each investment type serves a distinct purpose in your financial plan, offering varying levels of risk, return, and alignment with your goals. Whether you focus on accumulating wealth, generating passive income, or diversifying your portfolio, selecting the right mix of investments is critical to achieving your objectives.

Let's explore the main types of investments and how they fit into these wealth-building strategies:

1. **Fixed interest/bonds:** A lower-risk option that provides predictable returns through interest payments.
2. **Cash:** Includes high-interest savings accounts, term deposits, and cash management accounts.
3. **Direct property:** Our preferred investment type, covering residential and commercial properties.

4. **Superannuation:** A tax-advantaged, government-enforced long-term savings and investment vehicle, typically accessible only at retirement.

5. **Direct shares/equities:** Investing in Australian or international companies through publicly traded stocks.

6. **Private equity:** Investing directly in private businesses or syndicates that take direct equity stakes in non-publicly listed companies.

7. **Alternative investments:** Includes Real Estate Investment Trusts (REITs), agribusiness, art, antiques, coins, wine, and other collectables.

8. **Cryptocurrency and emerging assets:** Digital assets such as Bitcoin, Non-Fungible Tokens (NFTs), and other blockchain-based investments.

9. **Exchange Traded Funds (ETFs):** Diversified investment funds that trade like shares, offering liquidity, easy diversification, and lower fees than managed funds.

10. **Managed funds:** Pooled investments actively managed by a professional fund manager across shares, bonds, or property, with returns tied to overall fund performance.

11. **Debentures:** Unsecured fixed-income securities issued by companies or governments, offering regular interest payments based on the issuer's creditworthiness rather than collateral.

Each of these investment types carries a different balance of risk and potential reward. Some offer stability and predictable returns, while others come with higher volatility but greater upside potential.

The graphic below helps you understand where each asset class sits and how it aligns with different wealth-building strategies.

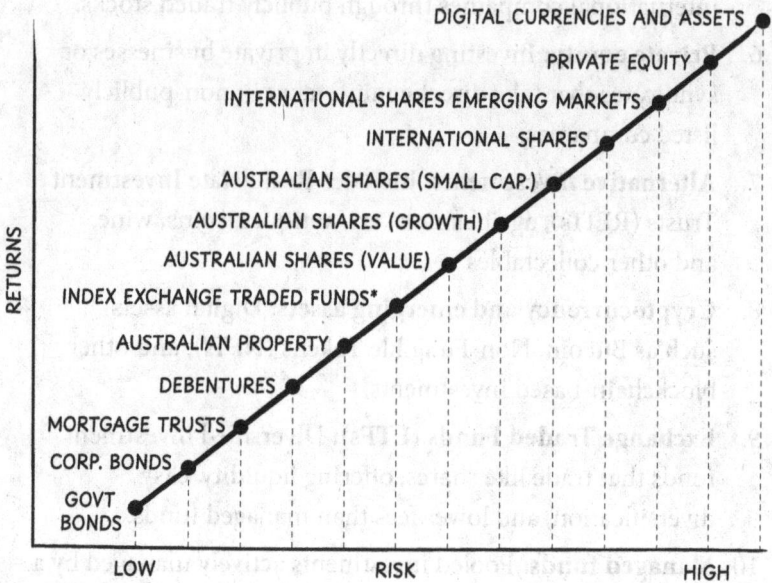

RETURNS

DIGITAL CURRENCIES AND ASSETS

PRIVATE EQUITY

INTERNATIONAL SHARES EMERGING MARKETS

INTERNATIONAL SHARES

AUSTRALIAN SHARES (SMALL CAP.)

AUSTRALIAN SHARES (GROWTH)

AUSTRALIAN SHARES (VALUE)

INDEX EXCHANGE TRADED FUNDS*

AUSTRALIAN PROPERTY

DEBENTURES

MORTGAGE TRUSTS

CORP. BONDS

GOVT BONDS

LOW   RISK   HIGH

*ETFs

RISK VERSUS RETURN BY INVESTMENT TYPE

With a clear understanding of wealth and the pathways to build it, the next question is: why property?

In the next chapter, we explore why it's our vehicle of choice for wealth creation.

Chapter 4

Why property?

When considering why property is such a powerful investment vehicle, it's essential to start with one undeniable truth: everyone needs a place to live. Shelter isn't just a want – it's a fundamental human necessity. This universal demand gives property a unique resilience and stability that sets it apart from other investment classes.

Furthermore, in Australia, property transcends necessity – it's woven into the fabric of our national identity as part of the Great Australian Dream. Let's backtrack for some context to understand how deeply this aspiration is rooted in our culture.

Australia was a young nation during World War II. When our soldiers returned home, it sparked a boom period that stretched into the 1950s and 1960s. Manufacturing jobs were plentiful, the standard of living was high, and for the first time, many Australians began to believe that owning their own home was achievable. This was a stark contrast to the Great Depression of the early 1930s, when only 30% of people owned their homes.

These post-war years gave birth to the suburbs, with houses springing up across the country. 'The Dream' took flight.

In wealthy countries like Australia, owning a home transcends practicality and becomes a powerful social symbol. It's where The Dream truly takes shape, offering more than just shelter – it's an expression of identity, success, and belonging.

There's a deep cultural love affair with property ownership, and for many Australians, a home represents much more than bricks and mortar. It's where people showcase their personal style, build lifelong memories, and reflect their aspirations and achievements. A home becomes a tangible statement to demonstrate where you stand in life.

This desire for self-expression, status, and even envy fuels a cycle of continuous improvement and one-upmanship. Home-owners aren't just maintaining their properties; they're upgrading them. From sleek new kitchens to elaborate outdoor entertaining spaces, these enhancements serve practical and social purposes. The land, its location, and the types of dwellings built, tell stories of neighbourhood formation, new friendships, family connections, and the pursuit of prestige and social status. These elements signal 'We've arrived' or 'We've made it'. While this might sound superficial, it's a powerful driver that keeps pushing land values higher and the overall property market thriving.

This constant reinvestment into properties creates a foundational strength in the market. Unlike other investments, property taps into the deep-seated human desire to belong, achieve, and improve. That's why the property market consistently demonstrates resilience over time.

Whether it's the allure of a prime location with multi-million-dollar views, the convenience of proximity to 'everything', the charm of a well-loved family home, or the pride of a stunning renovation, property offers far more than just shelter – it embodies aspiration and connection.

Who controls the market?

Beyond being a reflection of personal style and success, property also operates within a unique market dynamic that sets it apart from other asset classes. In Australia, this dynamic is largely shaped by the people who occupy the properties – approximately 70% of the residential property market is dominated by owner-occupiers, with investors making up the remaining 30%.

This balance holds important insights for anyone considering property as an investment. Unlike shares, property prices are predominantly influenced by everyday Australians making these deeply personal, emotional decisions about where they want to live, not necessarily about the properties' financial performance. This creates a unique opportunity for investors: a market led not by spreadsheets but by sentiment and lifestyle priorities.

As an investor, it might seem logical to focus on properties that are 'pitched' to investors, like National Disability Insurance Scheme (NDIS) or student accommodation, studio apartments, or holiday letting/motel/hotel accommodation. However, the opposite is true if you want sustained long-term property value growth. The smartest strategy is to target locations and properties with strong owner-occupier appeal – properties that resonate emotionally as homes and offer features that people genuinely aspire to. Why? Because owner-occupiers are the market's *price makers*. They're often willing to pay more than intrinsic value to secure their forever home, in a dream location, while investors should be *price takers*, calculating returns and following the trends set by these emotional decisions.

This is why investing in areas with a strong owner-occupier presence is our preferred focus. We are tapping into The Dream. These markets are more stable and less prone to the volatility seen in investor-driven locations like mining towns or types of properties that could be easily oversupplied. In such places, when investors become the price makers, markets can boom rapidly but are equally vulnerable to sudden downturns when external conditions change. On the other hand, established cities like Melbourne, Sydney, Brisbane, Adelaide, and Perth benefit from the stabilising influence of continually growing economies, attracting jobs, which in turn attracts owner-occupiers, who create consistent demand and reduce the likelihood of dramatic price swings.

As property investors, the goal is to be price takers, not price makers – understanding this dynamic is crucial. The key isn't to dominate the market but to align with it. By following the lead of owner-occupiers, investors can ride the wave of steady growth and long-term stability, leveraging the market's natural momentum rather than trying to force it.

This unique market dynamic is one of the many reasons property is such a resilient and rewarding investment. But there's another advantage that sets property apart: its incredible tax benefits, and we aren't talking about investor benefits here.

Home sweet (tax-free) home

For Australian homeowners, the Principal Place of Residence (PPR) isn't just a place to live – it's a powerful, tax-free wealth-building tool. The PPR offers one of the most significant advantages in the Australian tax system: unlike other invest-ments, your home is exempt from capital gains tax (CGT). This means that when your property appreciates in value and you sell, every cent of profit is yours to keep, *tax-free!* Whether you own a $400,000 home in a regional town or a $40 million estate in Toorak or Bellevue Hill, the rules are the same: no CGT upon sale. Additionally, the PPR is exempt from means-testing for the pension, and certain exemptions allow sale proceeds to be transferred tax-free into superannuation. These factors help us understand why property is such an attractive pathway to building and preserving wealth in Australia.

THE PPR ADVANTAGE

The Dream and these tax exemptions are powerful growth drivers within Australian residential property. Adding to this compelling appeal is the reality that property enjoys significant 'ballot box' support. In a country where residential real estate is the primary store of wealth for millions of Australians, governments are acutely aware of the political importance of protecting property values. While no market is entirely risk-free, property's deep economic and political significance provides an added layer of confidence for investors. Policies are frequently designed to maintain or even bolster property markets, offering a safety net that reinforces its robustness as an asset class.

Beyond individual benefits, this deeply entrenched owner-occupier base provides unparalleled market stability. According to the February 2025 CoreLogic Chart Pack, overall outstanding debt across the residential asset class stands at $2.4 trillion, representing less than 25% loan-to-value ratio (LVR) of its total $11.1 trillion value. This structure helps insulate property from extreme volatility and systemic risk, ensuring values remain resilient even in challenging economic conditions.

When you consider residential property alongside other asset classes, its dominance becomes even clearer:

- Residential real estate: $11.1 trillion
- Australian superannuation: $4.1 trillion
- Australian listed stocks: $3.3 trillion
- Commercial real estate: $1.3 trillion

This sheer scale – combined with tax-free growth, owner-occupier influence, and government support – cements property's unmatched resilience and potential.

Volatility

One of the most appealing aspects of property investing is its stability – it doesn't come with the rollercoaster volatility of other investments, like the share market, which can swing wildly and make your heart race.

In the share market, few things are more stressful than a margin call – i.e. when your investment value drops below a certain point, and your lender demands you either pay up or sell off assets, often at the worst possible time. The good news? Property doesn't come with that kind of stress. Even if the market dips or we hit an economic slowdown, your lender isn't likely to call demanding immediate repayment. This financial breathing room allows property owners to weather market fluctuations without scrambling for cash.

Sure, property isn't as liquid as shares – you can't sell it with a click of a button. But that's actually one of its strengths. The process of listing, marketing, negotiating, and closing a property sale acts as a natural safeguard against impulsive, fear-driven decisions. While shares can be sold in seconds during a moment of panic, selling a property requires thought, planning, time and a fair bit of effort. This built-in buffer discourages snap decisions based on short-term market noise and encourages a long-term perspective.

And that long-term mindset is essential. While property values may experience short-term ups and downs, history shows a consistent upward trend over a longer time horizon.

Of course, property isn't without its challenges – interest rate changes, government policies, vacancies, and maintenance costs can all impact returns. But without margin calls, you're less likely to react to every market blip. Next, we'll explore how leverage amplifies these foundational advantages, making property one of the most powerful asset classes available.

The power of leverage

The shares versus property debate is a long-standing one, but comparing these asset classes isn't as simple as looking at growth percentages or historical performance. The real game-changer is leverage – and how it transforms the profitability equation.

One key concept that clarifies this is cash-on-cash return. This metric highlights the true power of leverage, showing how borrowed capital can amplify returns, often allowing leveraged investments to outperform non-leveraged assets when measured against the cash or equity you personally invest.

Let's break it down with a simple comparison:

- **Investment #1:** A higher growth investment operating without leverage.
- **Investment #2:** A slightly lower growth investment leveraging up to 80%.

CASH-ON-CASH RETURN AND THE POWER OF LEVERAGE

Example	Investment #1	Investment #2	
Capital gain	8%	6%	
Yield	4%	4%	
Return	12%	10%	
Cash invested	$100,000	$100,000	
Leverage	0%	80%	
Could buy in value	$100,000	$500,000	
Debt	$0	$400,000	
Return on investment (ROI)	$12,000	$50,000	
Interest costs (7%)	$0	$28,000	
Return ($)	$12,000	$22,000	
Cash-on-cash return (%)	**12.00%**	**22.00%**	Difference of 10%

The results are striking – in simple terms it's a 10% difference, but in relative terms – 12% vs 22% return – it's an 83% improvement. Leverage magnifies the cash-on-cash returns, and when combined with property's low volatility (discussed earlier), it strengthens the case for real estate as a wealth-building powerhouse. This is why, when structured correctly, property can become an unparalleled vehicle for creating long-term financial security.

Paul Clitheroe, highly respected financial commentator and former host of Channel 9's *Money* show, weighed in on the shares versus property debate when he joined us on Episode 200 of *The Property Couch* podcast, 'Timeless Wisdom from the Original "Money" Guru'. When asked which option was better, he responded emphatically, 'I don't care! If you have shares, get a property; if you have property, get some shares.' His refreshing and balanced perspective reinforces a timeless truth: diversification matters. However, understanding how leverage works and why property allows you to use it effectively makes residential real estate a standout for us as personal and professional investors.

To be clear, we're not here to pick sides or spark debates. In fact, we have both property and shares in our personal portfolios. Nevertheless, we've chosen property as our primary vehicle because of its unparalleled leverage advantage. It's a fact: property offers the most optimal and stable leverage opportunities, making it the ideal vehicle for building wealth in a risk-adjusted way that aligns with our conservative personalities.

We don't love property *per se* – we love what it enables: passive income leading to lifestyle design. For us, property is simply the best means to that end. In our view, leverage is the ultimate umpire in the property versus shares debate. So, we don't argue about which vehicle is better – we just focus on getting to the goal on time. And with leverage as our ally, property becomes the standout choice for us.

Chapter 5

The magic of compounding

Imagine planting a tiny seed in the ground and watching it grow into a massive tree – not because you watered it endlessly, but because time and nature did their work. That's the magic of compounding. It's a financial principle that's as simple as it is powerful: let your investments earn returns, and then let those returns start earning returns too. Over time, this cycle repeats, creating a snowball effect that can turn even modest investments into substantial wealth.

While compounding sounds straightforward on paper, the real challenge lies in behaviour. As financial expert Dave Ramsey aptly puts it, 'Money is simple, but behaviour is hard.' It's not about finding the perfect investment strategy or nailing market timing – it's about mastering the habits that keep you consistent. The people who benefit most from compounding aren't the ones chasing the next quick win but those who stay calm during market wobbles and stick with their plan over the long haul.

And here's the secret ingredient that makes compounding truly magical: time. The longer you stay in the game, the greater the potential payoff. Even Warren Buffett – one of the greatest investors in history – credits time as his greatest ally. Patience is what allows your investments to grow and compound, turning small efforts into extraordinary results.

From our own experiences and the countless success stories we've seen through our podcast and business, one thing is clear: compounding isn't a get-rich-quick scheme. It's a get-rich-slow plan – a steady, reliable path to financial freedom. In a world dominated by social media and instant gratification, waiting for compounding to work its magic can feel frustrating. The social media generation glorifies fast success, making it even harder to stay patient when progress feels slow. But here's the truth: while compounding might take time, it's one of the most dependable ways to build wealth.

With compounding, patience isn't just a virtue – it's a requirement. The biggest rewards go to those who stay the course, ride out market swings, and resist the urge to act on short-term impulses that betray common sense. Charlie Munger, the late investor, billionaire, and longtime business partner of Warren Buffett, put it best: 'It's waiting that helps you as an investor, and a lot of people just can't stand to wait.' It's a game of waiting, but the payoff is well worth it for those who hold their ground. Every decision you make today – every seed you plant – has the potential to create security and financial freedom for your future.

So, start planting seeds now, trust the process, and let time do the rest. The journey might not be flashy or fast, but compounding is the ultimate proof that patience pays off – not just in wealth but in life.

Take a look at the following graph, which highlights the real cost of waiting. If you decided today that you wanted to buy an investment property *one day* but procrastinated for five years, that hesitation would cost you $759,315. Yep, just five years on the sidelines could set you back over three quarters of a million dollars!

SAME $700,000 INVESTMENT MADE 5 YEARS APART
6% CAPITAL GROWTH PER ANNUM

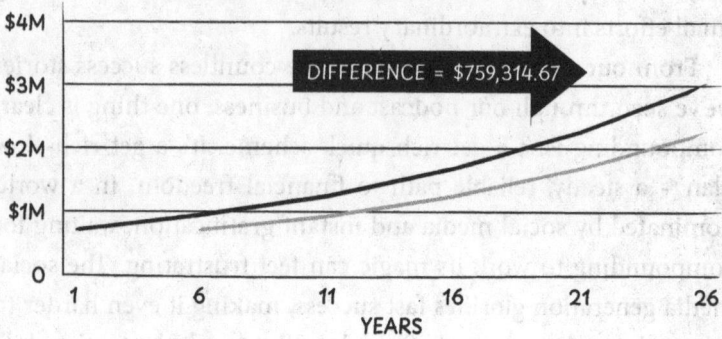

DIFFERENCE = $759,314.67

THE IMPACT OF DELAYED INVESTMENT ON GROWTH

Now, what if you had the capacity and ability to buy a $700,000 property but played it a little too safe and bought a different property for $600,000 instead? That decision alone, compounded over 25 years, would cost you $429,187.

$700,000 vs $600,000
6% CAPITAL GROWTH PER ANNUM

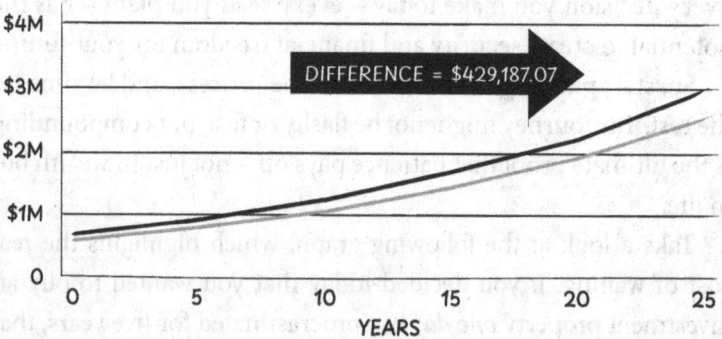

DIFFERENCE = $429,187.07

THE IMPACT OF INITIAL INVESTMENT SIZE ON LONG-TERM GROWTH

But here's where it gets really staggering – what if you did both? Wait five years AND underinvest? That combined decision would likely cost you $1,188,502 – that's over a million dollars in lost net worth! That's the power of compounding – and the cost of procrastination.

How does this play out in the real world? What does it actually look like to stay the course and let time do the heavy lifting? Next, we'll explore two powerful market reflections that showcase the transformative impact of patience, action, and consistency.

You're about to see just how rewarding it can be to get in the game *and* stay there.

Compounding in action

Compounding isn't just a theoretical concept – it's a strategy that transforms potential into reality. To see this in action, let's begin with property, the cornerstone of our personal wealth-building and the focus of this book, before broadening the lens to see how the same principles apply to shares.

The long game in real estate

Cotality's (formerly CoreLogic's) 30-year property performance chart (see pages 52–53) vividly illustrates how time and consistency can turn property investments into powerful wealth-building tools.

SCAN FOR A
LARGER DIAGRAM

You can view a clearer and more detailed version of this chart at www.thepropertycouch.com.au/ playbook.

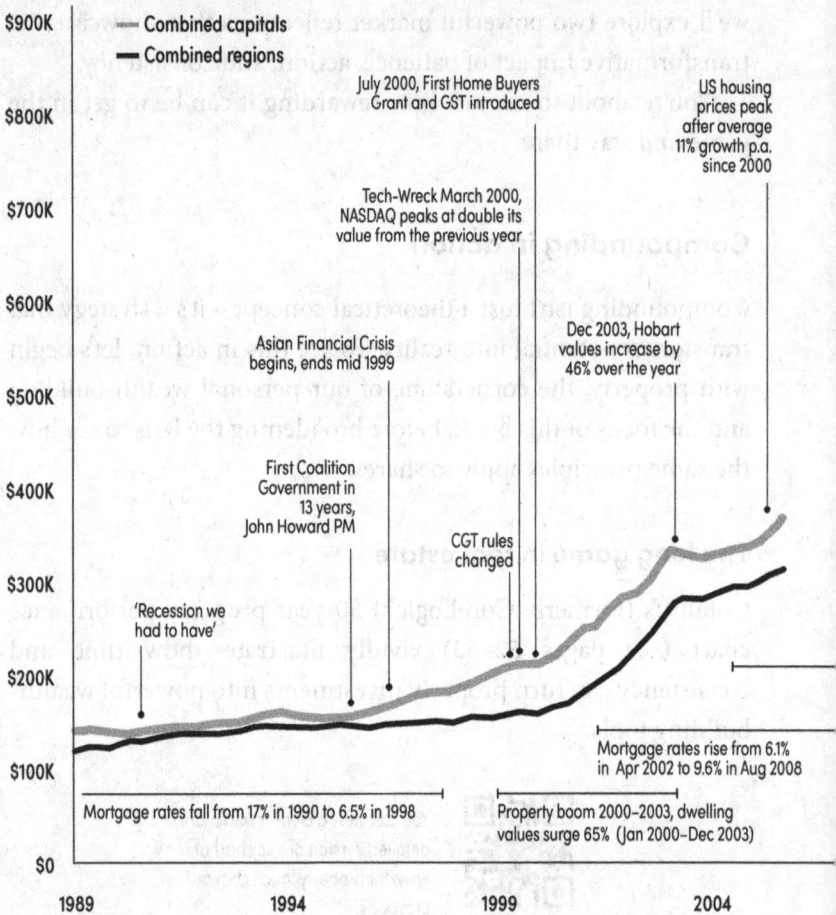

MEDIAN DWELLING VALUES OVER THE PAST 30 YEARS

The magic of compounding

Perth housing values up 41% in a year on the back of booming mining sector

Brisbane and Melbourne dwelling values up 22% in a year

GFC, housing values fall 7.5% over 2008. US values down 17%, UK down 11% and NZ down 8%

First Home Buyers Grant Boost, Oct 2008

APRA announced 30% limit on IO loan originations

Record high proportion of investor lending – 46% of mortgage demand nationally

APRA announces 10% speed limit on investment lending

Perth and Darwin housing values peak as mining boom winds down

Tony Abbott elected Coalition PM

Nov 2011, RBA cuts cash rate from 4.75%

APRA removes macro-prudential policies

Sydney and Melbourne housing values peak after rising 72% and 56% over past 5 years

Dec 21 qtrly inflation rises >1%

Headline inflation below 3%, core inflation falls to 3.5%

Fiscal support expired. Fixed mortgage rates rising. Consumer sentiment peaks

COVID declared a global pandemic

Cash rates start to rise May 2022, reaches 4.35% Nov 2023

New listings drop to below the 5-year average and hold low

Coalition retains government

Oct 2021 APRA tightens serviceability buffer by 50bps to 3%

Oct 2009 to Dec 2010 cash rate rises from 3.0% to 4.75% in Dec 2010

Resources boom, commodity prices climb 215% between 2004 and 2011

Cash rate drops to 0.1% and $291 billion in COVID-related fiscal support

RBA commences interest easing cycle, cuts cash rate from 7.25% to 3.0% between Sep 2008 and Apr 2009

Banking Royal Commision Dec 2017 to final report on Feb 2019

| 2009 | 2014 | 2019 | 2024 |

The chart shows:

- **Steady appreciation:** Despite economic downturns, housing market corrections, and interest rate hikes, Australian property values have marched upward over the long term. Compounding works its magic through capital appreciation and reinvested rental income, creating a snowball effect off the back of economic, population, and broader wealth growth and purchasing power.

- **Resilience in the face of uncertainty:** From the Global Financial Crisis (GFC) to rising interest rates, the chart highlights significant market events that tested the resolve of investors and homeowners. Yet, those who held onto their properties emerged with substantial long-term gains because the resistant and downward forces weren't enough to overpower the broader longer-term market demand and sentiment.

- **Time as the secret ingredient:** Warren Buffett famously said, 'Someone is sitting in the shade today because someone planted a seed 20 years ago'. The longer your money is left to compound, the more significant the results become as each year builds upon the last.

This is the essence of compounding: staying invested through the market's inevitable ups and downs. Property's tangible and 'expressive status' nature makes it an ideal example of how holding assets over time creates wealth, especially when coupled with patience and a sound strategy.

The broader picture of compounding

Compounding isn't exclusive to property – it's a universal principle that applies to most investments. Vanguard's 30-year index chart (see pages 56–57) showcases the growth of $10,000 invested across Australian shares, U.S. shares, international shares, bonds, and cash from 1994 to 2024.

SCAN FOR A
LARGER DIAGRAM

You can view a clearer and more detailed version of this chart at www.thepropertycouch.com.au/ playbook.

The results are equally compelling:

- **Growth across asset classes:** Australian shares grew to $135,165 (9.1% p.a.), while U.S. shares soared to $237,318 (11.1% p.a.). Even cash, the most conservative option, reached $34,552 (4.2% p.a.), given Vanguard results assume 100% of income is reinvested. This demonstrates the power of compounding regardless of the vehicle.

- **Patience over perfection:** The chart highlights market shocks like the dot-com bubble, the GFC, and the COVID-19 pandemic. While each event sparked panic for many investors, those who stayed the course and avoided emotional reactions saw their portfolios recover and thrive over time. This example reinforces a key truth – over time, the collective power and performance of great businesses outweigh short-term market sentiment and the decline of companies exiting these indexes.

2024 Vanguard Index Chart

Market returns – 1 July 1994 to 30 June 2024

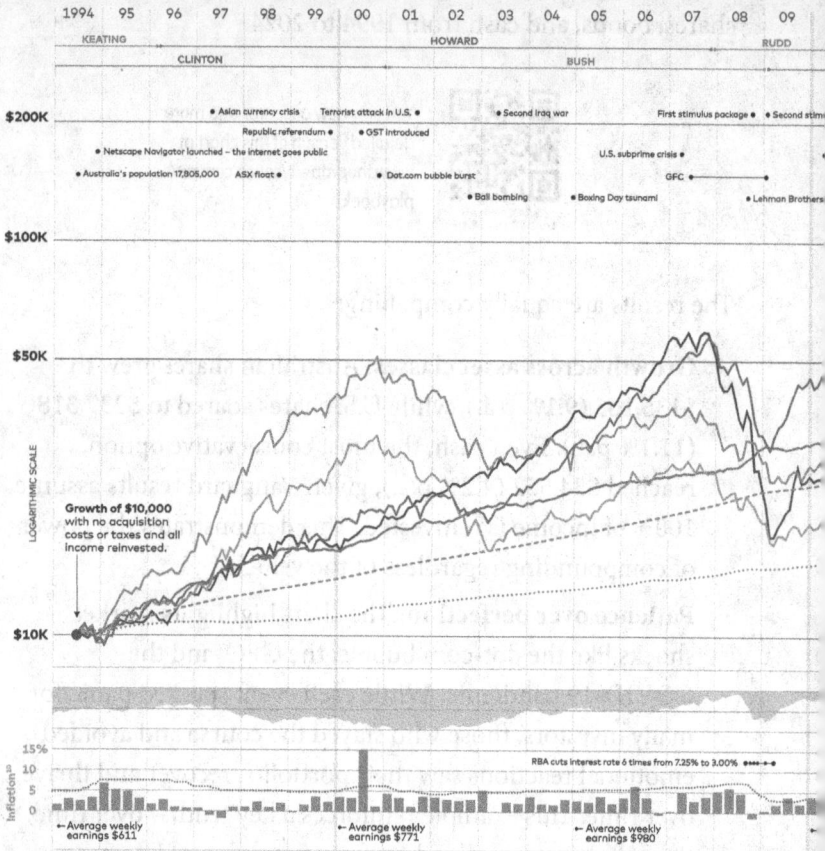

| 1994 | 95 | 96 | 97 | 98 | 99 | 00 | 01 | 02 | 03 | 04 | 05 | 06 | 07 | 08 | 09 |

KEATING
CLINTON
HOWARD
BUSH
RUDD

$200K

- Asian currency crisis
- Terrorist attack in U.S. ●
- Second Iraq war ●
- First stimulus package ●
- Second stim...
- Republic referendum ●
- GST introduced ●
- Netscape Navigator launched – the internet goes public ●
- U.S. subprime crisis ●
- Australia's population 17,905,000 ●
- ASX float ●
- Dot.com bubble burst ●
- GFC ●
- Ball bombing ●
- Boxing Day tsunami ●
- Lehman Brothers ●

$100K

$50K

LOGARITHMIC SCALE

Growth of $10,000
with no acquisition
costs or taxes and all
income reinvested.

$10K

Inflation

15%
10
5

RBA cuts interest rate 6 times from 7.25% to 3.00% ●●●●-●-●

← Average weekly
earnings $611

← Average weekly
earnings $771

← Average weekly
earnings $980

Connect with Vanguard™

vanguard.com.au

Sources: Australian Bureau of Statistics, Bloomberg Finance L.P, Melbourne Institute of Applied Economic & Social Research, MSCI Inc., Standard & Poor's, WM Reuters. **Notes:** 1. Per annum total returns to 30 June 2024. 2. S&P 500 Total Return Index (in AUD). 3. S&P/ASX All Ordinaries Total Return Index. 4. MSCI World ex-Australia Net Total Return Index AUD Index. 5. S&P/ASX 200 A-REIT Total Return Index. 6. Bloomberg AusBond Composite 0+ Yr Index. 7. Bloomberg AusBond Bank Bill Index. 8. ABS Consumer Price Index. 9. Recessions as defined by the Melbourne Institute of Applied Economic and Social Research. 10. Annualised Rate of Inflation. 11. Interest Rate is the Reserve Bank of Australia's Official Cash Rate. All figures are in Australian dollars. All marks are the exclusive property of their respective owners. **Disclaimer:** This publication contains factual information only that is of a general nature. It does not contain financial product advice. We have not taken your objectives, financial situation or needs into account when preparing the information so it may not be applicable to your circumstances. Vanguard Investments Australia Ltd (ABN 72 072 881 086 AFSL 227263) recommends that, before you make any financial decision about whether to invest in any financial product, you seek professional advice from a suitably qualified adviser. Past performance information is given for illustrative purposes only and should not be relied upon as, and is not, an indication of future performance. This publication was prepared in good faith and we accept no liability for any errors or omissions. © 2024 Vanguard Investments Australia Ltd. All rights reserved. Vanguard Investments Australia Ltd pays a subscription fee to Andex Charts Pty Ltd.
INDPOST_072023

56

Vanguard

Strong and Steady

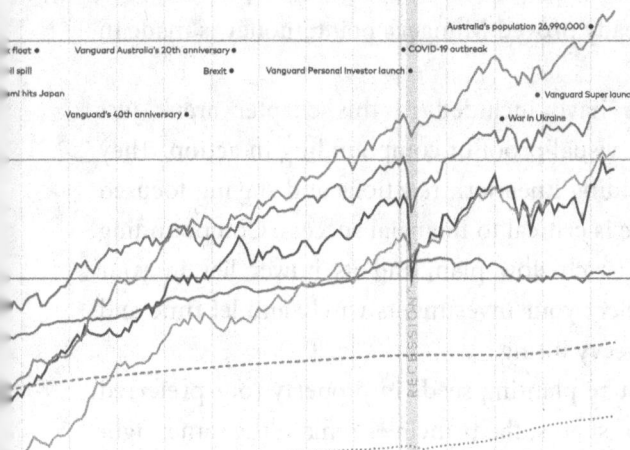

| | 12 | 13 | 14 | 15 | 16 | 17 | 18 | 19 | 20 | 21 | 22 | 23 | 2024 |

Australian Prime Ministers: LLARD · RUDD · ABBOTT · TURNBULL · MORRISON · ALBANESE

U.S. Presidents: OBAMA · TRUMP · BIDEN

U.S. Shares
$237,318 | 11.1% p.a.

Australian Shares
$135,165 | 9.1% p.a.

International Shares
$105,082 | 8.2% p.a.

Australian Listed Property
$94,587 | 7.8% p.a.

Australian Bonds
$51,797 | 5.6% p.a.

Cash
$34,552 | 4.2% p.a.

CPI
$22,428 | 2.7% p.a.

Chart annotations:
- x float
- Vanguard Australia's 20th anniversary
- ll spill
- Brexit
- mi hits Japan
- Vanguard Personal Investor launch
- Vanguard's 40th anniversary
- Australia's population 26,990,000
- COVID-19 outbreak
- Vanguard Super launch
- War in Ukraine
- RECESSION

Returns % per annum		1 Year	5 Years	10 Years	20 Years	30 Years
—	U.S. Shares[1]	24.1	16.2	16.8	10.5	11.1
—	Australian Shares[3]	12.5	7.6	8.3	8.6	9.1
—	International Shares[4]	19.9	13.0	13.1	8.4	8.2
—	Australian Listed Property[5]	24.6	4.4	8.9	5.6	7.8
—	Australian Bonds[6]	3.7	-0.6	2.2	4.3	5.6
--	Cash[7]	4.4	1.6	1.9	3.4	4.2
...	CPI[8]	3.8	3.9	2.7	2.8	2.7

As at 30 June 2024[1]

U.S. dollar: 1.25 / 1.00 / 0.75

Interest rate: 20% / 15 / 10 / 5 / 0

RBA hikes interest rate 13 times from 0.10% to 4.35%

← Average weekly earnings $1,483

Average weekly earnings $1,714

Average weekly → earnings $1,889

Andex Charts Pty Ltd

VANGUARD'S 30-YEAR INDEX CHART

Decades not years

The universal truth is that compounding rewards patience.

Whether you're investing in property, shares, or both, the lesson is clear: time and consistency are your greatest allies. Compounding rewards those who embrace the wait, turning even modest investments into substantial wealth. Each dip on the chart represents a moment when many might have panicked, but those who held steady proved Munger's point: money is made in the waiting.

The charts we have included in this chapter aren't just historical data but visual proof of compounding in action. They highlight why avoiding knee-jerk reactions and staying focused on long-term goals is critical to financial success. Compounding is the ultimate get-rich-slow plan, and its power lies in your commitment to select your investments wisely and let time and discipline do the heavy lifting.

So, whether you're planting seeds in property (our preferred primary vehicle) or shares, the principles remain the same: right assets, stay invested, remain patient, and allow compounding to do its thing!

PLANT A SEED AND WATCH IT GROW

The secret sauce: time

Let's explore further why time is the ultimate weapon in property investing. Take a look at the table below, which shows the value of a $700,000 property growing at a compounding rate of 6% per annum. After 10 years, the property is worth $1,253,593. At 20 years, it hits $2,244,995. And by 30 years, it reaches a staggering $4,020,444.

PROJECTED GROWTH OF A $700K PROPERTY AT 6% ANNUAL GROWTH

Year	Value	Year	Value	Year	Value
1	$742,000	11	$1,328,809	21	$2,379,695
2	$786,520	12	$1,408,538	22	$2,522,476
3	$833,711	13	$1,493,050	23	$2,673,825
4	$883,734	14	$1,582,633	24	$2,834,254
5	$936,758	15	$1,677,591	25	$3,004,310
6	$992,963	16	$1,778,246	26	$3,184,568
7	$1,052,541	17	$1,884,941	27	$3,375,642
8	$1,115,694	18	$1,998,037	28	$3,578,181
9	$1,182,635	19	$2,117,920	29	$3,792,872
10	$1,253,593	20	$2,244,995	30	$4,020,444

Now, this often sparks a few common reactions:

1. 'I can't imagine a $700,000 property ever being worth $4,020,444!'

2. 'Property doesn't grow in a perfect straight line like this every year.'

3. 'Why does every property investment book have one of these tables?'

Let's address these one by one.

1. The mind-boggling growth

It's natural to struggle with the idea of exponential growth, even though history consistently proves it. Ask your grandparents what they paid for their first home – they'll likely tell you they never imagined it would be worth what it is today!

While some people argue that current incomes can't support ever-rising prices, they often overlook a key factor: not all purchases are debt-funded. For example, as Baby Boomers pass down significant wealth, much of it can be reinvested into property.

Also, keep in mind that $4,000,000+ homes already exist in premium suburbs today. Given enough time, it's not such a stretch that we'll see properties in other areas follow a similar trajectory.

2. Growth isn't linear

Property prices typically don't grow in a smooth, linear fashion. As we illustrated in the charts earlier, the journey is often jagged, with ups and downs along the way. The secret is thinking in decades, not years.

3. Another chart? Guilty as charged!

Yep, it's a classic for a reason. Numbers and spreadsheets tell the story of growth best; this example is no exception.

Now, here's the point we really want to drive home: *it's about the decades, not the years.*

Take that same $700,000 property:

- **First decade:** $553,593 in growth. Not bad.
- **Second decade:** $991,401 in growth. Impressive!
- **Third decade:** $1,775,449 in growth. Now, that's extraordinary!

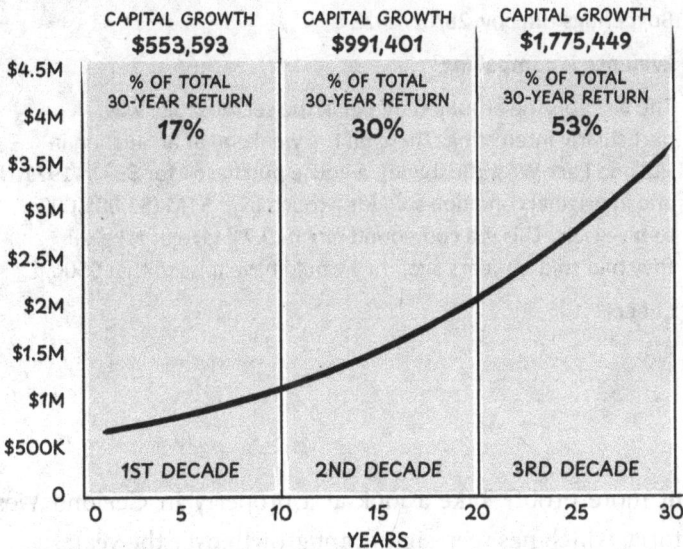

CAPITAL GROWTH $553,593	CAPITAL GROWTH $991,401	CAPITAL GROWTH $1,775,449
% OF TOTAL 30-YEAR RETURN 17%	% OF TOTAL 30-YEAR RETURN 30%	% OF TOTAL 30-YEAR RETURN 53%

THE POWER OF TIME IN PROPERTY GROWTH

Here's the kicker:

- In percentage terms, the first decade gives you 17% of the 30-year growth.
- The second decade delivers 30%.
- The third decade? A whopping 53%!

This is why Charlie Munger said, 'You don't make your money in the buying, you don't make your money in the selling; you make your money in the waiting.' After discussing this concept on Episode 379 of *The Property Couch* podcast, 'Why Time is the Secret Sauce', a listener shared this powerful story:

☆☆☆☆☆

Buggerlugs the boy, 28/02/2022

Evidence is compelling

The last episode around time being the secret sauce was particularly interesting. Then, on the weekend at an auction in Holland Park West [Brisbane], a house purchased for $9k in 1971 and in original condition sold for a touch over $1M ($1,005,000 to be exact). This is a compound rate of 9.7% give or take... if they had sold 10 years ago, they would have missed that $500k!

Cheers

Rob

Want more proof? Take a look at a property in Geelong West, Victoria, which has seen significant growth over the years:

- Sold in 1991 for $54,000
- Sold again in 2002 for $163,000
- Sold in 2012 for $408,000
- Sold in 2022 for $792,500

LONG-TERM GROWTH OF A GEELONG WEST PROPERTY

Date	Sale price	Growth %	Growth $	% of total growth
6 June 1991	$54,000	–	–	–
13 May 2002	$163,000	10.62%	$109,000	14.8%
13 June 2012	$408,000	9.52%	$245,000	33.2%
27 May 2022	$792,500	6.89%	$384,500	52.1%

Here's how the growth played out:

- **First decade:** 15% of its 30-year growth
- **Second decade:** 33%
- **Third decade:** 52%

This example drives home the power of expanding your time horizon.

All successful property investors think in decades, not years. Their language is always about waiting 10 years or more before assessing the outcome of a property. BE – DO – HAVE: if you want to 'BE' a successful investor, then 'DO' what they do, and you 'HAVE' what they have! Commit to the decades game, and you'll harness the undeniable power of compounding growth.

Time is the secret sauce. Let time do the work. Patience isn't just a virtue – it's your greatest asset.

The future

The future of Australia's property market will be shaped by powerful demographic and economic forces. Population growth, housing supply constraints, shifting social dynamics, and the rise of new urban centres will all play a role in defining where and how Australians live in the coming decades.

For investors, understanding these trends today presents an opportunity to position themselves ahead of the curve. With careful planning, strategic investment selections, and a long-term perspective, the changing landscape could unlock significant opportunities for wealth creation and financial security.

Now, let's explore the key forces shaping the future of property in Australia.

Population growth

Unlike many developed nations grappling with stagnant or declining populations, Australia's steady population growth is a defining advantage. As renowned demographer Bernard Salt describes, this is our 'superpower', fuelling economic vitality and sustaining long-term demand for housing.

Despite being one of the world's top economies, Australia's relatively small population presents unique expansion opportunities. More people mean more homes, driving demand and reinforcing market stability. For many immigrants, owning property in Australia is a milestone achievement. This sentiment is captured beautifully in taking the symbolic 'selfie' photo in front of their first Australian home to send back to their family overseas to let them know they've 'made it'!

This consistent influx of new Australians ensures that property remains a fundamental necessity and a culturally significant and resilient asset for decades to come.

Supply constraints: A perfect storm

Post-COVID, Australia faced a perfect storm of record low interest rates and supply constraints – low listing levels, skyrocketing construction costs, building company insolvencies, and labour shortages. Compounding the issue was the reopening of Australia's borders, which triggered a surge in immigration and intensified the demand-supply imbalance. At its core, our immigration policy was out of sync with housing policy, leading to a significant shortfall in available homes.

Picture a bathtub with the tap running nonstop, water spilling over the edges. That's a snapshot of Australia's housing market: relentless demand outpacing limited supply. For those who understand market dynamics, this mismatch presents an opportunity, as it's a challenge unlikely to resolve quickly.

Fixing this issue isn't straightforward either. Tim Reardon, HIA Chief Economist, explained in Episode 512 of *The Property Couch* podcast, 'Solving Australia's Housing Crisis', that addressing supply constraints is like trying to push water uphill. Historically, infrastructure costs for new developments were subsidised by government revenue, making projects more feasible for developers and affordable for buyers. However, today, there is a shift to a user-pays system, which has placed these significant costs – covering utilities and community amenities – on new homeowners already burdened with taxes. This shift has squeezed developers and homebuyers alike, reducing new housing projects, exacerbating rental shortages, and driving prices higher.

For investors, this ongoing imbalance highlights the resilience of residential property as an asset class.

POPULATION GROWTH VS HOUSING SUPPLY

Class divide: A shifting landscape?

Australia has long prided itself on being a society less defined by rigid class systems, unlike parts of Europe, where the feudal system historically drew a clear line between the 'haves' and the 'have-nots'. A significant part of this distinction has been the Great Australian Dream – the idea that homeownership is achievable for anyone willing to put in the effort. Historically, this accessibility has been a cornerstone of Australian life, fostering a sense of equality and opportunity.

Yet, this landscape is shifting. The once-assumed trajectory of homeownership that defined 20th century Australia is no longer guaranteed. Housing affordability is an increasingly pressing concern, and entering the property market has become more challenging. As prices continue to rise, the risk emerges that property ownership could become the defining line of social status – a divide reminiscent of the class systems Australia has worked hard to avoid.

For investors, this shifting landscape serves as a canary in the coal mine – a clear signal to stay ahead of the curve and position yourself proactively before the full impact unfolds. Building a property portfolio while homeownership remains within reach could place you on the right side of this emerging divide. Investing early allows you to capitalise on stability and long-term growth, securing wealth and a strong foothold in a changing economic and social landscape.

The rise of future satellite cities

The future of Australian cities is also changing – our population is growing, and with it comes the need to rethink where and how people live. The question isn't *if* this shift will happen but *how* we handle it when it does. Will our existing cities stretch to accommodate the growth, or will we need entirely new urban hubs to keep up?

As demographer Simon Kuestenmacher highlighted in numerous interviews on the podcast, Australia is at the edge of a transformation. Looking ahead to the 2080s, when the population is expected to double to in excess of 50 million people, he paints a compelling picture: Australians will remain drawn to the coast, driving the development of new and existing urban centres in places like Wollongong, Newcastle, the Central Coast, the Gold Coast, the Surf Coast, and other coastal regions that combine growth potential with a desirable lifestyle.

Here's the challenge: developing these areas requires far more than building a few extra houses. It demands major infrastructure projects – think high-speed rail, upgraded transport networks, and carefully planned housing supply. And it all has to be done sustainably to avoid stretching our current capital cities to breaking point.

This alignment between housing, infrastructure, and migration policies is crucial. If we get it wrong, we'll face worsening housing shortages and affordability pressures. But if we get it right, these future coastal hubs could redefine how Australians live and work – boosting the economy, creating new lifestyle opportunities, and easing the strain on our major cities.

For investors, these emerging satellite cities represent a horizon of potential. With proper planning and forward thinking, they could offer significant long-term opportunities in residential property as Australians seek new spaces to call home.

The key takeaways for the future are clear:

- **Population growth** → Continues to underpin long-term demand.
- **Supply constraints** → Reinforce market stability.
- **Class divide** → Signals emerging exclusivity.
- **Future satellite cities** → Coastal hubs provide expansion outlets for overcrowded major cities.

Part I – Wrap

The foundations: your base camp for wealth

Every climb begins with a strong foundation. Now that yours is in place, you're equipped with the fundamental truths about wealth, lifestyle, and why property is the most powerful vehicle to take you where you want to go.

✓ **The goal:** Wealth without a clear destination is just wandering. Now, you know exactly what you're aiming for – whether that's $1,000, $2,000, or $3,000 a week.

✓ **Lifestyle by design:** It's not about money for money's sake. It's about freedom – to work because you want to, not because you have to.

✓ **Defining wealth:** True wealth isn't just about dollars. It's time, choice, and control over your life.

✓ **The power of property:** No other asset class offers the leverage, stability, and long-term growth of real estate. It's demand-driven, bank-backed, and deeply embedded in Australian wealth creation.

The groundwork is done. You've set up base camp. Now, it's time to climb higher.

In the next part, we move beyond theory and into the Property Investment Formula – your blueprint for building a portfolio that delivers real financial peace.

The summit is still ahead, but you've taken the most important step – starting.

Let's keep climbing.

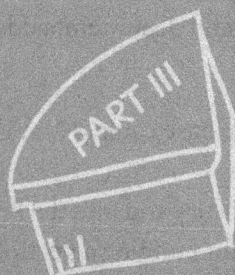

PART II
The Property Investment Formula

When we started teaching property investing, we noticed a recurring challenge: people felt overwhelmed. They didn't know where to start, what to focus on, or how to navigate the maze of property investing without a clear path. It was like trying to solve a puzzle with pieces scattered everywhere. We knew there had to be a better way – something simply organised but powerful that could take the guesswork out of property investing.

That's why we created the Property Investment Formula – a big-picture step-by-step guide to bring clarity and confidence to the process. This formula tells you where to start and what to master. Because the truth is, the secret to property investing success lies in knowing what truly matters and ignoring what doesn't.

Here's the challenge: property investing can feel like a short-term popularity contest driven by hype, trends, and buzzwords like 'hotspots' and 'next big areas'. It's easy to get distracted, chasing quick wins and hoping to ride the wave before it crashes.

Benjamin Graham, the father of value investing, summed it up perfectly: 'In the short term, the market is a voting machine, but in the long term, it's a weighing machine.'

This principle applies just as much to property as it does to shares. In the short term, the market 'votes' for what's hot, but in the long term, it rewards the fundamentals – economic activity, location, infrastructure, and population growth. Smart property investors know the real wins don't come from chasing hype; they come from choosing quality locations (land) and assets that compound value steadily over years and decades.

But here's where most people get stuck: they don't know how to focus on these fundamentals. Property feels confusing, and without a clear structure, it's easy to be swayed by the noise. Enter the Property Investment Formula. It's designed to simplify the process, cut through the mystery, and guide you toward long-term success.

We call it **the ABCD of Property Investing**, a framework built on four critical pillars:

- **A is for asset selection:** Picking the best-suited property in the right location is critical, as well as understanding what types of properties perform best and why they stand the test of time.

- **B is for borrowing capacity:** Finance is the engine behind your portfolio, and knowing how much you can borrow, how to structure loans, and how to optimise your borrowing capacity is crucial for growth.

- **C is for cashflow management:** Effectively managing your income and expenses ensures your investments are sustainable. It's not just about what you earn but what you keep and how you put that surplus to work.

- **D is for defence:** Defence is about protecting what you've built through buffers, insurance, and risk management.

Think of it like a four-legged stool – if you remove just one leg, the whole thing becomes wobbly. Ignore two, and it's bound to topple. A solid investment strategy needs all four pillars firmly in place. Take defence, for instance – one of the most overlooked pillars. Many investors focus on growth and borrowing power but fail to safeguard their portfolios against unexpected challenges (more on that later).

When all four pillars are in place, you create a strategy that's not just strong and stable but built to last. Here's how to approach it: start with cashflow management, then assess your borrowing power in conjunction with your cashflow to determine what you can afford. Next, move to asset selection, and finally, put your defences in place to minimise risk.

This formula turns property investing from a confusing maze into a clear roadmap, keeping you focused on fundamentals and cutting out distractions.

The key is that property investing is a long game. It rewards patience, discipline, and the consistent application of proven principles. Chasing short-term hype might feel exciting, but it rarely leads to lasting success.

The Property Investment Formula is your compass, steering you away from fleeting trends and toward long-term growth. Whether you're just starting out or fine-tuning your strategy, this framework gives you the clarity and confidence to build wealth with purpose.

Let's dive in. It's time to master the ABCD of Property Investing.

Chapter 6

Asset selection

When I (Bryce) bought my first property in 1999 – a three-bedroom apartment in a 110-unit complex in Victoria Park, Perth – I was thrilled to finally be in the game. At 24, it felt like I'd just climbed Everest, hitting a major milestone after dreaming about this moment since I first read *Building Wealth Through Investment Property* by Jan Somers at 19.

Looking back, though, it's definitely not a property I'd buy again. I don't own it anymore, but I still check on its performance from time to time – and over 25+ years, its capital growth has been a disappointing 2.77% per year. Yet, despite being the worst-performing property I've ever bought, I still consider it the best investment decision I've ever made.

Wait… what?! How does that even make sense?

It's simple. Because most people never actually start in the first place, that property got me in the game and set the foundation for everything that followed. I have since gone on to purchase many more properties and build a multi-million-dollar portfolio. But without that first leap of faith, I wouldn't have created the momentum to get where I am today. While most people are Mr or Mrs 'Wait-and-See', I chose to be Mr 'Do-It-Now'.

Sure, it wasn't the best purchase I could've made, but it taught me one of the most valuable lessons in property investing: it's not just about putting your name on a title but putting your name on the *right* title.

When I (Ben) bought my first property at 23 in 1994, I was a complete novice. I paid $120,000 for a 1970s three-bedroom brick house with a games room extension. All I really understood was that property was an appreciating asset over the long term. Its location – just across the road from my mum and dad's house – sealed the deal. They had bought their land in 1971 and built their home for $14,000. Plus, the bonus of home-cooked meals and easy access to Dad's lawnmower didn't hurt!

Fast forward to 2000, I was working in Sydney and looking to buy another property – this time in the Sydney market. Thinking I was doing the right thing, I sought 'professional' property investment advice. I was referred to a local accountant who viewed property primarily through the lens of saving tax rather than long-term price growth. The accountant fixated on *new* stock, emphasising depreciation and negative gearing benefits as ways to reduce tax.

Following the accountant's advice, I sold this Melbourne property, which had become cashflow positive, to avoid paying extra tax. I sold it for $165,000. Today, that property is worth over $850,000, making it a $730,000 mistake – and counting. I didn't need to sell; I could've leveraged its equity, combined with my savings, to purchase the Sydney property instead.

Lesson learned: don't take property investment advice from just anyone – whether it's an accountant, mortgage broker, buyer's agent, or anyone else who may benefit from the transaction. Get organised. Make a detailed, long-term plan tailored to your unique needs – ideally crafted by a Qualified Property Investment Adviser (QPIA). Then, put that plan into action.

There is a silver lining to my story. That mistake motivated me to get better educated and qualified to give property investment advice so others wouldn't have to make the same costly errors.

We're sharing these stories because we want to let you know that we're human, we've made mistakes, and we want to help you avoid making the same ones. We've been there – focused on just getting into the game without fully understanding the importance of asset selection or opportunity cost.

Your goal is to build a portfolio that works hard for you, not just one that looks impressive on paper. It's not about how many properties you own but about owning the right ones. A few high-quality properties, carefully chosen to align with your plan, can easily outperform a dozen mediocre ones.

Too often, we see people caught up in the idea that more is better – chasing property accumulation as if 'he or she who dies with the most properties wins'. But investing isn't about chasing bragging rights. It's about being crystal clear on how many properties you actually need to achieve your goals – no more, no less. Think of it like fishing: the goal isn't to catch as many fish as possible but to catch just enough to feed yourself and thrive.

So, how do you make sure you're choosing the right properties? In this pillar, we'll dive into exactly what you should be looking for to maximise your portfolio's potential. This section will guide you through the fundamentals of asset selection, the types of properties that perform well, and how to align your choices with your financial goals.

Asset selection strategy: growth, balance, or yield?

There's often a fierce debate between two camps: the capital growth champions who see appreciation as the holy grail and the cashflow die-hards who argue that income is king. Both sides have a point, and honestly, we still lean more towards the capital growth camp. Why? Because the power of compounding growth helps build greater equity and then greater income over time as part of our long-term wealth creation plans.

But, as we have matured into 'multi-decade' investors and as property prices have compounded (as predicted), we see more emerging investment opportunities in entry-level locations as another way to achieve suitable investment returns (more on that shortly). Hence, these days, it's not about picking sides; it's about picking the right strategy for you.

Here's the reality: your strategy should be shaped by your unique financial circumstances and capacity to invest safely instead of just someone else's opinion – it's better to be in the game than forever sitting on the sidelines. While chasing growth might look ideal on paper, not everyone can afford the cashflow deficit that often comes with high-growth properties. On the flip side, prioritising cashflow alone might slow down your ability to scale your portfolio. It's not a one-size-fits-all game.

Before we go further, let's clarify something: we're talking about residential property here. While commercial property has its merits for experienced investors, our focus for this book is on residential because of its necessity-driven demand, broad market appeal, and proven track record as a wealth-building vehicle.

So, with that foundation in place, let's explore how we categorise properties into three groups based on the combination of capital growth and rental yield they offer and how they fit into different strategies.

1. **Growth properties:** These are the properties that prioritise capital appreciation over rental yield. For example, you might see returns of 7% growth and 2% yield. They're the heavy lifters in your wealth-building journey, delivering significant

long-term gains. But here's the trade-off: they often run at a cashflow deficit, so you'll need surplus cashflow to hold them. Growth properties are perfect for investors who can afford to play the long game and have the financial capacity to weather short-term costs for big future rewards.

2. **Balanced properties:** Balanced properties offer a sweet spot between growth and yield – something like 4.5% growth and 4.5% yield. They're the steady performers that don't lean too heavily in one direction. If you're looking for capital gains but need a more manageable cashflow, these are your go-to. Balanced properties provide a mix of both worlds, making them ideal for investors who want to grow wealth steadily without over-stretching their finances.

3. **Yield properties (cash cows):** These properties focus on cashflow first, with returns like 5.5% yield and 3.5% growth. They're perfect for investors who need to prioritise income to cover expenses, build buffers, or reduce debt – especially in the later stages of their property journey. While these cash cows won't deliver explosive growth, they bring stability and financial breathing room. They're particularly valuable for retirees or those looking to strengthen their position before diving into higher growth opportunities.

GROWTH   BALANCED   YIELD

Here's the kicker: the total return in each scenario is still 9%. What changes is the composition of that return. Whether you focus on growth, balance, or yield depends entirely on your circumstances – your cashflow position, long-term goals, and risk tolerance.

It's easy to get caught up in the noise of growth evangelists and cashflow fanatics. But as seasoned investors, we remain agnostic. Instead of picking sides, we focus on what delivers the best outcomes for each investor.

The truth is most people jump straight into the doing – making a purchase – without first mapping out the strategy. That's a mistake. Property investing isn't about buying a house and hoping it works out. It's about making sure every purchase fits into your broader plan.

Fail to plan, and you're planning to fail. It's as simple as that. You've got to plan to become what you plan to become.

We'll dive deeper into this in Chapter 8, 'Cashflow management', but for now, keep this in mind: every successful property journey starts with a clear, deliberate roadmap.

Property prices: a balance of supply and demand

Property prices don't rise or fall in isolation – they're shaped by a complex interplay of factors that influence shorter and longer term supply and demand. Since more supply is the enemy of future capital growth, understanding these forces is essential to navigating the property market. By doing so, you can ensure you invest in a market poised to ride a wave of growth rather than risk price stagnation or a downturn in value.

Supply: The push for housing

On the supply side, the availability of new and existing housing significantly impacts the market. Key factors include:

- **Construction activity:** The pace of new housing completions and building approvals signals how quickly supply is increasing.

- **Properties on the market:** Auction and private sale listings reflect current supply levels, helping gauge competition, days on the market, overall stock on the market and the pace at which this stock is being absorbed.

- **Land availability:** Undeveloped or zoned land availability for future subdivision is shaped by policies and planning regulations, directly influencing housing supply.

- **Government regulation:** Planning laws, zoning changes, and infrastructure decisions affect how and where housing supply can be developed and delivered.

- **Taxes and charges:** Government-imposed fees such as development duties and civil works charges, as well as windfall taxes on development and transactions, can deter or disincentivise housing supply.

Demand: The pull for housing

On the demand side, factors like population sizes and movements, buyer capacity, and economic conditions drive competition for available properties. Key drivers include:

- **Local economy:** Strong local economies create jobs, which drives population growth and higher living standards, boosting land and housing demand.

- **Population growth:** Immigration, natural increases, and interstate migration increase the need for housing.
- **Location desirability:** Human behaviours, such as social connection and social status, often concentrate demand in popular areas, creating scarcity and inflating prices.
- **Household size:** Trends like smaller households or multigenerational living influence household composition, which in turn affects the demand for the numbers and types of dwellings required.
- **Relative returns:** From an investor's perspective, comparisons with other investments, like shares or bonds, influence demand.
- **Government regulations:** The more the government tries to control the free market, the greater the impact on confidence and sentiment, which ultimately impacts demand.
- **Taxes and charges:** Policies such as principal place of residence (PPR) capital gains exceptions, negative gearing or capital gains tax concessions can drive housing demand.

Ability to buy: buyer capacity

When we drill a little deeper, we see that demand is also shaped by the financial capacity of buyers, influenced by factors such as:

- **Interest rates:** Lower interest rates improve affordability and increase borrowing power.
- **Regulatory settings:** The Australian Prudential Regulation Authority (APRA) enforces macro-prudential lending measures, such as buffer rates or limits on certain types of lending, which impacts borrowing power and potential access to lending.

- **Tax settings:** Policies such as negative gearing or capital gains tax concessions can drive investor demand.
- **Household income:** Higher income levels boost purchasing power, enabling buyers to compete for higher priced properties.
- **Bank credit policies:** Lender policy settings directly affect borrowing risk tolerance. Some lenders are willing to lend more than others.
- **Funds to complete:** About a quarter of all property purchases in Australia are made in cash, usually by those downsizing, receiving family gifts, or using existing equity releases or inheritances.
- **Tenants in common:** Shared ownership structures, such as buying with family or friends through a joint venture or partnership, impact buying capacity.
- **Government incentives:** Beyond tax incentives, government home building initiatives also influence demand.

Understanding these supply and demand drivers is key to navigating the property market with confidence. By recognising how these forces shape property price movements, you're better positioned to pinpoint markets primed for growth and steer clear of those vulnerable to stagnation or decline.

In the following sections, we'll dive deeper into these dynamics.

Finding the right fit for your strategy

To craft a sustainable and financially rewarding property investment strategy, one of the first steps is deciding which target market and demand cohort you're aiming for. This decision is integral to your investment planning process and is heavily influenced by your cashflow and purchasing power at the time. The key here is choosing the right **investment lens** to apply – either a **prime location lens** or an **entry-level location lens**. Let's explore both in detail.

Prime location lens

This lens focuses on demand driven by the aspirational Australian cohort – those striving for a better life and an improved standard of living, as well as the status and prestige that comes with it. These buyers are drawn to city-fringe living or waterside access locations, where exclusivity, convenience, and lifestyle are premium offerings. They're willing to pay a significant price to secure properties in these areas or to gentrify the next most affordable neighbouring suburb.

- **Key characteristics:** These prime locations are established, high-demand areas with strong owner-occupier appeal. These markets attract those who value lifestyle and location, often creating a 'price taker' environment for investors. Investors in prime location areas should align their expectations with the enduring demand driven by these aspirational buyers.
- **The approach:** Investing through a prime location lens taps into long-term capital growth driven by sustained demand and continuous reinvestment by existing house-proud owners seeking lifestyle and prestige. This ongoing investment pushes underlying land values higher. These locations historically outperform in dollar terms over the long run due to their inherent scarcity and desirability.

Entry-level location lens

This lens caters to first home buyers and budget-conscious cohorts, where demand is driven by affordability and necessity rather than aspirational wants. Although these markets may not have the status, scarcity, and prestige of prime locations, they offer significant opportunities for shorter term growth spikes and higher percentage yields as population increases and the demand for homeownership rises in cyclical waves over time. However, with rapid price spikes, investors must be prepared for longer dormant price periods and the risk of prices occasionally overshooting fair value in the long term.

- **Key characteristics:** Entry-level locations attract demand from two competing groups:
  - First home buyers and price-constrained owner-occupiers who are bottlenecked by affordability.
  - Investors chasing strong yields or quick equity gains to fast-track their next purchase. This supply-demand tension fuels price growth as both sides compete for limited properties. Over the long term, sustained value growth depends on continued population and economic growth. Success in these areas requires strategic timing and a discerning approach to location, land size, and property type selection.
- **The approach:** The important focus here is not on buying new or near new properties but much older established ones, where land value as an overall percentage of what you are buying is key. Strong returns are achieved by evaluating:
  - **Land-to-asset ratios (LAR):** Maximising land value versus building value.

- **Replacement costs:** Comparing the cost of purchasing versus building new.
- **Healthy rental yields:** Ensuring the property offers strong cashflow potential.

Critical filters for entry-level location investments

Once you've chosen an entry-level location, every decision must pass through the following three filters:

1. **Price point:** Stick close to the median price or just below, ensuring most of the value is in the land. Avoid properties priced as the 'best in the worst area'. Instead, target properties with strong land value and/or cosmetic improvement potential. Keep in mind that older properties may require more maintenance, but it's the *land value* you're really investing in.

2. **Limited vacant land:** Prioritise areas with little or no vacant land in established housing estates to avoid competing with new developments. Proximity to new estates can potentially work in your favour, as this new investment in local infrastructure will help lift your land value over time. However, *don't* buy in the new estate – opt for the neighbouring older estate instead, ensuring the price per square metre of land in the new development is at a significant premium to what you're paying.

3. **Age of the estate:** Older estates typically show stronger land appreciation because the improvement on the land (the dwelling itself) depreciates over time. Compared to nearby new stock, older properties offer greater land value bang for your buck.

Why the right lens matters

Choosing the right lens – prime location or entry-level location – sets the foundation for your journey as a property investor. Each approach offers distinct advantages and reasons to take action, but the ultimate decision should reflect your financial capacity, long-term goals, and risk tolerance.

By applying the appropriate lens and integrating critical filters, you can make confident decisions about where to focus your attention in terms of location – something we'll explore next. Remember, investing isn't just about putting your name on a title; it's about selecting the right properties in the right markets at the right time – that is, putting your name on the *right* title!

PRIME
LOCATION

ENTRY-
LEVEL
LOCATION

APPLY THE RIGHT LENS

Location: The heart of property performance

With property investing, one truth stands tall: **location is the engine that drives success**. It's not just a factor – it's *the* factor. For us, location always comes first because, as a simple rule of thumb, it does **80% of the heavy lifting** when it comes to a property's growth potential. The remaining 20%? That comes from the property itself.

This means an average property in a great location will almost always outperform a great property in an average location. It's easy to get caught up in focusing on the property, but that's not where the real value lies most of the time.

Take this example: during the gold rush of the 1860s, Melbourne became a hotbed of development. The proliferation of gold wealth saw stately homes spring up across Victoria – both in Melbourne's now-iconic blue-chip inner urban suburbs and in regional gold-rush townships such as Ballarat, Bendigo, and Castlemaine. Built at the same time, with the same craftsmanship and style, you'd expect these properties to hold similar values today, right? Sadly, this is not true, as these same homes in Ballarat, Bendigo, and Castlemaine now range from $1.5 million to $4 million, while their counterparts in Melbourne's inner suburbs can fetch anywhere between $4 million to $15 million.

Why the difference? Well, the secret lies in the location – not the property itself. This story is a powerful reminder of our 80% rule of thumb that location – proximity, land size, and scarcity – not bricks and mortar, determines a property's long-term value and growth potential.

The point is simple: even if your property isn't the cream of the crop, the right location can elevate its performance. We call this the land value 'drag-up effect'. However, there is a very important exception to this: medium-to-high-density housing often underperforms due to oversupply and reduced land value, which undermines growth. Scarcity matters. Locations where demand consistently exceeds supply will always win out in the long run.

So, what is it about location that is so pivotal? Well, it comes down to understanding the true demand drivers – the factors that shape where people want to live and how much they're willing to pay for it. These drivers fall into three key elements:

1. Economic activity

A strong economy creates work and play opportunities, which attracts more people. Locations with job growth, economic stability, and secure employment will always see higher demand for housing. People need jobs, and jobs drive migration and population growth to specific areas. Generally speaking, the larger and more diverse the economy, the greater the potential for higher incomes, which in turn support stronger land and property values.

2. Human behaviour

This is about the emotional drivers of buyers – particularly owner-occupiers. Human behaviour determines where people aspire to live, influenced by:

- **Status:** Exclusive and desirable locations attract those who seek to reflect their own success. Prestige property is one of the ultimate ways to project this. Just like luxury brands, certain locations carry a cachet that people aspire to be associated with, driving sustained demand over time.

- **Stigma:** Some locations carry a negative 'brand' image due to associations with crime, socioeconomic challenges, or lack of infrastructure. This perception dampens long-term demand as these areas struggle to attract aspirational buyers. Instead, demand tends to be cyclical, driven primarily by affordability rather than desirability.

- **Lifestyle:** Life isn't just about work – people gravitate toward places that align with their lifestyle aspirations and values. A compelling mix of natural and built amenities, convenience, and cultural, sporting, or business hubs create strong demand, drawing like-minded individuals who want to live, work, and play in an environment that reflects their ambitions.

3. Human interest

The benefits and joy of living in a particular area can't be overstated. Features like access to good, high-paying jobs, good schools, transport options, shopping, dining precincts, beaches, sporting and leisure facilities, and green spaces all drive demand.

*

A suburb's demographics – such as its family appeal or aspirational and property-proud residents – can elevate its desirability and growth prospects. When all three align – economic activity, human behaviour, and human interest – you've got the recipe for a winning suburb.

Building on this important point, it's worth noting that, unlike shares where past performance is no guarantee of future results, property offers a more stable narrative. Decades of past performance in property often serve as a reliable indicator of future success. Locations that have historically performed well tend to continue to do so because of three key factors: economic growth, deeply ingrained human behaviour, and enduring human-interest drivers. These elements create sustained demand, which in turn applies consistent upward pressure on property values over the long term. In fact, many suburbs improve over time through gentrification, further bolstering their appeal. Even when a location faces short-term adversity – like a rare, unexpected event that temporarily affects its reputation – strong fundamentals usually win out, and the suburb returns to its growth trajectory over time.

Investing based on familiarity rather than fundamentals is a common trap. The reality is that opportunity doesn't always lie in your own backyard. By applying the location learnings outlined above and embracing the concept of borderless investing – researching locations across Australia irrespective of where you live – you can access areas with superior growth drivers, stronger yields, or better overall fundamentals. Why settle for 'average' in your local area when better opportunities are available elsewhere? Property investing isn't about staying local; it's about achieving the best possible results, with the lowest possible risk.

Focus on the location drivers, and you're already 80% of the way there.

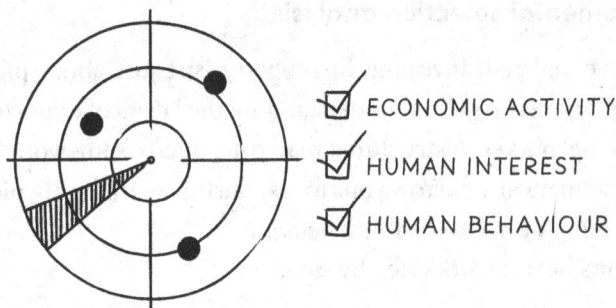

ECONOMIC ACTIVITY

HUMAN INTEREST

HUMAN BEHAVIOUR

THE 3 DEMAND DRIVERS OF A WINNING LOCATION

Property research

When it comes to property research, there are two distinct approaches: **long-term fundamental analysis** and **short-term technical analysis**. The philosophy we've adopted in our own investing and in the property advisory work we do for our clients centres on the premise that we are investing for decades and not chasing quick wins. That's why we prioritise **fundamental analysis – a macro-to-micro framework** that uncovers areas with strong long-term potential.

That said, short-term trends still play a role. By overlaying **technical analysis**, such as demand versus supply, we can help identify potential short-term waves of demand pressure in comparison to supply. However, a word of caution: a lot of new property spruikers focus solely on short-term trends to make their strategies sizzle. The problem? Short-term gains can quickly evaporate if the long-term location fundamentals are weak, so beware.

In the following sections, we'll unpack how both approaches – fundamental and technical – shape a robust property investment strategy.

Fundamental selection analysis

As we've covered, investing in property isn't just about picking the right house; it's about understanding the layers of opportunity within the market. A structured macro-to-micro framework helps you systematically narrow your focus, starting with the big picture and drilling down to the finest details.

Here's how it works step by step:

1. **Australia:** Start at the national level, analysing the federal government's agenda on economic policy, taxes, regulations,

infrastructure spending, housing policy and incentives, as well as immigration policies and trends on where new arrivals are settling. Additionally, consider other macro settings such as housing approvals, lending activity and conditions, interest rates, and the interplay between these factors and national consumer and business sentiment, as they collectively influence overall economic activity.

2. **State:** Next, evaluate the performance of individual states (or territories) with the macro-economic lens. Consider factors such as overall current economic performance, i.e. Gross State Product (GSP). Where is the future economic growth going to come from? What is the population story? What is the employment story? How much debt do they have to pay off? What are the state taxes and charges like? What is the state government doing to attract new business and investment to grow the economic pie? Focusing on property – what rules and regulations are currently in place for property investment, e.g. rental laws and minimum property standards? Broadly speaking, where is the state's property cycle at? What incentives (if any) are being offered to attract property investors to run their small private rental accommodation businesses?

3. **City/town:** Focus on economic performance by examining the diversity of industries and businesses, as well as the wage profiles they offer. Assess climate – extreme weather event risk. How much job demand exists, and what does the current unemployment story look like? For towns, assess their location in relation to larger employment centres – is it within a commutable distance? Also, analyse the population trend and the demographic breakdown, including age and housing profiles.

Shift the focus to the demand versus supply story. What stage of the property cycle is this market in? Evaluate the levels of stock on the market and how quickly that stock is being absorbed. Who or what is driving this demand? What human behaviour or interests make this property market attractive today and into the future?

4. **Suburb:** It is time to move beyond the economic activity and government influences and focus on human (buyer) behaviour and interests, aligning this with your investment strategy. Are you looking through a prime or entry-level location lens? Dive deeper into suburb selection by exploring demand drivers such as status, lifestyle, infrastructure, affordability, scarcity, available supply, and underlying demand. Key factors include amenities, school zones, transport access, proximity to shops and cafes, commutability to job centres, access to knowledge-based or higher-wage jobs, and the overall community vibe. On the property front, consider land sizes, dwelling profiles, and historical performance. By understanding who lives in a suburb and why, you can better assess its growth and rental potential.

5. **Street:** Here's where precision truly matters – not all streets are created equal. Factors like elevation, street appeal, flood risk, accessibility, orientation, traffic, parking availability, noise levels, and housing stock consistency can all impact a property's long-term performance. The key is to sift through A, B, and C-grade streets and steer clear of the Cs. These details can be the difference between an average investment and a high-performing asset.

6. **Property:** At this level, evaluate the individual property itself. Consider its historical growth, land size, land-to-asset

ratio, liveability, floor plan, flood risk, easements, character, charm, uniqueness, overall condition, owner-occupier buyer appeal, and how it compares in desirability to other properties in the local market.

7. **Due diligence:** Before purchasing, conduct thorough due diligence. Examine zoning laws, obtain building inspections, review building permits, and assess potential risks. Ensure you understand any conditions related to the property's future maintenance and upkeep.

8. **Negotiation:** Finally, secure the property through effective negotiation. Ensure the price aligns with your criteria, the current market conditions, recent comparable property prices, and your overall strategy and budget.

This step-by-step approach ensures a logical, methodical path for property selection – from the national outlook right down to the finer details of your purchase.

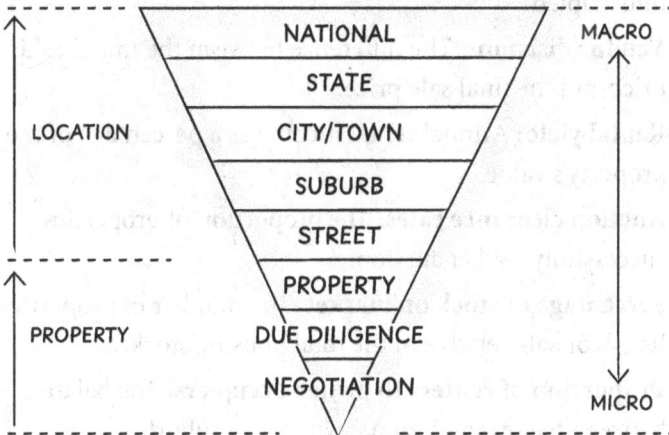

ASSET SELECTION FRAMEWORK

Technical selection analysis: Current demand versus supply

Our technical analysis is powered by extensive data collection. Each month, we gather millions of data points to evaluate variables and indicators that highlight potential demand-supply imbalances. This analysis spans cities, towns, local government areas (LGAs), suburbs and even street mass-block clusters, assessing both houses and units.

To make more informed decisions, we prioritise certain variables over others, combining them to score each market in detail. This approach provides the confidence that short-term indicators align with our longer term fundamental assessments. To give you a clearer picture, here's a summary of some of the key short-term technical indicators we evaluate:

1. **Days on market:** The average time properties remain listed for sale.
2. **Vacancy rate:** The percentage of rental properties that are unoccupied.
3. **Vendor discount:** The difference between the initial asking price and the final sale price.
4. **Rental yield:** Annual rental income as a percentage of the property's value.
5. **Auction clearance rates:** The proportion of properties successfully sold at auction.
6. **Percentage of stock on market:** The number of properties listed for sale relative to the total housing stock.
7. **Proportion of renters to owner-occupiers:** The balance between tenants and homeowners in a suburb.
8. **Online search interest:** The level of online search activity compared to available listings.

Each indicator is weighted based on its significance and combined to generate a demand versus supply score for each suburb we analyse. A higher score signals stronger demand relative to supply, suggesting a greater likelihood of short-term price growth, while a lower score indicates potential price declines.

If you'd like to see our technical analysis in action, where we illustrate our demand versus supply score for these and other indicators, along with other rich demographic and housing data, you can download a FREE report for any suburb in Australia at thepropertycouch.com.au/propertyreport.

It's all about stacking the odds in your favour. A methodical, step-by-step approach – combining both fundamental and technical analysis – gives you the best chance of securing a sound property in a strong location. At the very least, it helps you avoid a poor property or location selection. And reducing risk is what it's all about, which leads us to another powerful strategy: building in a **margin of safety** – a buffer that not only protects you but could also amplify your future returns.

Margin of safety: Your investment buffer

The concept of margin of safety, first introduced by Benjamin Graham in his seminal works *Security Analysis* (1934, co-authored with David Dodd) and *The Intelligent Investor* (1949), emphasises building a safety net into both short- and long-term investment decisions. Instead of merely chasing upside potential, the focus is on actively mitigating risk from the outset. The critical question to continually ask is: 'Is there a margin of safety in this decision?'

This principle becomes even more vital when helping others invest. Managing your own risks and rewards is one thing, but when advising others – as we do – the responsibility to safeguard against potential downsides takes on an added dimension of importance. That's where this concept of margin of safety truly stands out and why it is such a critical component of long-term value investing.

Understanding productive use of land

Understanding margin of safety becomes easier when you consider the productive use of land. In Episode 418 of *The Property Couch*, 'The Hidden Forces Driving Property Values', we explained the seven types of land use in Australia, ranked from least to most valuable:

1. **Desert land:** With minimal rainfall and a poor vegetation profile, this land has virtually no productive use, making it of very low value.

2. **Semi-arid land:** Limited rainfall and sparse vegetation make this land suitable mainly for extensive cattle farming, resulting in low per-acre value due to its restricted agricultural potential.

3. **Broad acre farming land:** Regular rainfall and suitable soil provide potential for commercial use, supporting large-scale grain, crop, and grazing activities. This type of land is recognised for its higher productivity and value.

4. **High-intensity farming land:** High rainfall and fertile soil enable intensive farming activities, such as vegetable cultivation and high-intensity beef farming, yielding greater outputs and commercial value.

5. **Rural hobby lot:** Smaller plots within driving distance of urban centres, often used for light farming and lifestyle purposes. These lots combine residential and productive appeal.

6. **Lifestyle lots:** These lots, located closer to urban fringes, offer privacy, proximity to services, and lifestyle benefits. Their urban accessibility and amenity appeal significantly enhance their value.

7. **Residential lots:** These include land for single dwellings, as well as options for higher productive use like townhouses and medium- to high-density developments. They represent the highest value due to their location in densely populated areas, ensuring proximity to infrastructure and economic hubs, and scarcity-driven investment return potential for developers.

Here's where it gets interesting for investors: the transition of land from lower value use to higher value use – such as farmland becoming residential lots – is where value is created. However, once a property's productive use has been maximised – like converting a single house into multiple townhouses or high-density apartments – there's little room left for further enhancement, reducing the margin of safety.

Investing in properties with potential for future productive use, such as a single dwelling on a potential future sub-dividable lot, provides a crucial buffer and a future value-added opportunity. In contrast, properties where all potential has already been extracted, such as high-density apartments, lack a healthy land-to-asset ratio and opportunities for adding value, ultimately eroding the margin of safety.

Why margin of safety matters

Most first-time investors overlook the margin of safety, often because they are overwhelmed by emotions and inexperience or seduced by new and shiny offerings. To emphasise its importance,

Warren Buffett, an avid student of Benjamin Graham, says it best: 'On the margin of safety… don't try and drive a 9,800-pound truck over a bridge that says "Capacity: 10,000 pounds". Go down the road a little bit and find one that says "Capacity: 15,000 pounds".'

That's clear.

But let's drive the point home with a property example. Who really wins in the productive use and margin of safety battle when a developer maximises every inch of land, and you buy their finished product? It's them, not you. They've extracted all the value – leaving you with minimal land component and virtually no margin of safety. The upside has already been realised… just not by you.

New versus established

One of the most important decisions you'll make – as you just glimpsed in margin of safety – is choosing between brand-new and established property. Why? While shiny new builds are often marketed as the ultimate investment – offering tax benefits, depreciation claims, and modern finishes – the reality is they rarely stack up for long-term wealth creation. It's the difference between buying **investment stock** and securing **investment-grade property**.

There's a whole industry out there pushing new properties (more on that later), often prioritising sales targets over your needs. Our goal is simple: to help you cut through the white noise and make informed decisions that align with your goals – not someone else's.

All things being equal, a new property simply can't outperform an older property mathematically. Let's break this down with a simple example using two comparable properties – each with four bedrooms, two bathrooms, and two car spaces. One is an established property, the other brand new. Now, let's dissect their values into **land** (the appreciating asset) and **improvements** (the building on the land, which depreciates).

Property #1 – Established	Property #2 – Brand new
Value: $650,000 Land value: $450,000 Improvements (building): $200,000	Value: $650,000 Land value: $300,000 Improvements (building): $350,000

What do we know about property? Land appreciates, and improvements depreciate.

Now, let's fast forward 10 years. Assume the **land value** has appreciated by 6% per annum while the **improvements** (the building itself) have 'technically' depreciated by 25% over this period.

So, how has each property performed? Let's break it down.

Property #1 – Established	Property #2 – Brand new
Value: $955,881 Land value: $805,881 Improvements (building): $150,000	Value: $799,754 Land value: $537,254 Improvements (building): $262,500

- Total technical value growth for Property 1 = $305,881 or 47%
- Total technical value growth for Property 2 = $149,754 or 23%

Even factoring in the additional maintenance costs of the older property, the overall return is still far superior – simply because of the stronger land value component at the time of purchase. **Land does the heavy lifting, and that's where the real wealth is built.**

By understanding the differences between new and established properties, you can avoid the trap of **investment stock** – properties built to be sold, not to perform – and instead focus on securing **investment-grade property** that drives long-term, sustainable success.

Investment-grade property

When deciding on an investment-grade property, we also evaluate every choice through three critical filters:

1. **Scarcity:** A scarce property stands out in the market because of its unique appeal – whether it is location, architectural charm, or limited availability. Scarcity creates a dynamic where demand outpaces supply, fuelling long-term price growth. But scarcity isn't just about today; its real value lies in future desirability. Will the property remain sought after as market trends evolve? Properties in tightly held suburbs or those with distinctive, hard-to-replicate features often capture this enduring scarcity.

2. **Owner-occupier appeal:** Owner-occupiers are usually the long-term price makers in a sound market, and they drive demand based on emotion, lifestyle aspirations, and long-term goals. A property that appeals to owner-occupiers will often experience more consistent price growth than one targeted solely at investors.

3. **Investment worthiness:** An investment-worthy property has two key features:

    a. **Proven growth history:** A track record of capital growth confirms the property's potential to perform over time if the economic growth fundamentals also remain sound.

    b. **High land-to-asset ratio (LAR):** As we just highlighted, the majority of the property's value lies in its land, which appreciates, rather than the building, which depreciates.

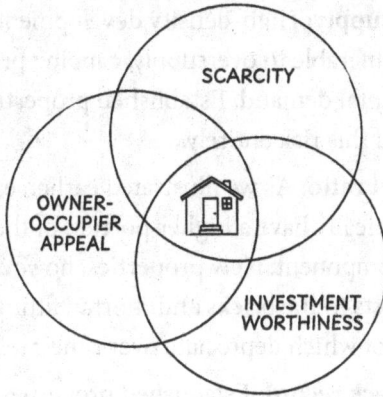

THE INVESTMENT-GRADE PROPERTY SWEET SPOT

By filtering investment opportunities through these criteria and the investment lenses described earlier, new properties consistently fall short. Here's why:

· **Scarcity factor:** New properties lack uniqueness, particularly in high-density developments or new house-and-land estates, where hundreds of identical properties saturate the market. This oversupply limits demand and stifles growth potential.

- **Location stability:** Established properties are typically located in areas with well-established infrastructure – schools, transport, shops, and lifestyle amenities that reliably drive demand and underpin long-term value. In contrast, new properties are often positioned in 'emerging' suburbs with developing infrastructure and abundant greenfield supply. While marketers promote these as 'growth' suburbs, they 'forget' to highlight that this refers to population growth, not capital growth – a crucial distinction for investors seeking sustainable returns.

- **Risk of oversupply:** High-density developments and new estates are vulnerable to oversupply, capping price growth and weakening rental demand. Established properties in built-out suburbs avoid this risk entirely.

- **Land-to-asset ratio:** As we illustrated earlier, established properties typically have a higher portion of their value tied to the land component. New properties, however, allocate significant costs to the bricks and mortar, fittings, and finishes – all of which depreciate over time.

- **Historical track record:** Established properties have a proven performance history you can back-test and judge, whereas new properties lack any re-sale market testing or track record, making it a blind date at best.

- **Developer margins:** New properties often carry inflated prices due to marketing costs, buyer incentives, and developer profits. This 'new premium' is like the higher price paid for a brand-new car that is no longer new once you drive it off the lot.

- **Depreciation:** While new properties offer short-term tax benefits through depreciation, this is a false economy. Again, buildings depreciate, tax benefits fade, and you're left with hope that it won't lose value.

While new properties may attract owner-occupiers, they rarely meet the mark for sensible investment. If you're focused on building a high-performing, wealth-generating portfolio, investment-grade properties – not just investment stock – are where the real opportunities lie. That's why, both personally and professionally, we continue to champion established properties as the smarter choice for long-term success.

Houses versus units

The debate between houses and units is timeless. Each offers distinct advantages and drawbacks, and the right choice depends on your goals, financial position, and the specific market you're targeting.

The primary difference lies in the nature of the asset: houses typically come with exclusive land ownership, while units are part of a larger complex with shared ownership of common areas.

As with most investment decisions, the details matter. We'll break down the pros and cons of each.

Key benefits of investing in houses

- **Higher land-to-asset ratio (LAR):**
  - Houses derive much of their value from the land they sit on, which appreciates over time.
  - A higher land-to-asset ratio provides a margin of safety, ensuring long-term value regardless of the property's age.
- **Opportunities for adding value:**
  - Houses allow for renovations, extensions, or redevelopment (increase in productive use) to actively increase their value.
  - Projects like subdividing land or adding a granny flat can create additional income streams.

- **Owner-occupier appeal:**
  - Houses attract owner-occupiers, who are the price makers in the property market. Their demand drives steady price growth.
  - Families, in particular, value the space, privacy, and lifestyle benefits houses offer.
- **Flexibility of use:**
  - Houses can be used for residential living, rental income, or even business purposes, subject to zoning regulations.
- **Greater privacy:**
  - Standalone houses provide more privacy and freedom compared to units, which involve shared walls, common areas, and strata management.
- **Superior perceived status:**
  - Broadly speaking, owning a house carries more social status and significance than owning an apartment does, which helps underpin some of its demand factor.
- **Margin of safety protections:**
  - Because the productive use of the land typically hasn't yet been fully realised, houses with land can offer higher levels of protection.
- **Complete control:**
  - Decisions about the land and its improvements, such as repairs and upgrades, rest entirely with the owner.

Challenges of investing in houses

- **Higher price point:**
  - Houses usually require a larger upfront investment, making them less accessible for first-time buyers or budget-conscious investors.

- Higher prices also translate to larger loans and greater financial risk if cashflow isn't managed well.

- **Increased maintenance costs:**
  - As the sole owner, you are responsible for all maintenance, repairs, and upgrades.

- **Lower rental yields:**
  - Houses often generate lower rental yields compared to units, impacting cashflow.

- **Affordability in prime locations:**
  - Houses in high-demand urban areas can be prohibitively expensive, limiting opportunities to invest in prime locations.

- **Higher land taxes:**
  - Depending on which state your house is in, the land value portion, compared to an apartment land portion, will always bear a higher land tax cost.

Key benefits of investing in units

- **Lower entry point:**
  - Units are generally more affordable, making them ideal for first-time investors or those with smaller budgets.
  - This lower price point also reduces financial exposure and loan obligations.

- **Higher rental yields:**
  - Units tend to deliver stronger rental yields, providing better cashflow.

- **Prime urban locations:**
  - Units are often located in city centres or high-demand suburbs with access to amenities, public transport, and employment hubs.

- Their proximity to lifestyle features ensures consistent rental demand.
- **Reduced maintenance responsibilities:**
  - Strata management takes care of common areas, reducing the maintenance burden on individual owners.
- **Lifestyle appeal:**
  - Units in premium complexes with amenities like pools, gyms, and concierge services can attract tenants willing to pay a premium.
- **Lower or no land tax:**
  - Lower land value restricts or removes the obligation to pay land tax, depending on the state/territory.
- **Potential exclusivity (margin of safety):**
  - Rather than deriving value from the productive use of land, exclusivity can act as a margin of safety. This comes in the form of tightly held or protected locations that cannot be built out – think absolute beachfront, properties overlooking significant landmarks, or areas safeguarded by strict planning overlays and regulations.

Challenges of investing in units

- **Lower land component:**
  - Units have a much smaller land-to-asset ratio, tying less of their value to appreciating land. This limits future productive use and may limit their long-term growth prospects.
- **Risk of oversupply:**
  - High-density developments are particularly vulnerable to oversupply, which can cap price growth and reduce rental demand.

- **Strata fees:**
  - Unit owners must pay strata fees for the maintenance of common areas, which can eat into rental income.
  - Special levies for major repairs or upgrades may add unexpected costs.
- **Limited customisation:**
  - Strata by-laws restrict the ability to renovate or add value to units, limiting opportunities to manufacture capital growth.
- **Slower capital growth:**
  - Units typically experience slower capital growth than houses.
- **Limited control and decision-making:**
  - Decisions about common property, repairs, and upgrades are made collectively by the owners' corporation, which means individual unit owners have limited influence. Disputes or inefficiencies within the owners' corporation can delay important decisions and increase costs, reducing overall control.

So, which one should you buy?

Think about it this way: ask a Baby Boomer what they picture as the Great Australian Dream, and they'll likely describe a detached house on a quarter-acre block, surrounded by a garden with a Hills Hoist and BBQ in the backyard. Contrast that with Millennials, who've grown up with apartment living normalised by U.S. sitcoms like *Friends* and *Seinfeld*. To them, it's no longer, 'Jack and Jill went up the hill to fetch a pail of water'; it's more like, 'Jack and Jill went down the lift to fetch a babycino'. Times have changed, but how does this shape property investment decisions?

Well, let's look at the facts. The figure below shows that houses have outperformed units over the long term – a result that complements our filters of scarcity, owner-occupier appeal, and investment worthiness.

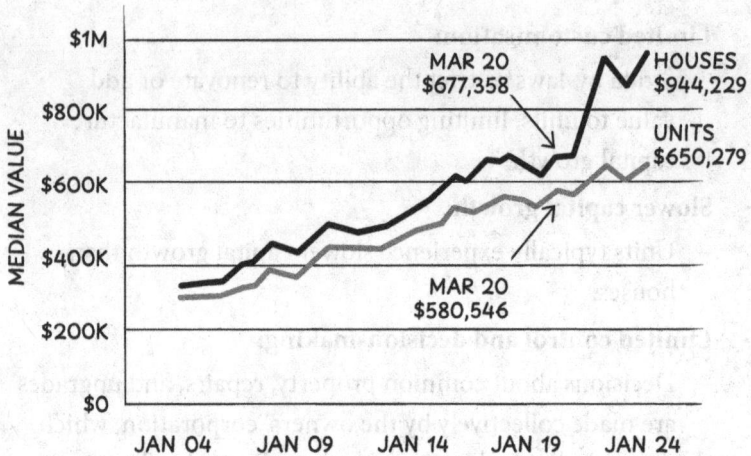

MAR 20
$677,358

HOUSES
$944,229

UNITS
$650,279

MAR 20
$580,546

MEDIAN VALUE

$1M
$800K
$600K
$400K
$200K
$0

JAN 04   JAN 09   JAN 14   JAN 19   JAN 24

COMBINED AUSTRALIAN CAPITAL CITIES

Does this mean units are a bad investment? Not necessarily. For some, units represent the most realistic way to enter the property market.

Our take is clear: wherever possible, buy an established house. Houses align more closely with long-term growth fundamentals and the key drivers of price performance.

If you can't buy a house in an investable location, explore a townhouse or villa unit within your budget and within your identified purchase area(s). Note: property terminology varies across Australia – what's called a villa in one state might be a unit or flat in another. The best rule of thumb? Prioritise land content and opt for properties with fewer dwellings on the same land lot to maximise scarcity and value.

However, if purchasing a unit is your best option to get you diversified exposure into a significant capital city market in a great location, ensure it still meets our critical filters: scarcity, owner-occupier appeal, and investment worthiness. Focus on buying only in prime locations to maximise your chances of success. For entry-level areas, we generally advise against buying a single unit, but we would consider acquiring an entire apartment block under the right circumstances.

It's rare that buying property results in the perfect purchase – it's a balancing act. To help you navigate compromises, use the Buyer's Decision Quadrant framework, which we'll cover next.

The Buyer's Decision Quadrant

The Buyer's Decision Quadrant, introduced on *The Property Couch* in Episode 20, 'Science of Asset Selection – The Buyer's Decision Quadrant', is our framework designed to help you strategically navigate the inevitable trade-offs you'll face when buying a property. Unless your budget is limitless, a 'best-suited' approach means compromises are unavoidable, and this quadrant provides clarity to make informed decisions that align with your goals.

The Buyer's Decision Quadrant breaks the decision into four key areas.

1. Price

Unless you're fortunate enough to inherit wealth or win the lottery, price is often the most immovable piece of the puzzle. Most buyers work within a budget dictated by their borrowing capacity, savings, and current financial situation. This sets the boundaries for what's realistically achievable. If the price is fixed – and for most people, it is – then compromises must be made elsewhere in the quadrant.

2. Location

'Location, location, location' isn't just a cliché; we've reinforced it as the cornerstone of property investing and established that it does 80% of the heavy lifting. That's why, when it comes to making trade-offs, location is usually the last thing buyers want to compromise on, with other factors being more flexible.

3. Size of the land

As you've been learning, land is the foundation of long-term value, but when price and location are relatively fixed, land content is often the first area where compromises begin. Will you settle for a smaller block, or will you consider a townhouse or even an apartment? With rising urban density, the dream of a sprawling backyard may need to be re-evaluated. The size and usability of the land component remain critical, but flexibility here often becomes necessary.

4. Quality of the dwelling

Finally, we come to the dwelling itself – the physical property you're buying. What level of quality are you willing to accept? This is where many compromises take place, starting with the type of property and working down to its condition. How much 'property' are you getting for your money? The vision of an ideal home – whether it's a specific property type or the allure of shiny new taps and a turnkey-ready finish – often shifts toward a more practical mindset. You might find yourself considering DIY projects or even major renovations. For many, the priority is securing the right location and land size while accepting a property that needs work. A less-than-perfect property in a great location will often outperform a pristine home in a poor location – making this one of the most common and impactful trade-offs.

WHICH ONE ARE YOU WILLING TO COMPROMISE ON?

Buying a property is an emotional journey, and it's easy to let excitement cloud judgment. That's why understanding the Buyer's Decision Quadrant before you start shopping is crucial – it prepares you for the compromises you'll face and prevents emotional hooks from derailing your investment decisions.

Deciding in advance which factors are non-negotiable and where you're willing to compromise removes much of the on-the-spot anxiety. It helps you make trade-offs confidently – whether it's on price, location, land content, or dwelling quality. This clarity reduces stress, curbs emotional decisions, and ensures your purchase aligns with your goals and financial capacity.

Why it matters to investors

The Buyer's Decision Quadrant is just as vital for investors as it is for homeowners. The difference? Investors have a clear endgame: building wealth and achieving financial freedom. If you prioritise location (as we've emphasised earlier), your investment decisions will be sharper and more focused.

This framework helps investors eliminate emotions and stay grounded, even when budgets are tight. It prevents them from chasing properties with higher land components in poor locations, and reinforces why location drives better long-term performance.

When using this framework, you'll explore various combinations and trade-offs, as your budget will inevitably limit your options in some way. If you feel uncertain or overwhelmed, that's perfectly normal. Stay focused on your plan, revisit the data, and, if needed, consider enlisting the help of a buyer's agent to overcome any procrastination or analysis paralysis and move forward confidently.

When approaching a purchase as an investor, remember: you're not the one living there. Your tenants simply need a safe, clean, and quiet property to enjoy. This means 'clean and tidy' can often be sufficient. However, it's important to factor in maintenance and upkeep for older properties – it's a given, and planning for these costs is essential to your strategy and budget.

By using the Buyer's Decision Quadrant, you're making decisions based on strategy, not emotion. But even the best property means nothing if you can't fund it.

*

The next pillar of mastery is borrowing power – the fuel that keeps your investment journey moving.

Chapter 7

Borrowing power

Property investing isn't just about bricks and mortar; it's a game of finance. As we often remind people, the key to long-term success in property investment lies not just in the physical properties themselves but in mastering financial strategies. We recently spoke to a client, Anthony, who's built an impressive portfolio, who summed it up perfectly: 'The more I invest, the more I realise property investing is less about real estate and more about lending.'

This mindset shift is crucial. While the properties are the visible pieces on your board that help you win the game, the gamification happens behind the scenes – loan structures, cashflow management, and borrowing strategies. And just like chess, the best players are always thinking two or three moves ahead. Each decision you make today – whether it's how you structure your loans or how you leverage equity – sets up your next move. It's not just about winning the moment; it's about positioning yourself to win the game.

One of the most important lessons in this game is understanding the different types of debt and how they impact your financial future. Most people grow up believing all debt is bad, but as they learn more, they graduate to the idea that there's good debt and bad debt. However, we have an alternative perspective that brings greater clarity – one that's critical for building wealth. It revolves around defining three distinct types of debt.

THREE TYPES OF DEBT

Let's break them down:

1. **Horrible debt:** This is debt incurred for consumer items and things that lose value over time – credit cards, personal loans, or store finance debt. It's the kind of debt you want to avoid at all costs because it takes you further from your financial goals.

2. **Tolerable debt:** This is the mortgage on your family home. It's tolerable because you're carrying this debt alone, with no financial assistance, but it serves an essential need as well as being a stepping stone toward greater financial security.

3. **Productive debt:** This is the golden ticket. Productive debt is incurred to acquire income-producing assets, such as investment properties, that appreciate in value over time. This type of debt is a tool for wealth creation, enabling you to leverage your borrowing power to generate returns far beyond what you could achieve by simply saving.

The story of two boys in the playground captures this concept perfectly. One boy sat on a bench crying. When his concerned friend asked what was wrong, he said, 'We're so poor – we owe the bank $50,000.' The other boy grinned and replied, 'Well, we're so rich… we owe the bank $5,000,000!' The difference? It's all about the type of debt you carry. Productive debt, when used wisely, can unlock incredible opportunities.

This is why having an investment-savvy mortgage broker on your team is non-negotiable. Think of them as the anaesthetist in the operating room. When your portfolio's health is at stake, you want a specialist who understands exactly what's required to keep things running smoothly – not a generalist who might unintentionally put you on life support. Their expertise ensures your borrowing power is optimised with productive debt when investing.

Ultimately, property investing is a game of finance, strategy, and foresight. Ignore this truth at your own peril. Embrace it, and you're moving towards mastery.

The changing landscape of property investment

In the early 2000s, building an extensive property portfolio was surprisingly straightforward for those willing to take the risk. Investors leveraged lenient lending conditions, including low-doc and no-doc loans, which allowed for minimal regulatory oversight and greater financial flexibility. These loans were particularly popular among self-employed individuals and small business owners who lacked traditional income documentation.

Low-doc loans allowed borrowers to provide alternative proof of income, such as business activity statements (BAS), business bank statements, or an accountant's declaration, instead of full tax returns or payslips. While these loans required a larger deposit (typically 20% or more), they enabled rapid portfolio expansion.

Even more flexible were no-doc loans, which required little to no proof of income, relying instead on the borrower's credit history and property equity. While these loans came with higher interest rates and stricter terms, they made it possible for investors to acquire properties with minimal financial disclosure.

Fast forward to today, and the story is entirely different. Regulatory changes now prioritise financial stability and responsible lending practices, significantly reducing access to debt. Low-doc loans remain available but under stricter conditions, while no-doc loans have largely disappeared from the market. As a direct consequence, the bar for property investors has been raised. Strategies that once seemed easily replicable have become far more challenging to execute, requiring a greater focus on financial planning, income verification, and long-term stability.

How APRA transformed the lending landscape

The Australian Prudential Regulation Authority (APRA) has been pivotal in reshaping lending practices and implementing policies designed to protect the financial system. As a result, these measures aim to mitigate the risk of further rapid property price growth. These macro-prudential measures have fundamentally altered how investors approach financing:

- **Serviceability buffers:** Since 2021, lenders must assess borrowing capacity with a 3% buffer above the current interest rate. This adjustment has notably reduced borrowing power, sometimes making it feel like driving with the handbrake on.

- **Investor and interest-only loan restrictions:** Temporary caps on investor loan growth and the proportion of interest-only lending reshaped loan offerings. While these restrictions were eventually lifted, they ushered in tighter scrutiny and higher rates for these products, creating lasting effects, and there are no guarantees they won't use these types of policies again in the future.

- **Focus on responsible lending:** Today's lending environment involves mortgage brokers having to undertake thorough assessments of borrowers' financial situations, including existing debts and living expenses. While these measures promote financial responsibility, they also make securing multiple properties far more challenging.

The path forward

The takeaway is clear: the lending landscape is ever-changing, and getting ahead requires staying informed and flexible. Building a portfolio in today's regulatory environment demands more than just ambition – it calls for mastering this financial pillar of borrowing.

By understanding how lending policies evolve and leveraging smart strategies, you can position yourself to overcome hurdles and continue building wealth through property.

Strategy versus capacity

For most aspiring property investors, the first question is, 'How much can I borrow right now?' This focus on borrowing capacity makes sense – it's the starting point for planning your next move. But professional investors take it further. They shift their focus from borrowing capacity to borrowing strategy.

Borrowing capacity is a snapshot in time. It's what you can borrow today based on your current income, expenses, and lender policies. However, borrowing strategy is like the chess game we referred to earlier. Without a well-thought-out borrowing strategy, you risk blocking yourself with glass ceilings, unable to grow your portfolio later.

This is where an investment-savvy mortgage broker becomes essential. Unlike brokers or banks who focus solely on securing your immediate loan or finding the lowest interest rate, an investment-focused broker takes a portfolio-wide approach. They understand that today's loan structure has a direct impact on your ability to expand your portfolio tomorrow.

The key differences

1. **Standard brokers or direct-to-bank lending:** Walk into your bank, and they'll offer the best product from their limited range. Even if another lender has a better option for your goals, they won't mention it. Similarly, generalist mortgage brokers might shop around across lenders, but without expertise in property investment portfolios, their focus is often on interest rates rather than loan structuring that supports long-term growth.

2. **Investment-focused (a.k.a. investment-savvy) brokers:** These brokers think beyond the immediate loan.

Their strategies and lending structures are optimised across your whole property and lending portfolios. They might:

- Avoid cross-securitisation of your loans to increase your lending flexibility
- Spread lending across different banks to improve borrowing power options and avoid lender concentration risk
- Use interest-only loans for investment properties to improve cashflow
- Leverage package offers and offset accounts to enhance flexibility and manage cash buffers and risk
- Structure your lending to reduce LMI exposure or higher insurance premiums
- Initiate lender valuation reviews as part of lending portfolio negotiations to release equity or more competitive interest rate pricing
- Focus on long-term growth, ensuring you can keep building your portfolio beyond today's loan.

Why structure beats rate

As professional investors, we learned long ago that loan structure is far more important than finding the lowest interest rate. Sure, chasing the cheapest interest rate is important, and it might save some costs, but it could end up costing us more in missed opportunities later.

The takeaway is simple: strategy trumps capacity. While getting your next loan might feel like the priority, successful property investing is all about the way your loans are structured, as it's what sustains and scales your portfolio over time. Don't underestimate its importance.

We think it best serves you to partner with the right investment-savvy mortgage broker, but it's equally important to equip yourself with the knowledge to identify an investment-savvy professional. In the next section, we'll break down the key insights you need to have meaningful conversations with brokers, ensuring they align with your investment goals and strategy.

The foundations of smart borrowing

Mastering property investing requires a solid understanding of key lending concepts that shape your borrowing strategy. While this is far from a complete and comprehensive lending playbook – as lending is a complex and ever-changing landscape – these fundamentals will guide you through the borrowing process and help you navigate this pillar.

Following are 12 essential concepts every property investor should understand:

1. **Borrowing strategy:** Your borrowing strategy is the blueprint for building a sustainable, multi-property portfolio. Again, it's not just about securing loans – it's about setting the foundation for smart, strategic investing.

2. **Loan structure:** A well-designed loan structure is integral to your borrowing strategy. This includes loan splits that avoid cross-collateralisation, as well as factoring in additional borrowing for costs like stamp duty rather than using cash (explained further a bit later).

3. **Borrowing capacity:** This represents how much you can borrow based on your income, expenses, and current debt. It reflects what you can borrow now, but if done right, it should be shaped by an overall strategy rather than short-term tactics aimed at maximising capacity at all costs.

4. **Principal and interest repayment type and terms:**
A mortgage typically has a loan term of 25 to 30 years, with repayments set on a monthly basis. For example, a 30-year loan consists of 360 monthly repayments. Each repayment covers both the principal (the loan amount) and interest owed to the lender. Standard practice is to use principal and interest (P&I) repayments for personal property loans, such as your principal place of residence and holiday homes.

5. **Interest-only repayment type and terms:** Building on the understanding of a P&I loan, an interest-only (IO) repayment term is typically applied at the start of a 25 or 30-year mortgage for a set period – usually 3 to 5 years – before reverting to P&I repayments. As highlighted in the previous section, investment-savvy mortgage brokers outline the pros and cons of IO lending, including the benefit of lower initial repayments during the IO period, which can significantly assist investors in the early stages of property ownership.

6. **Interest rates:** Interest rates play a pivotal role in shaping your cashflow, directly influencing the cost of borrowing. Lower rates mean smaller repayments, while fluctuations can significantly impact your financial strategy:

   - **Variable rates** adjust monthly based on Reserve Bank of Australia (RBA) decisions, offering flexibility but also uncertainty.

   - **Fixed rates** lock in a set rate for a specific period – typically 1 to 5 years, though some lenders offer terms up to 15 years. In most cases, we recommend fixing for no longer than 5 years, with 2- to 3-year terms being the most common choice, as personal circumstances can and often do change. At the time of writing, lenders apply different interest rates based on factors such as security type, repayment structure, and loan-to-value ratio (LVR). For example:

- A 60% LVR loan secured against your personal home with P&I repayments would attract a lower interest rate.
- Meanwhile, an 80% LVR investment mortgage with IO repayments would typically have a higher rate.

Our tip? Stay in regular contact with your investment-savvy mortgage broker to ensure your lending remains competitive and aligned with your strategy.

7. **Loan-to-value ratio (LVR):** LVR measures the loan amount relative to the property's value. A lower LVR requires a larger deposit, reducing risk for both you and the lender. For example, a $560,000 loan on a $700,000 property equates to an 80% LVR. Understanding LVR is crucial for determining your deposit size, current and future equity releases, and whether lenders mortgage insurance (LMI) applies.

8. **Lenders mortgage insurance (LMI):** In most cases, LMI applies when your deposit is less than 20% of the property's value, but ask your broker for further guidance. It enables market entry with a smaller deposit but adds an expense that impacts borrowing power. It is insurance that protects the bank, not you. Our advice: avoid it if you can but embrace it if you must use it to get ahead.

9. **Equity:** Equity is the difference between your property's market value and the outstanding loan balance. As you pay down your loan and/or your property appreciates, you build equity. This becomes a powerful tool for funding future purchases and accelerating your portfolio growth, minimising the need for cash deposits.

10. **Offset account:** Offset accounts are accounts that you can request to be linked to your home loan. The balance offsets your loan principal, reducing the interest calculated each day. For example, if you have a $300,000 loan and $50,000 in your offset, interest is only charged on $250,000 instead of $300,000 – saving you daily interest on the $50,000 offset amount. This is a powerful tool for reducing interest costs and paying off your loan faster, all while preserving access to your cash. Unlike regular savings accounts (where 'earned' interest is taxed), offset accounts simply reduce the 'expense' instead. Check the table overleaf to see how much interest you could save.

11. **Assessment rate:** Lenders evaluate your ability to repay a loan using an assessment rate, which includes a servicing buffer usually between 2% to 3% above the lender's market interest rate, but can on occasion with some lenders be as low as 1% for special refinancing situations. This buffer helps protect against potential interest rate increases but also reduces your borrowing capacity. The assessment rate acts as a safeguard, ensuring both you and the lender can manage future financial risks.

12. **Personal buffer:** A buffer is your financial safety net – extra cash on hand or borrowed funds set aside to manage unexpected expenses, rising interest rates, or any short-term rental vacancies. This liquidity ensures financial resilience and, importantly, peace of mind, allowing you to navigate market changes without derailing your strategy.

These 12 essentials form the backbone of smart borrowing, helping you to master this pillar and ensuring your team is aligned with your strategy.

MONTHLY SAVINGS FROM USING A 100% OFFSET ACCOUNT

Interest rate	$1,000	$5,000	$50,000	$100,000
3.00%	$2.50	$12.50	$125.00	$250.00
3.50%	$2.92	$14.58	$145.83	$291.67
4.00%	$3.33	$16.67	$166.67	$333.33
4.50%	$3.75	$18.75	$187.50	$375.00
5.00%	$4.17	$20.83	$208.33	$416.67
5.50%	$4.58	$22.92	$229.17	$458.33
6.00%	$5.00	$25.00	$250.00	$500.00
6.50%	$5.42	$27.08	$270.83	$541.67
7.00%	$5.83	$29.17	$291.67	$583.33
7.50%	$6.25	$31.25	$312.50	$625.00
8.00%	$6.67	$33.33	$333.33	$666.67
8.50%	$7.08	$35.42	$354.17	$708.33
9.00%	$7.50	$37.50	$375.00	$750.00
9.50%	$7.92	$39.58	$395.83	$791.67
10.00%	$8.33	$41.67	$416.67	$833.33

(Assumes the benefit is based on the monthly interest saving on an interest-only loan.)

Best practices and pitfalls to avoid

To take this further, let's walk through a typical loan structure. As we've mentioned, property investing is a game of finance, and nailing your loan structure is critical. While banks may present convenient solutions, it's essential to recognise their motivations – spotting a wolf in sheep's clothing – to ensure your long-term strategy remains intact.

Here's what you need to know.

Banks often suggest cross-securitising your loans. This means they use multiple properties as collateral for a single loan, entangling your investments into one complex web. While it might seem simple and more convenient at first, make no mistake, it's designed to create inertia – making it cumbersome for you to move away or negotiate with other lenders.

Cross-securitisation limits your flexibility, increases your risk of hitting borrowing glass ceilings, and reduces your leverage when dealing with competing banks. As a savvy investor, you must avoid this trap and instead maintain control of your portfolio. Here's what a cross-securitised structure might look like.

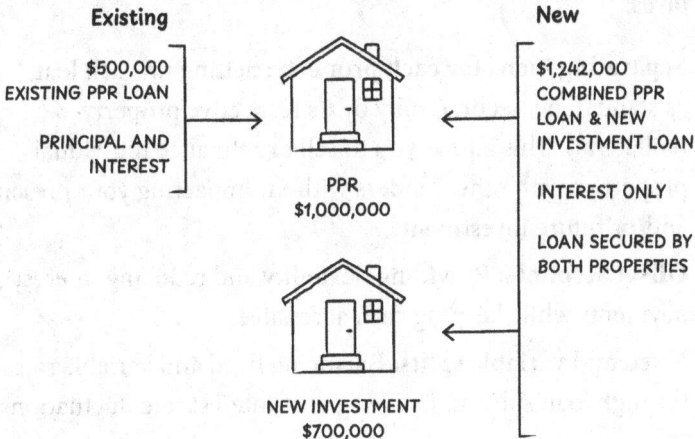

Existing

$500,000
EXISTING PPR LOAN

PRINCIPAL AND
INTEREST

PPR
$1,000,000

New

$1,242,000
COMBINED PPR
LOAN & NEW
INVESTMENT LOAN

INTEREST ONLY

LOAN SECURED BY
BOTH PROPERTIES

NEW INVESTMENT
$700,000

EXAMPLE OF A CROSS-SECURITISED LOAN STRUCTURE

In this loan structure, both properties are being used as security for a new loan on an investment property purchase. Loan 1 is the existing loan (i.e. the mortgage on the PPR), while Loan 2 is the new loan to cover the $700,000 purchase price of the investment property and settlement costs (6% of purchase price). However, the security for Loan 2 is tied to both the PPR and the investment property – this is how the bank creates cross-securitisation (also referred to as cross-collateralisation). This structure demonstrates either a lack of understanding of correct property investing structuring by the bank's lending representative or is intentionally designed to make you more reliant on a single lender – something we want to avoid in the majority of cases.

The savvy investor's approach

An investment-savvy mortgage broker will structure your loans to maximise flexibility and prepare for future purchases. This involves:

- **Separating loans for each property:** Setting up each loan as standalone, secured only by its respective property (collateral). This allows you to sell or refinance individual properties with other lenders without impacting your present and/or future investments.

- **Offset accounts:** Providing flexibility and reducing interest payments while keeping cash accessible.

- **Fixed and variable splits:** Balancing fixed and variable rates through loan splits to hedge against interest rate fluctuations.

- **Valuation independence:** Keeping properties uncrossed to allow for independent valuations and the potential for new equity release. If properties are crossed, an increase in one property's value combined with a decrease in another can prevent access to new equity.

· **Combining lenders:** Maintaining standalone properties allows you to explore different borrowing power combinations, helping to maximise overall borrowing capacity.

By structuring your loans correctly from the start, you retain control, avoid unnecessary risk, and keep lenders competing for your business.

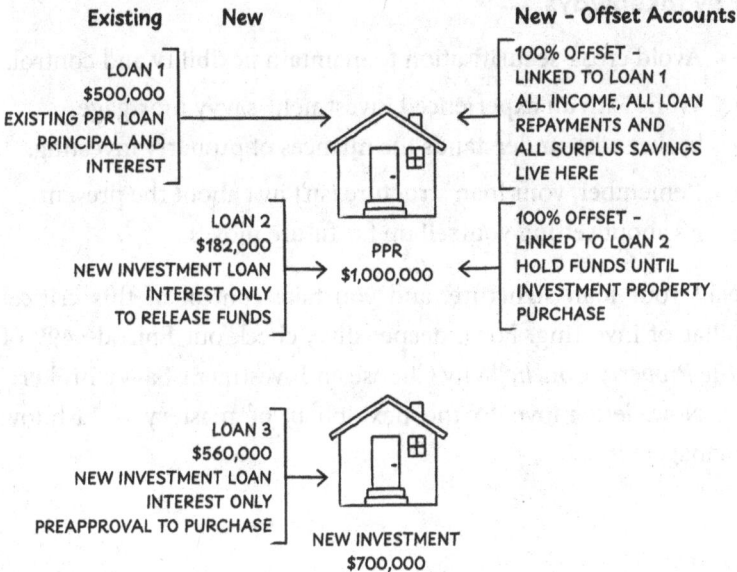

EXAMPLE OF AN INVESTMENT-SAVVY LOAN STRUCTURE

In this preferred loan structure, Loan 1 remains the existing loan (i.e. the mortgage on the PPR). Loan 2 is a standalone loan secured solely against the PPR, used to cover the 20% deposit and associated costs for the investment property. Loan 3 is also a standalone loan, but it is secured exclusively against the new investment property. Together, the funds from Loan 2 and Loan 3 ensure sufficient resources are available to complete the purchase at settlement.

Crucially, the funds released in Loan 2 are held in an offset account against that loan until a suitable investment property is identified.

Key takeaways

- Avoid cross-securitisation to maintain flexibility and control.
- Work with an experienced investment-savvy mortgage broker who understands the nuances of property investing.
- Remember, your loan structure isn't just about the present – it's about setting yourself up for future moves.

Nail your loan structure, and you take control of this critical pillar of investing. For a deeper dive, check out Episode 499 of *The Property Couch*, 'Why Choose an Investment-Savvy Broker?'

Now, let's move to the next pillar of mastery – cashflow management.

Chapter 8

Cashflow management

Of all the pillars in the Property Investment Formula, cashflow management is hands down the toughest to master for many. Why? Because it's not just about crunching today's numbers – it's about projecting into a future filled with uncertainty. Most people struggle to think five years ahead, let alone account for all the moving parts like taxation and inflation impacts, present value versus future value, and how to prioritise their financial goals for the next 30+ years. It's a delicate juggling act: balancing basic needs with bucket-list dreams while optimising the sequence in which you make those moves.

Enter Ben and his Excel spreadsheet back in 2011. When I first met Ben, he introduced me to a cashflow modelling simulator that completely blew my mind. Up until then, I'd spent 13 years helping investors buy property, often witnessing an industry that relied on basic spreadsheets – or worse, financial plans scribbled on the back of a napkin. The typical approach was: 'Do you have an income? Do you have equity? Great, let's buy a property!' Thankfully, what Ben and his right-hand man (the late and very great!) Michael Pope had created was next level.

It didn't just crunch numbers – it painted a clear roadmap for lifestyle by design. For the first time, there was a tool that could show exactly how today's decisions would ripple through the years ahead. That was the moment I realised I wanted to team up with Ben and help property investors move away from guesswork and make data-driven decisions. We've been working together ever since!

Now, to be clear, this simulator wasn't the only tool out there. Another software program had existed for some time, but unfortunately, it approached property investment decisions in isolation from every other financial decision an investor was making. Sure, it could give you the numbers for one property, but it failed to integrate the bigger picture. Not to mention, analysing multiple properties required you to panel-beat the results of one property into the second scenario model – clunky at best.

Ben's updated approach was different. It factored in your entire life: paying the mortgage, with offset and tax impacts, renovating the kitchen, upgrading the car, and even weighing up the cost of public versus private school for the kids.

What made it truly revolutionary was how it integrated real-world finances with property investing. It treated your home, investments, and lifestyle choices as interconnected pieces of the same puzzle. That was the missing link I was searching for. Thank God for Ben and Michael's vision here.

To state the obvious: most people park a large portion of their income into residential real estate, typically through their principal place of residence (PPR). But treating property investing as if it exists in its own bubble – independent of the major financial commitment of a mortgage on your home – is like trying to drive a car without a steering wheel. Sure, you can move forward, but you have no control. This new simulator became the steering wheel, giving investors clarity, control, and the confidence to make decisions that aligned with their bigger life plans.

So yes, cashflow management is the hardest pillar to master – but master it you must if you want to optimise your hard-earned money and make it work harder to build your wealth base.

The good news? What started as a simple Excel spreadsheet has now evolved into a cloud-based powerhouse, serving as the engine behind the real-world scenarios showcased in the case studies at the back of the book, where we demonstrate exactly how to bring it all together.

Now that we've explored the role that a cashflow modelling simulator can play, let's break down the practicalities of cashflow management and how to apply it to your own finances.

At its core, if you want to achieve the likes of $3,000 a week in passive income, cashflow management means understanding your income and expenses and optimising the surplus to fuel your savings and investments. For property investors, this involves covering essential costs like living expenses, mortgage repayments, maintenance, and property expenses while also accounting for personal outlays such as school fees, holidays, and home improvements. Without surplus cashflow, you risk overextending yourself and stalling your financial progress.

The first step in cashflow management is understanding the flow of money in your household:

1. **Sources of money:**
   - Wages or self-employment income.
   - Investment income, such as rental returns.
   - Government handouts or charity.
   - Borrowings, including loans or lines of credit.

2. **Committed money:**

   - Fixed payments like mortgage or rent.
   - Essential living expenses, including utilities, groceries, and insurance.
   - Provisioning for irregular costs like holidays or gifts.
   - Discretionary spending on lifestyle choices such as dining out or entertainment.

3. **Surplus money:**

   - The remaining funds after covering all commitments – this is where wealth-building begins and it's your key to financial independence.
   - By identifying areas where money slips through the cracks, you can redirect it toward reducing debt, saving, or investing.

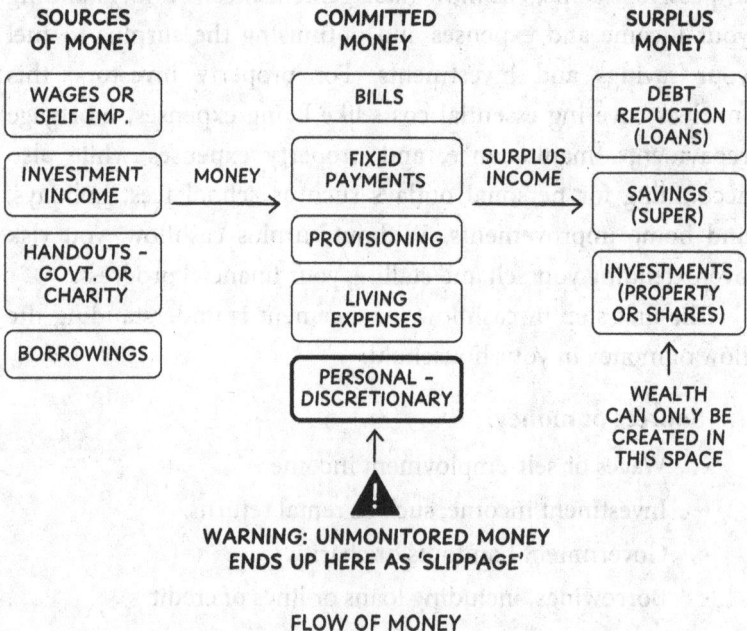

SOURCES OF MONEY	COMMITTED MONEY	SURPLUS MONEY
WAGES OR SELF EMP.	BILLS	DEBT REDUCTION (LOANS)
INVESTMENT INCOME	FIXED PAYMENTS	SAVINGS (SUPER)
HANDOUTS – GOVT. OR CHARITY	PROVISIONING	INVESTMENTS (PROPERTY OR SHARES)
BORROWINGS	LIVING EXPENSES	
	PERSONAL – DISCRETIONARY	

MONEY → SURPLUS INCOME →

WEALTH CAN ONLY BE CREATED IN THIS SPACE

⚠ WARNING: UNMONITORED MONEY ENDS UP HERE AS 'SLIPPAGE'

FLOW OF MONEY

Good versus great cashflow management

There's a significant difference between good and great cashflow management, and if you ever want to move to the top of the seven grades of financial well-being, managing cashflow is a must.

- **Good cashflow management** focuses on tracking your spending, adhering to a budget, and ensuring your expenses stay within your income. It's a strong starting point, but it's not enough to secure long-term success.

- **Great cashflow management** involves planning for the future, projecting your income and expenses, and preparing for life's inevitable surprises. Whether it's managing rising interest rates, funding a renovation, or navigating a career change, great money managers anticipate these challenges and adapt accordingly.

Mastering cashflow management

Mastering cashflow requires adopting the mindset of a business owner – thinking strategically, applying proven operational principles, and using data-driven planning to guide decisions. Great cashflow managers leverage tools like cashflow models to align every decision with their long-term goals, maintaining control even when faced with the unexpected.

Like a business owner who uses budgets and forecasts before making any decision about what's best for the business, you can leverage a cashflow modelling simulator to map out scenarios, test strategies, and make informed choices to determine what's best for your household. This data-driven approach allows you to allocate money where it creates the greatest impact.

The power of surplus

Trapping surplus cashflow is the secret weapon for wealth creation. It's the money left over after covering all your expenses, and it's what allows you to grow your property portfolio. But surplus doesn't appear by accident – it's the result of careful planning and disciplined spending.

Today, however, we're constantly challenged by social media platforms showcasing people 'investing' in lifestyle now – lavish vacations, luxury purchases, and dining at the latest hotspots. These platforms, fuelled by social envy, create a powerful Fear of Missing Out (FOMO) that tempts impulsive spending. It's easy to get caught in a never-ending cycle of lifestyle upgrades. Without a plan, these decisions can derail your ability to build wealth and, ultimately, your goal to retire on $3,000 per week.

The first rule of effective money management is simple: spend less than you earn. I know – it seems obvious, right? But it's surprisingly uncommon. Our grandparents did this by default, but now many people spend more than they earn, thanks to horrible debt with credit cards, fast credit, and buy-now-pay-later options that make overspending all too easy.

Once you trap surplus cashflow, you have three choices for how to use it:

1. **Invest in lifestyle now:** This is the path most people take, living for the here and now. It means using your surplus to enhance your lifestyle immediately – whether through experiences, luxury purchases, or personal indulgences. While it offers instant gratification, it often leaves little room for building long-term wealth and can delay or even prevent financial independence.

2. **Invest in lifestyle now and into your future:** A more balanced approach, this choice allows you to enjoy some of life's pleasures today while also setting aside part of your surplus for future investments. It involves moderate sacrifices – enough to live a little now while still maintaining a clear focus on your future. This path is about striking a balance and preparing for both the present and the long term. This is our preferred approach.

3. **Invest into your future:** This option is for those laser-focused on their financial goals, often needing to address past financial challenges or build wealth quickly. With gazelle-like dedication, they direct the majority of their surplus toward future-oriented goals. This strategy demands high levels of sacrifice and discipline today in exchange for significant rewards tomorrow.

But if we know we need to trap surplus, then how do we do it? We'll cover that next.

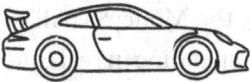

INVEST IN
LIFESTYLE NOW
(LUXURY)

INVEST IN
LIFESTYLE NOW AND
FOR THE FUTURE
(PRACTICAL)

INVEST FOR
YOUR FUTURE
(BUDGET)

Why budgets don't work

Yep, you heard us right. We take a contrarian view on classic budgets – that they simply don't work! Well, unless they're supported by a rules-based system to guide you when it matters most – at the point of sale. To be clear, we believe that budgets have their place, but if left alone without a supporting system, they're like a boat lost at sea without a rudder – directionless and ineffective. As James Clear wisely says in *Atomic Habits*, 'You do not rise to the level of your goals, you fall to the level of your systems.'

Classic budgeting – with its multiple rows and columns in spreadsheets and generic and limited categories – often fails because, let's face it, no one's pulling out their budget at the checkout or when deciding on that extra coffee. In the heat of the moment, it's easy to forget your goals. Without a system to back it up, a budget becomes little more than a static document based on wishful thinking. Before you know it, unconscious overspending creeps in, and you're left wondering why your money didn't stretch as far as you expected.

That's where our MoneySMARTS system comes in. Instead of relying on willpower or endless tracking, the MoneySMARTS system puts guardrails in place to guide your spending in real time to trap more surplus savings. Think of it as swimming between the flags – a practical, automated way to keep your finances on track without constant effort. This isn't about restricting your life; it's about structuring your money to put it on autopilot.

Here's how it works:

1. **Primary account:** This is the foundation of your financial system. If you have a mortgage, it's an offset account where all your income flows to reduce interest costs. If you don't,

it's an everyday high-interest savings account generating income. Either way, it serves as your financial HQ.

2. **Weekly living and lifestyle account (a seven-day float):** Each week, a set amount moves here for day-to-day spending on a debit card. It's like having bumpers in a bowling alley – keeping your spending in line with your goals.

3. **Fixed costs:** Regular expenses go on a credit card with interest-free days, allowing your cash to work harder in the offset account or savings account. If you're not a credit card person, you can direct debit the primary account or use a second debit card linked to your primary account instead – it serves the same purpose.

4. **10 minutes a month check-ups:** As a rules-based system, it's designed to be quick and easy to set up and take control of your finances on a monthly basis.

5. **Trapping surplus for wealth:** This isn't just about tracking expenses. It's about freeing up cash for wealth-building, like investing in property.

6. **Leveraging technology:** Built-in historical and current-day tracking and reporting tools do the heavy lifting, so you have on-the-go access – good-bye old spreadsheet.

It's important to say that this book isn't here to teach you every detail of MoneySMARTS – that's what we cover in depth in our book, *Make Money Simple Again*. Here, we're introducing it as a game-changing way to manage money. If 80% of winning is beginning, then simply restructuring your banking as shown in the following figure will make a profound difference to how you spend your money and ultimately reap more surplus savings.

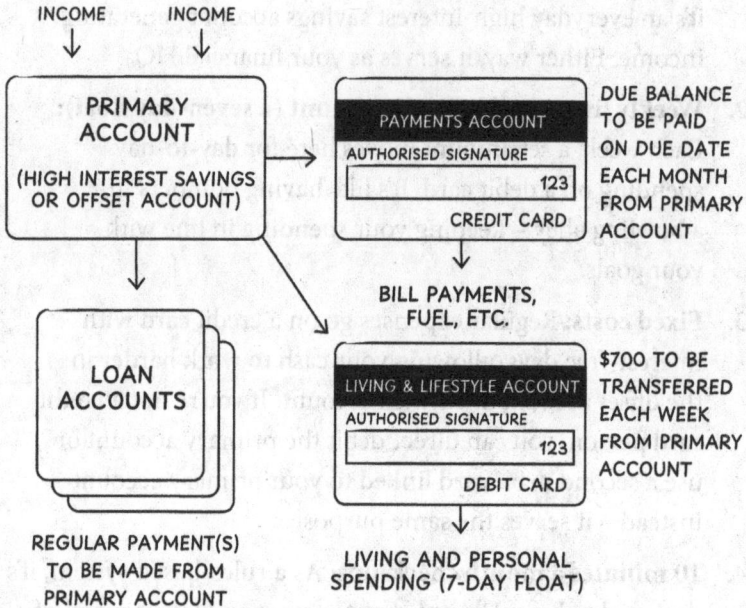

INCOME   INCOME

PRIMARY ACCOUNT
(HIGH INTEREST SAVINGS OR OFFSET ACCOUNT)

PAYMENTS ACCOUNT
AUTHORISED SIGNATURE
123
CREDIT CARD

DUE BALANCE TO BE PAID ON DUE DATE EACH MONTH FROM PRIMARY ACCOUNT

BILL PAYMENTS, FUEL, ETC.

LOAN ACCOUNTS

LIVING & LIFESTYLE ACCOUNT
AUTHORISED SIGNATURE
123
DEBIT CARD

$700 TO BE TRANSFERRED EACH WEEK FROM PRIMARY ACCOUNT

REGULAR PAYMENT(S) TO BE MADE FROM PRIMARY ACCOUNT

LIVING AND PERSONAL SPENDING (7-DAY FLOAT)

THE MoneySMARTS ACCOUNT STRUCTURE

With MoneySMARTS, you're no longer crossing your fingers and hoping your budget will stick. Instead, you're in the driver's seat, directing your money to where it matters most. If you don't already have a system, we recommend giving this one a try. And if you do, how does yours stack up? Does it actually work, or is it a system that allows a lot of slippage or unconscious overspending? Remember, we're talking about your financial future here – it's important. Is your system simple, effective, and consistently capturing surplus? If you're being honest, it might be time for an upgrade, right? Why settle for less when your financial future is on the line?

The Five Essential Steps

When we first started out, property investing wasn't the BBQ conversation starter it is today. There were no podcasts, no YouTube tutorials, and no social media gurus offering advice at every turn. Figuring out how to invest in property was more trial and error than tried and tested. Back then, the common approach for most investors was to start by looking at the property itself, with little thought given to the preparation required for optimal outcomes – not just in terms of property performance but also for aligning investments with your personality, risk profile, and long-term goals.

That's why we created a process: the **Five Essential Steps** to property investing. Whether you're just starting out or already building your portfolio, these steps provide the foundation for every property investor. Think of it like tailoring a suit – it ensures your strategy fits your unique circumstances perfectly. Unlike the one-size-fits-all approach that plagues much of the property industry, this process is designed to customise your strategy, helping you avoid generic advice and missteps. It's not about throwing darts at a map or blindly following cookie-cutter recommendations. It's about following a structured, proven process that sets you up for success.

Imagine you're feeling unwell and walk into a doctor's office. Without asking you a single question about your symptoms, they scribble out a prescription, hand it over, and usher you out the door so they can move on to the next patient. Sounds absurd, right? You'd walk out feeling completely ripped off, thinking, 'How could they possibly know what's best for me when they didn't even take the time to understand my situation?'

Yet, this kind of approach happens all too often in the property investment industry. So-called advisers offer recommendations without any consideration for your unique circumstances, goals, or financial position. They skip the crucial steps of clarifying your needs, evaluating your opportunities, and creating a tailored plan. Instead, they jump straight to the 'prescription' – a property in a location that may be completely wrong for you – because their primary interest is often their own commission, not your success.

Property investing deserves the same level of care and thoughtfulness as a doctor applies to their practice. While it's not about your physical health – which is undeniably vital – it's about your financial health, which is equally critical in its own right. The Five Essential Steps mirror a doctor's process:

1. **Clarify** your situation by asking the right questions.
2. **Evaluate** the information to diagnose where you stand and what's possible.
3. **Plan** a tailored strategy that aligns with your needs and goals.
4. **Implement** the plan through decisive action.
5. **Manage** your progress with ongoing reviews and adjustments as needed.

Skipping these steps is like handing out the doctor's prescription without a proper diagnosis – it's reckless and ineffective. By following the Five Essential Steps, you ensure your investment journey is intentional, informed, and aligned with your goals. This process helps you avoid costly mistakes and provides a clear roadmap to long-term success.

These steps form the backbone of our advisory work and have been tested by thousands of successful property investors. They're not just principles we believe in – they're principles that work. By following this proven process, you're in charge, and you can confidently take control of your property journey, prioritise your goals (lifestyle by design), avoid unnecessary risks, and create lasting value – not just for today but for your future self as well.

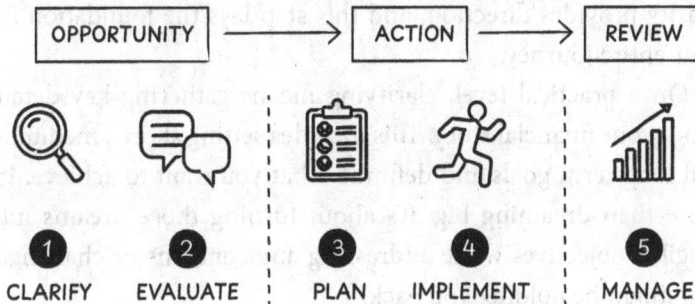

| OPPORTUNITY | → | ACTION | → | REVIEW |

① CLARIFY   ② EVALUATE   ③ PLAN   ④ IMPLEMENT   ⑤ MANAGE

THE FIVE ESSENTIAL STEPS

In essence, property investing is a **process**, not an event.

You will have noticed from the diagram that the Five Essential Steps are grouped into three key phases:

1. **Opportunity (Steps 1 and 2):** These steps focus on the bigger picture, giving you a clear understanding of where you are now and uncovering potential opportunities.

2. **Action (Steps 3 and 4):** This phase is about execution – the doing and implementation of your plan.

3. **Review (Step 5):** This final step brings it all together, allowing for reflection and fine-tuning to ensure you stay on track toward your goals.

With this process in mind, let's explore the Five Essential Steps in detail.

Step 1: Clarify

The first step is all about understanding you and your household's potential. It's about preparing for tomorrow by taking a deep dive into where you stand today – both personally and financially. Clarity provides direction, and this step lays the foundation for your entire journey.

On a practical level, clarifying means gathering key details about your financial story. This includes setting short-, medium-, and long-term goals and defining what you want to achieve. It's more than dreaming big; it's about turning those dreams into tangible objectives while addressing any concerns or challenges that might be holding you back.

We often say the state of your wallet plays with your state of mind, so this step is about more than just numbers. It's about uncovering where your money is going, down to the last detail:

- What do you spend on household bills, food, and essentials?
- What are your car and transport costs?
- What are your regular commitments, like phone bills and gym memberships?
- Where else is your money going, and what's left over at the end of the day?

Unfortunately, many people skip this crucial step and fail to begin with the end in mind – a concept highlighted in Stephen Covey's *7 Habits of Highly Effective People*. To clarify, you need to start with the 'destination'.

Ask yourself:

- What's your dream? Financial security or freedom? Retiring early? Being debt-free? Retiring at 50?

- What's your goal? Saving for a wedding, spending more time with family, or building wealth?
- What's your strategy and preferred investment vehicle to get there?

By taking the time to clarify your goals and dreams, you're creating a roadmap for your future. Once you've defined the destination, you're ready to move on.

Step 2: Evaluate

This step is where your goals meet reality. It's all about crunching the numbers to determine your opportunity and potential, and we believe everyone has the potential, so this might be your opportunity. Success in property investing isn't guesswork – it's a science.

Evaluation means assessing your cashflow, identifying challenges, and understanding the resources you'll need to succeed. This step involves forecasting cashflow movements every month for at least 40 years into your retirement. Why such a long horizon? Because successful property investment hinges on effective debt management and balancing income and expenses over the long term.

Key questions to address during this step include:

- How much surplus cashflow do you have to invest?
- What kind of property performance do you need – growth, cashflow, or a mix of both?
- How will major current and future planned life events like starting a family or retiring impact your cashflow and overall financial trajectory?

For instance, we often see clients delay investing while focusing on milestones like raising a family, only to scramble to catch up in their 40s or 50s. A thorough evaluation can help you achieve both goals simultaneously – building wealth while enjoying life's milestones.

To evaluate effectively, focus on these three areas:

1. **The committed money basics:** Cover everyday essentials like shelter, food, and clothing.

2. **The surplus money:** Determine what's left after expenses to direct toward lifestyle, savings, or investments.

3. **The bucket list:** Identify your 'big rocks', like early retirement, a dream holiday, or funding your child's education.

Step 3: Plan

With clarity and evaluation in hand, it's time to create a plan. Without one, you're leaving your financial future to chance. The route isn't one-size-fits-all. Your property investing journey must be uniquely tailored to your circumstances and goals. As the saying goes, *if you fail to plan, you plan to fail.*

This stage has two components:

1. **Strategy:** A fully tailored and optimised financial roadmap that clearly defines and documents your goals, objectives, and the reasons behind them.

2. **Tactics:** A well-timed sequence of actionable steps that guide you through each milestone, ensuring you stay on course while providing the flexibility to handle any challenges that arise along the way.

As illustrated in the case studies later in this book, a customised plan is critical. Every household has unique incomes, aspirations, and risk profiles, so applying a cookie-cutter approach simply won't work.

Your plan should include:

- **Surplus cashflow:** The fuel for your investment journey.
- **Household liquidity:** A cash reserve buffer to cover at least six months of current spending (12 months if you cut spending to essentials only) to handle unexpected bumps on the journey.

Your plan must be realistic, measurable, and adaptable. A solid plan is your best defence against the challenges of property investing, and it's the difference between reactive decision-making and confident, informed, and planned choices.

Step 4: Implement

This step transforms your plan into reality. It's where preparation meets execution.

This is where most people get it wrong – instead of working through the crucial groundwork in the first three steps, they dive headfirst into online property portals, scrolling through listings and hoping to spot 'the one'. DIY investors often make the mistake of searching *before* researching, risking their financial future on hunches. Others fall prey to industry 'professionals' who push properties and locations without understanding the investor's needs (we'll cover this in Chapter 11).

'Implement' ensures every decision is informed and sequenced within your plan. With a clear roadmap in hand, you can take confident steps towards your goals while avoiding the guesswork that leads to very costly financial mistakes.

Step 5: Manage

The final step is about measuring and monitoring your progress. Managing is often overlooked, but it's critical for keeping your investments on track – what gets managed gets done.

Think of this as your regular check-up. If you are working with a team of trusted professional advisers, they should be proactively performing annual reviews for you to ensure you remain on track towards your goals. Property investing isn't a set-and-forget strategy, but it doesn't require micromanaging either. For most investors, it takes about 10 hours per property per year to ensure everything is running smoothly.

Here's how to manage effectively:

- **Track your budgeted surpluses:** Make sure you're capturing the monthly surpluses you planned for.
- **Use MoneySMARTS:** Leverage its monthly check-up feature to track your financial performance as part of its operating rhythms.
- **Stay connected with your property manager:** Regular communication ensures any issues are addressed promptly.
- **Confirm tenant satisfaction:** Happy tenants are more likely to stay longer, reducing vacancy rates.
- **Monitor local rental markets:** Check current asking rents to ensure your property remains competitive.
- **Conduct debt reviews:** Have your investment-savvy broker review your lending annually to optimise your financial structure.
- **Track rental income and expenses:** Keep detailed records for each property to maintain profitability.

- **Work with a property-savvy tax accountant:** Ensure all claimable deductions are accurately reported to maximise tax efficiency.

Great money management and property investing are about balance – keeping your portfolio aligned with your goals while allowing you to enjoy the benefits of passive income.

The Five Essential Steps separate successful investors from those who fall short. This process isn't just for beginners – it's a proven method that seasoned investors rely on to consistently achieve success and build a portfolio that supports their dream lifestyle. Remember, as we said earlier, property investing isn't an event; it's a process. Embrace the steps, and you'll set yourself up for long-term success.

At this point, you might be thinking, 'This all sounds logical and sensible, but how do I pull it together?' Great question.

Through years of professional advisory work with our valued clients, we've created a cloud-based platform called Moorr (moorr.com.au). And here's the exciting news for you: we've made a host of **FREE tools and resources** available for our community to use. By implementing the knowledge from this book, you can:

- Evaluate and manage your household finances, including running our popular MoneySMARTS money management system.
- Follow our proven Five Essential Steps process for building wealth through property investing.
- Manage and review individual investment properties and your overall portfolio.
- Expand your education and knowledge about property, finance, and money management.

Join over 60,000 registered Moorr users to access a suite of practical tools designed to simplify your journey. From managing your finances to tracking your property portfolio, Moorr provides the insights and structure to help you stay on course. These resources are here to support your goals and make implementing the strategies in this book easier and more effective. Why not explore what's possible?

The builder versus the architect

We hear clients ask, 'Why do I need a property portfolio plan if I'm using your buyer's agency? Aren't they the best people to help me?' The answer is nuanced – sure, our buyer's agents are highly skilled professionals, but they play a specific role in the bigger picture. Think of them as the builder in the builder-versus-architect analogy.

If you ask a builder to construct a house, they'll deliver exceptional craftsmanship. But they're working to your brief – they're not considering the engineering requirements, the orientation, your future family needs, or the overall design strategy. That's where the architect comes in.

The architect's role is strategic. They design a plan that considers your present needs and future aspirations. They'll ask questions like, 'Where does the sun hit? What will your family need in five years? How do we make the space flow seamlessly with your lifestyle?' The builder, by contrast, focuses on execution. They bring the vision to life with precision and skill, but their work relies on the roadmap created by the architect.

This analogy perfectly mirrors the property investment journey. Many people skip the planning phase entirely – they want to dive straight into action, buying a property to get the ball rolling. But just as building a house without a plan can lead to costly mistakes, jumping into property investing without a tailored strategy can derail your long-term goals.

Think of planning your property portfolio like using Google Maps. You start with your current location – let's say Melbourne – and enter your destination, Sydney. The journey isn't one-size-fits-all. Some people want the fastest route, prioritising efficiency and speed. Others prefer the scenic route, taking their time and enjoying the journey. Then, there are those who need stops along the way to visit family or take a break.

For property investors, the destination is often clear – $3,000 per week in passive income. But the route to get there depends entirely on your unique circumstances. These might include 'stops' like raising a family, saving for a big event, or taking a career break. The 'architect' maps out the best route for your journey, considering variables like your income, risk profile, lifestyle goals, and potential roadblocks. Once the plan is set, the 'builder' – your buyer's agent – takes over, using the roadmap to find locations and properties that fit seamlessly into your strategy.

Without this tailored plan, you risk ending up on the wrong road entirely, wasting time, money, and opportunities.

Planning also allows you to 'paper trade' your life before you live it. On paper, you can test different scenarios, adjust if something doesn't work, and refine your decisions before they become costly commitments.

In property investing, the consequences of mistakes often don't surface until a decade later – a decade of lost time and missed compounding benefits. Proper planning ensures you avoid these pitfalls, giving you the confidence to move forward with clarity and precision.

Cost versus benefit of a plan

Remember the example from the compounding section (page 51), where delaying a purchase by five years and under-optimising the purchase cost over $1 million ($1,188,502 to be exact)? Now, compare that to the approximate $3,000 to $5,500 you'd spend on a professional to design a personalised and fully tailored plan. The cost of expert guidance is minimal compared to the potential financial impact of poor timing and decision-making.

We're strong advocates of planning first because it's proven to work in pretty much every discipline in life, work, business and other forms of investing. Success leaves clues. Later in this book, you'll find case studies showing exactly what needs to be done and when to achieve $3,000 per week in passive income. The mystery is removed, and the process becomes predictable. By starting with the end goal in mind and working backwards, as property investment advisers, we take on the role of the architect – designing the dream home, solving roadblocks on paper, and then engaging the builder to execute the plan.

We'd like to think we know what we're talking about on this topic – at the time of writing this book, we've developed over 4,929 tailored plans and recommended over $10,453,053,160 (i.e. $10.4B+) in future property investments. Not to mention the 2,000+ properties we've purchased with our team on behalf of our clients.

We'll say it one more time: property investing isn't an event – it's a process. At the heart of every successful property portfolio, where mistakes are minimised, is a tailored, personalised plan. Start with the architect: design a plan tailored to your unique circumstances. Then, bring in the builder to execute it. This approach ensures that every decision is intentional, strategic, and aligned with your ultimate goal.

Learning about you

Hopefully, we've convinced you that having a plan is essential. Now it's time to dig deeper into what makes that plan truly effective – you. Property investing isn't a one-size-fits-all game; your plan needs to reflect your unique goals, preferences, and circumstances. This is where understanding yourself becomes critical. After all, there's no point in planning a renovation-heavy strategy if you're risk-averse or time-poor.

Understanding who you are as an investor significantly shapes the decisions you make when building a plan. Your investor type, risk tolerance, financial position, and even time availability all influence the options that need to be considered.

Type of investor

Understanding your investor type is crucial for tailoring your approach. It's not just about what you want to achieve but also how much time and energy you're willing to commit.

Here's how we define property investor types:

1. **Active worker:** Property investment is your full-time job. You're hands-on, managing every detail, from the tools to the project itself.

2. **Active weekend worker:** While it's not your primary focus, you spend significant time in the evenings and on weekends renovating or working on your properties.

3. **Active manager:** You oversee projects and remain involved in decision-making, but property investment isn't consuming all your free time – just a reasonable portion of it.

4. **Passive investor:** You rely on professionals to manage the details, freeing up your time to live life and focus on other priorities while still keeping an eye on results.

5.   **Pure investor:** Property investment is purely financial
     and completely hands-off. You entrust professionals to
     manage everything, and your involvement is limited
     to reviewing performance.

Knowing where you sit on this spectrum will help you determine
the level of outsourcing or involvement required for your strategy
to succeed. From our experience, most people lean toward being
passive investors – they want to build wealth while getting on
with and enjoying their everyday lives. After all, it's not 'whoever
dies with the most properties wins'; it's about creating a lifestyle
that works for you.

Investment horizon

How long you plan to hold your property plays a massive role in
your investment strategy. Property is not a short-term game: as we
discussed in Chapter 5, 'The magic of compounding', entry, exit,
and holding costs mean the longer you hold an investment-grade
property, the more likely it will deliver the returns you're after.

Here's how we classify investment horizons:

·   **Short-term (7 to 15 years):** This is not ideal due to
    high transaction costs and shorter timeframes to ride
    market cycles.

·   **Medium-term (16 to 25 years):** This is better but still
    limiting when aiming for meaningful wealth-building.

·   **Long-term (25+ years):** This is the gold standard.
    Holding for decades or indefinitely allows you to benefit
    from capital growth, passive income, and the potential to
    create intergenerational wealth.

Most of our strategies are built for the long game – think decades, not months. This is the opposite of a get-rich-quick approach. It's about leveraging compounding growth and steady cashflow to create lasting wealth.

Skills and ability

Your skills and abilities directly impact your capacity to implement a strategy. To help you assess this, we use a 1 to 10 rating scale, with 1 being the minimal ability (i.e. it would require full outsourcing) and 10 being highly skilled (i.e. it could confidently be executed without any professional assistance).

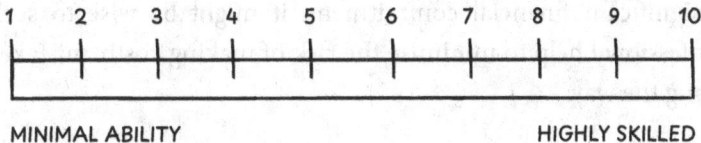

```
 1    2    3    4    5    6    7    8    9    10
 ├────┼────┼────┼────┼────┼────┼────┼────┼────┤
```

MINIMAL ABILITY   HIGHLY SKILLED

Think about your qualifications, experience, and general confidence in managing tasks. For example:

- A licensed builder or tradesperson might score higher for hands-on renovations.
- A professional with financial qualifications may excel at managing cashflow or tax planning.
- For others, outsourcing to one or more specialists may be the most efficient path.

By recognising your strengths and limitations, you can decide when and where to seek help to optimise your outcomes.

Level of knowledge

The more you know, the better decisions you'll make. Property investing, like any skill, rewards those who do their homework.

Solid research is essential. This doesn't mean you need to become an expert overnight, but taking the time to learn about the factors that drive property performance – such as economic activity, location, supply and demand, productive use of land, and cashflow – will put you ahead of the game.

If you're not confident or feel there are still gaps in your knowledge – understandably, this isn't something you do for a living – keep referring to the frameworks we're sharing and supplement them by listening to our podcast for more detailed explanations. Alternatively, given that property investing is a significant financial commitment, it might be wise to seek professional help to minimise the risk of making costly mistakes along the way.

Level of risk

All investments carry risk, and property is no exception. While residential property is generally considered a lower-risk investment, factors like location, leverage, and strategy can increase risk levels.

We classify risk tolerance into five categories:

1. **Low risk:** Proven locations and long-term horizons.
2. **Low to moderate risk:** Slightly more speculative but still stable areas.
3. **Moderate risk:** Potential for higher returns but requires deeper analysis.
4. **Moderate to high risk:** Growth areas or specific property types with more volatility.

5. **High risk:** Mining towns, speculative developments, or strategies reliant on timing.

Your personal risk tolerance will determine the strategies and properties suitable for you. A conservative approach often wins the long game, but the choice ultimately depends on your goals, comfort level, and retirement time horizons.

WHAT'S YOUR TOLERANCE FOR RISK?

Time allocation

Time is one of the most valuable resources in property investing, shaping the type of investor you can be.

If you're time-poor, outsourcing is likely your best option. Conversely, if you have the capacity and willingness to dedicate significant hours to research, management, or renovations, you can take a more active role. However, your time commitment should always align with your goals, lifestyle, and expertise.

In our experience, the level of time and attention dedicated often correlates with the results achieved. If time is a constraint, outsourcing some or all aspects of the process is a worthwhile consideration to ensure you stay on track.

Current capital and wealth position

Your financial starting point plays a critical role in shaping your strategy. For example:

- **First-time investors:** Likely to start conservatively, focusing on building capital through high-performing but low-risk properties.
- **Experienced investors:** May take a more aggressive approach, leveraging existing equity or diversifying their portfolio.

*

Understanding yourself as an investor isn't just self-awareness – it's the key to building a plan that actually works for you. When your plan aligns with who you are, decisions feel natural, challenges become manageable, and the journey ahead is one you're excited to take. It's no longer just a generic formula – it's YOUR roadmap to success, built on your terms.

The Four Foundation Levers

Now that you're clear on who you are as an investor, the next step in building your plan is understanding the Four Foundation Levers – income, expenditure, time, and target.

When we sit down with a client to design their property investment plan, we focus on working the Four Foundation Levers. Think of these levers as the controls on a bulldozer, each one fine-tuning the position of the bucket in front. Just as a skilled operator uses these controls to navigate complex terrain, you can adjust these financial levers to align with your unique retirement goals. There's no single 'right' setting for everyone – it all depends on your personal circumstances and what you want to achieve.

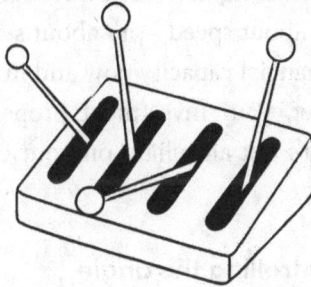

THE FOUR FONDATIONAL LEVERS:
INCOME, EXPENDITURE, TIME AND TARGET

Let's explore these levers and how adjusting them can shape your financial blueprint.

Income: Powering the bulldozer forward

Income is the fuel that powers your bulldozer – it determines how far you can go and how quickly. But it's not just about the money coming in today; it's about understanding how your income will evolve over time. Property investing is a long game, and knowing your income timeline helps you plan better.

Ask yourself:

- Is my income steady, or do I expect increases over time?
- Are there possible disruptions, like taking a career break or starting a family?

- Is my job secure, and could bonuses or commissions boost my earnings?

For example, someone working in a corporate job with steady pay rises might approach their investment strategy differently from a contractor with fluctuating income. Understanding your income trajectory isn't just about speed – it's about setting a course that aligns with your financial capacity now and in the future.

And don't forget, your investment property also generates rental income, so it's not all reliant on your exertion or regular working income!

Expenditure: Controlling the angle

Expenditure is the lever that controls your financial tilt. A steep angle – where your spending is high – makes it harder to move forward, while a shallower angle – where spending is carefully managed – makes it easier to save and invest. Balancing this lever is crucial to avoid tipping too far into indulgence or excessive restraint.

Consider:

- Which expenses are essential, and which are discretionary (lifestyle spending) choices?
- Can I reduce discretionary spending without sacrificing my quality of life or lifestyle choices?
- How do I strike a balance between enjoying today and saving for tomorrow?

Think of it like choosing a scenic route that uses more fuel versus a direct path that conserves resources. Both approaches are valid, but understanding your spending habits ensures you're driving toward your destination efficiently.

Time: Setting the distance

Time sets the bulldozer's path – the distance it needs to cover to reach your goal. The earlier you start, the more time your investments have to grow, amplifying the impact of every decision. This lever is about aligning your investment timeline with your life goals.

Ask yourself:

- How long do I have before I need passive income to kick in?
- Does my timeline support the goals I've set?
- Would I consider working longer to reach a higher target or less to reach a lower target?

For instance, starting your property journey in your 30s gives you decades to build wealth, while starting in your 50s might require a more aggressive strategy, but be careful please. Time is your secret weapon, compounding the benefits of good decisions and allowing small steps to lead to big outcomes.

Target: Defining the destination

Your target is the ultimate destination – the spot where you want your bulldozer's 'bucket' to land. It's the level of passive income you want to generate to live the life you envision. In this book, we've set a benchmark of $3,000 per week or $156,000 per year, but your personal target might differ. What's important is that you define it clearly.

Ask yourself:

- What lifestyle do I want my target income to support?
- Is my target realistic given my income, expenditure, timeline, and what things are going to cost in the future?

- Do my partner and I share the same vision for this ultimate goal?
- How will my lifestyle and expenses change over time?

Why the Four Foundation Levers matter

The Four Foundation Levers – income, expenditure, time, and target – are the controls that allow you to craft a personalised financial plan tailored to your goals. Each lever interacts with the others, meaning a small adjustment to one can influence the balance of the others. For example, tightening your expenditure might free up cash to invest sooner, while setting a higher target income might require extending your time in the workforce or looking for ways to increase your income.

Think of these levers like the strings of a guitar: each one contributes to the melody, and the harmony comes from striking the right balance. There's no universal formula – it's about tuning these levers to match your unique situation and aspirations.

Achieving this balance is where most people struggle. As you progress through the case studies later in the book, you'll see how these levers come into play in real-life scenarios, helping you understand how they can shape your thinking and priorities when building out a plan.

Rentvesting

Rentvesting lets you live where you want – often in lifestyle-rich areas that may be out of reach to buy – while investing where you can afford. It's a strategy that gives you the best of both worlds: enjoying your ideal lifestyle without putting wealth-building on hold.

For example, you might rent a sleek apartment near the city, close to work and your favourite restaurants. Meanwhile, you purchase an investment property in an outer suburb or regional area, where the entry price is lower, the land component is higher, and rental income helps offset the costs.

This strategy has become increasingly popular, particularly among younger generations who value lifestyle flexibility. For many, living close to work, nightlife, or beaches is a non-negotiable, but so is getting a foot on the property ladder. Rentvesting offers a practical solution, allowing you to live where you love while making financially smart choices about where you invest.

Rentvesting also allows you to:

- Enter the property market sooner rather than later.
- Leverage the growth potential of areas with better affordability or strong investment fundamentals.
- Retain flexibility in where you live without the long-term commitment of owning your residence.

While rentvesting can be a smart way to balance lifestyle and investment, it's not without its challenges. A PPR is resource-heavy – it uses a significant chunk of your borrowing capacity because it's not income-producing. If you choose to rentvest and delay buying a family home, that's fine, but it's a decision that needs thoughtful consideration.

Here's why:

1. **Serviceability impact:** Your borrowing capacity is finite. If you prioritise investment properties now, adding a family home later could stretch your finances or require selling to make it work.

2. **Interrupting compounding:** Selling investment properties prematurely to fund a PPR disrupts the power of

compounding – one of the most important drivers of long-term wealth creation.

3. **Medium-term sustainability:** Rentvesting works best when it's part of a broader plan that considers not just your early lifestyle years but your medium- and long-term goals. Will you still want to rent in 10 to 15 years, or will you prefer the stability of owning your own home?

4. **Future affordability risk:** Property prices will continue to rise. If you plan to buy a home later, consider how much its value may increase over time – potentially outpacing the growth of an investment property in a more affordable area.

5. **Shorter loan repayment window:** If you delay purchasing a home, you'll likely buy at a higher price down the track. This means you'll have fewer working years left to pay down the debt before retirement.

6. **Holding period risk:** If you haven't held your investment property long enough to offset purchasing costs, selling fees, and periods of negative gearing, you may end up financially worse off when switching to a PPR.

Changing your mind during a rentvesting strategy is akin to trying to turn the *Titanic* at full steam. It can't be done easily and requires enormous resources, effort, and quite often sacrifice to make it happen. We know what happened to the *Titanic* when it needed to pivot at the last minute, so rentvesting needs to be a considered part of the planning process.

17 potential investment strategies

Not all strategies are created equal. To help you tailor your approach, we'll briefly showcase 17 potential investment strategies. To help better understand them, we have organised them into four key groups, each focused on specific outcomes:

1. Area strategies for capital growth
2. Property selection strategies for capital growth
3. Area strategies for yield/income
4. Property strategies for yield/income

In our professional advisory world, these strategies represent the sharp end of your property plan – actionable tools selected and fine-tuned during 'Step 2: Evaluate' of the Five Essential Steps. However, not every strategy will suit your situation. The key is to align your choices with your goals, financial position, and comfort with risk, creating a plan that truly works for you.

Let's break down each category and explore how these strategies can shape your investment plan.

Area strategies for growth

These strategies focus on identifying locations poised for long-term appreciation, considering demographic shifts, infrastructure development, and market dynamics.

- **Proven performer:** Target areas with a reliable history of delivering consistent capital growth due to established demand, quality infrastructure, and proven performance over time.
- **Million-dollar strip:** Invest in premium suburbs where property prices exceed the median, leveraging status, limited supply and strong demand to achieve sustained growth.
- **City fling:** Focus on inner-city locations that attract professionals and high-income earners due to their proximity to jobs, lifestyle amenities, and transport hubs.

- **Rare earth:** Secure properties in tightly held locations, such as waterfronts or heritage areas, where scarcity and exclusivity drive long-term appreciation.
- **Changing places:** Identify areas undergoing gentrification, benefiting from new infrastructure, improved amenities, and changing demographics that increase desirability.
- **Wave rider:** Invest in emerging suburbs experiencing ripple effects from neighbouring suburbs that have recent growth, offering affordability and potential for future growth.

Property selection strategies for growth

These strategies refine your focus within a chosen area, helping you select properties with the highest potential for appreciation.

- **Scarce diamond:** Choose high-quality properties in excellent condition that appeal to a wide range of buyers and tenants, ensuring long-term demand and steady growth.
- **Shoulder rider (units) and piggy-backer (houses):** Leverage the benefits of other properties in the area that have been recently developed or significantly renovated to offer more up-market or valuable property stock in the local area. These strategies capitalise on the uplift in local property values, as the improved stock makes surrounding land more valuable over time.
- **Reliable and durable:** Target practical, broadly appealing properties, such as family homes, to ensure consistent demand and resilient value over time.
- **Ugly duckling:** Acquire cosmetically outdated properties with sound structures to add value through simple yet effective renovations.

- **Reno mission:** Seek properties that offer substantial renovation opportunities to create equity and improve rental income through strategic upgrades.
- **Size matters:** Prioritise properties with larger land components and a high land-to-asset ratio (LAR). Land tends to appreciate more consistently, providing inherent long-term value.

Area strategies for yield

These strategies focus on identifying locations that maximise rental income potential by targeting specific tenant demand and market conditions.

- **No vacancies:** Focus on areas with high rental demand and consistently low vacancy rates to ensure stable cashflow and reliable tenant interest.
- **The boom towners:** Target towns experiencing rapid economic growth due to industries like mining or infrastructure projects while being mindful of inherent cyclical volatility.
- **The non-aspirers:** Invest in lower socio-economic areas with higher rental yields, leveraging affordable property prices to achieve strong income returns off the back of lower debt exposure.

Property strategies for yield

These approaches optimise income by focusing on property types or configurations that generate higher rental returns.

- **The double-up:** Invest in properties with dual-income streams, such as duplexes or homes with granny flats, to enhance cashflow and reduce reliance on a single tenant.
- **The slice and dice:** Subdivide properties or convert them into multiple rental units to maximise rental income through creative configurations and higher occupancy potential.

Understanding these strategies provides you with a toolkit to craft a plan tailored to your needs. Each strategy plays a distinct role in achieving growth, yield, or a balance of both.

For a deeper dive into these strategies, download our comprehensive guide at thepropertycouch.com.au/playbook.

17 POTENTIAL INVESTMENT STRATEGIES

Category	Strategy	Description
Area strategies for growth	Proven performer	Areas with a consistent track record of capital growth.
	Million-dollar strip	Premium suburbs with status, high demand and limited supply.
	City fling	Inner-city locations appealing to professionals and high earners.
	Rare earth	Scarce, exclusive locations like waterfronts or heritage zones.
	Changing places	Gentrifying areas boosted by new infrastructure and demographics.
	Wave rider	Emerging suburbs benefiting from ripple effects of nearby hot spots.

Category	Strategy	Description
Property strategies for growth	Diamond	High-quality properties in great condition with wide appeal.
	Shoulder rider	Neighbouring suburbs to growth areas with lower entry prices.
	Reliable and durable	Broadly appealing properties, like family homes, for steady demand.
	Ugly duckling	Outdated properties ready for value-adding renovations.
	Reno mission	Properties with substantial renovation potential for equity growth.
	Size matters	Properties with larger land components for stronger long-term value.
Area strategies for yield	No vacancies	High-demand rental markets with low vacancy rates.
	The boom towners	Towns experiencing economic booms, such as mining regions.
	The non-aspirers	Lower socio-economic areas with higher rental yields.
Property strategies for yield	The double-up	Properties with dual-income streams, like duplexes or granny flats.
	The slice and dice	Subdivided properties or multi-unit conversions for increased income.

Chapter 9

Defence

Living in Australia, we are fortunate to enjoy many privileges, including access to quality education and healthcare, giving us one of life's greatest gifts – the opportunity to create something meaningful for ourselves. In less developed countries, much of life is spent simply surviving. But here, we have the chance to dream, plan, and build our lifestyle by design.

Of course, our government safety net is one of the most generous in the world, providing support when things go wrong. However, relying on it as a fallback is a reactive approach, and aspiring Australians think differently. They think longer term, understanding the importance of protecting what they're building, even when life doesn't go as planned.

I (Ben) want to share a deeply personal story that underscores the importance of planning for the best while protecting against the worst.

My brother, Jeremy, was engaged to his long-term partner, Yvette. Together, they were raising three beautiful boys and building a life they loved. In their 30s, they worked hard to live their lifestyle by design.

But out of nowhere, tragedy struck.

While holidaying in Thailand with her boys, Yvette attended a family gathering. There, she tragically slipped down a steep set of stairs, hitting her head on the concrete wall at the bottom. She was rushed to a hospital for emergency surgery to address the bleeding and swelling in her brain. Yvette survived two initial operations and the Medivac flight back to Australia. But despite months in an induced coma, she never regained consciousness and passed away at just 37 years of age.

Yvette's memory lives on through her incredible family and three boys, who continue to make her proud. But her financial legacy has also been profound. After meeting with our financial planning team and me, Yvette and Jeremy put protective measures in place as their asset base grew, ensuring that if the unimaginable ever happened, they'd be prepared.

Because of their foresight, Yvette's life insurance, combined with their investments, has enabled Jeremy to renovate the family home to accommodate three active boys and provide them with financial security – a path that would have been far more challenging without their planning. (We miss you, Yvette.)

Beyond tragedies like this, the statistics are sobering: one in two Australians will face a life-threatening medical diagnosis before age 60 unless preventative measures or treatment are sought.

The message is clear: hope for the best and work hard for it, but also plan for the unexpected. Insurance isn't just a cost – it's an asset you're paying for, and from our family's deeply personal perspective, we hope you never have to call on it – but if you do, you'll be grateful you planned ahead.

This is exactly why defence matters – it's the final pillar of property mastery and the safeguard against life's unexpected challenges. Wealth-building isn't just about growing your portfolio – it's about protecting it. Defence is the fourth leg of the Property Investment Formula 'stool', the element that ensures all your hard work doesn't crumble when the unexpected strikes. It's often overlooked yet critical for protecting long-term financial success. Think of it as building a moat around your financial castle, safeguarding it from unforeseen threats.

At its heart, defence is about preserving the life you've worked so hard to design. After all, isn't that the ultimate goal of this journey – to create and sustain a lifestyle by design? This pillar brings the other wealth-building components full circle, focusing on three interconnected areas of protection: **lifestyle**, **income**, and **assets**. Together, they form a framework for what we call **complete resilience** – the sweet spot where all three intersect to provide lasting security and peace of mind.

Lifestyle: Protecting your way of life

Your lifestyle is the centrepiece of your wealth-building journey. It's why you've set financial goals, taken risks, and worked so hard. Protecting your lifestyle means ensuring that you and your family can maintain the life you've designed, even in the face of unexpected challenges.

The greatest threats to your lifestyle often come from sudden disruptive events, such as illness, injury, or loss of life. These events can dramatically affect your household income and force tough decisions – often at the worst possible time. Defence strategies for lifestyle protection include:

- **Income protection insurance:** Replaces a significant portion of your income if you're unable to work due to illness or injury, ensuring the bulk of your current lifestyle remains intact.

- **Total and permanent disability (TPD) insurance:** Provides financial support if you are no longer able to work, helping you avoid drastic lifestyle changes.
- **Trauma/critical illness insurance:** Covers critical illnesses with a lump sum payout, allowing you to focus on recovery without financial stress.
- **Life insurance:** Also paid in a lump sum form, it helps secure your family's future in the event of your death, ensuring they can continue the life you've envisioned.

Your lifestyle is your 'why'. It's the very reason you've embarked on this wealth-building journey – to create a life by design, not by chance. Protecting it means ensuring the choices you've worked so hard to achieve remain yours, no matter what life throws your way.

Income: The fuel you can't afford to lose

Your income is the lifeblood of your financial system. Without it, your ability to sustain your lifestyle or grow your wealth diminishes. Income defence is about ensuring continuity and resilience in the face of disruptions.

Key strategies include:

- **Emergency cash reserves:** A buffer of six months' worth of living expenses to cover unforeseen events like job loss or major repairs. Cash reserves buy you time to assess options.
- **Income protection insurance:** Plays a dual role in defending both your lifestyle and your income stream.
- **Diversified income streams:** Generating passive income from multiple sources, such as rental properties or share

investments, reduces dependency on a single salary, for example.

- **Debt management:** Keeping debt manageable ensures that unexpected changes in income don't derail your financial stability.

Income resilience is about preparation and creating a safety net that allows you to navigate life's uncertainties without sacrificing your long-term goals. It's the foundation that keeps your financial engine running, ensuring you remain in control no matter what comes your way.

Assets: Fortifying what you own

Your assets represent the foundation of your wealth. Whether it's your home, investment properties, or other investments, they need to be defended against risks that could erode their value or utility.

Key asset defence strategies include:

- **Building insurance:** Protects against damage from natural disasters, fires, or other unforeseen events.
- **Landlord protection insurance:** Covers rental properties against tenant-related risks like non-payment of rent or property damage.
- **Professional property management:** Ensures your investments are well-maintained and protected from costly mistakes.
- **Estate planning:** Creates a roadmap for passing your assets on to loved ones, minimising disputes and taxes.

- **Diversification:** Spreading investments across state borders and various asset types reduces risk exposure to any one market or event.

Defending your assets helps you avoid losses and ensures the assets continue to support your income, lifestyle, and legacy. This is how you create durability in your wealth-building strategy, ensuring that the foundation you've built remains solid for years to come.

Complete resilience: Where lifestyle, income, and assets intersect

At the heart of complete resilience lies your lifestyle – the life you've worked so hard to design. By balancing the protection of your income, assets, and lifestyle, you ensure your financial castle can weather any storm while allowing you to live the life you've envisioned.

Here's how they interact:

- **Protecting your lifestyle** ensures your family's well-being, even when disruptions arise.
- **Safeguarding your income** ensures the financial engine driving your goals remains intact.
- **Fortifying your assets** ensures the resources you've worked hard to accumulate continue to serve you.

By aligning these three areas, you build a financial moat that's robust and adaptable – allowing you to weather life's uncertainties while staying on track toward your goals.

Defence is what lets you sleep well at night, knowing your financial castle is fortified against whatever life throws at it.

Think of it as the seatbelt on your wealth-building journey. It may not feel as thrilling as hitting the accelerator, but when the unexpected happens, it's what keeps you safe and on course. By locking in your lifestyle, securing your income, and safeguarding your assets, you're not just building wealth – you're ensuring it lasts. This is the foundation of a life by design, not by default. Now that's a legacy worth protecting.

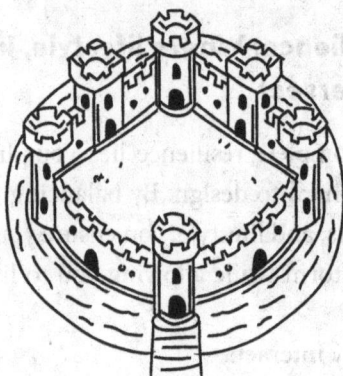

DOES YOUR CASTLE HAVE A MOAT?

Part II – Wrap

The Property Investment Formula: Your climbing ropes to the summit

You've now got what took us decades to develop and master – a proven formula for building a high-performing property portfolio. This isn't theory or guesswork. The ABCD of Property Investing framework is the result of:

✓ **Hard-won mastery** through real-world investing – our own wins, losses, and lessons.

✓ **Hundreds of hours** of expert conversations with the sharpest minds in property and finance.

✓ **Thousands of hours** at the coalface guiding investors through the highs, lows, and critical decisions.

✓ **Countless real-world insights** from everyday aspiring Australians actively building their portfolios.

It's been our life's work to decode the game of property investing and put it into a framework that cuts through the noise and actually works. This is the unlock we wish we'd had when we started investing back in the '90s. Now, you don't have to waste years learning through trial and error. You've collapsed time, taking 50+ years of experience and distilling it into a structured, repeatable process.

But here's the thing: mastery isn't just knowing the formula – it's applying it. If you can lock in these four pillars, you'll set yourself apart from the majority of investors:

✓ **Asset selection:** Picking the best-suited properties, in the right location that drives sustained growth.

✓ **Borrowing power:** Fuelling your journey with smart finance decisions.

✓ **Cashflow management:** Keeping your portfolio breathing and sustainable.

✓ **Defence:** Protecting your wealth from risk and setbacks.

You're now past base camp. You have the blueprint, the tools, and the strategy. The question is – what will you do with them? Because the truth is, even the best strategy is powerless without execution.

In the next part, we confront the final ascent – the point where most investors stall. This is not because they lack information, but because they hesitate to act. We'll unpack why that happens, how to move past fear, and what action actually looks like.

You'll also discover the key decision all investors must make: Will you invest actively or passively? We'll weigh the pros and cons, so you can decide what suits your life – not someone else's.

And, yes, we'll also touch on the boring-but-critical stuff – like tax. Because understanding how money works (and what the tax office takes) is essential if you want to keep more of what you earn.

Lastly, we'll help you zoom out and think long term – because knowing how to build wealth is only half the game. You also need to know how to land the plane.

The peak is within reach. Let's keep climbing.

PART III
Taking Action

OK, we've reached the final ascent – the 'how' of retiring on $3,000 per week. You've built your foundation, mapped out the right route, and gathered the tools to succeed. But before we push for the summit, we need to address the biggest obstacle standing between most investors and financial freedom. It's not a lack of knowledge. It's not bad luck. It's INACTION.

Over the past 25 years of personal investing and nearly 50 years of combined professional experience, we've seen it time and time again. Too many stop just short of the summit, hesitating, second-guessing, waiting for perfect conditions that never come. Taking action is the final frontier to success because, without it, all the knowledge and planning in the world is just a dream.

Learning, planning, setting goals – it's easy to get caught up in the preparation. But knowledge alone won't get you to the top. Only action will. Knowledge is empowering, but only if you act on it. Every week on the podcast, Ben signs off with this message, and for good reason. Time and time again, we've seen that the single most consistent trait of successful property investors isn't intelligence, luck, or resources – it's action. Those who succeed are the ones who step forward, make decisions, and take concrete steps toward their goals.

If taking action is so critical, why do so many people struggle with it? The answer often lies beneath the surface, in deeply ingrained limiting beliefs about money that act as invisible barriers to progress. These beliefs, often inherited from family or societal norms, can sabotage even the best-laid plans.

In her book *The Abundance Code*, Julie Ann Cairns outlines seven common money myths that hold people back:

1. **Scarcity:** The belief that resources are limited
   ('Money doesn't grow on trees').
2. **Time equals money:** The idea that earning more always
   requires working harder.
3. **Work equals worth:** Equating financial success with
   relentless effort.
4. **It takes money to make money:** Thinking wealth-building
   is impossible without a significant starting sum.
5. **Easy come, easy go:** Distrusting financial gains that feel
   'too easy'.
6. **Money won't make you happy:** Downplaying the role of
   financial stability in personal well-being.
7. **Money corrupts:** Associating wealth with moral decline.

Julie discussed these myths on Episode 219 of our podcast, 'How going from 30 properties to Bankruptcy shaped this riches to rags... and back again story!', explaining that they aren't just passing thoughts – they're deep-rooted subconscious scripts that dictate behaviour. They're the silent killers of financial freedom, undermining your progress without you even realising it.

While it's beyond the scope of this book to tackle these beliefs in depth, our goal here is to bring them to your awareness. Identifying and challenging these subconscious blockers is a crucial step toward adopting an investor's mindset – one that sees wealth-building as achievable and deserving.

Adopting an investor's mindset means challenging limiting beliefs and aligning your thoughts with your goals. Wealth-building isn't luck – it's a process. It's also about understanding that taking action doesn't mean perfection – it means progress.

Property investing isn't rocket science, but it does require consistent effort and decision-making. The people who've achieved financial freedom through property all took action (noticing a theme here!). Yes, they had knowledge. Yes, they made mistakes along the way. But they didn't let fear or limiting beliefs paralyse them.

You now have the strategies, frameworks, and insights. But, like climbing gear left in a backpack, they only work if you put them to use. Taking action is the moment when theory becomes a reality, plans transform into results, and personal and financial goals materialise.

This doesn't mean rushing into decisions without thought – it means intentional action guided by knowledge. It's about taking that first step, however small, and letting momentum build from there. Whether it's setting up a MoneySMARTS system, engaging a property investment adviser, or setting up your borrowing strategy, each action brings you closer to your goals.

As you prepare to move into action, take a moment to reflect on what's holding you back. Is it fear? Uncertainty? A belief that you're not ready or not capable? Recognise these as obstacles you can overcome. Start small if you need to, but start. Because in the end, success isn't just about knowing what to do – it's about doing it.

The strategies we've shared in this book are proven to work, but they only work if you use them. So here's our challenge: take the next step. Your $3,000-a-week lifestyle won't come to you – you have to climb toward it.

This is it – the final ascent of property investing mastery. The best part? You're ready. The plan is in place, and the path is clear. Now, take the last step. The summit is waiting.

THE YOUNG BOY WAITING FOR THE PRICE OF REAL ESTATE TO GO DOWN

Chapter 10

Active versus passive investing

In the property world, there's plenty of buzz around active investing. The active crew often flaunt their ability to 'manufacture' additional value and fast-track returns. They dive into renovations, subdivisions, and developments, turning 'apples into apple pie' to maximise profits. But let's take a step back – what do the stats tell us? According to the Australian Taxation Office (ATO), 71% of property investors in Australia stop at just one property (more on that later). Why? Most people simply don't have the time, energy, or resources to navigate the complexities of active investing.

So, which approach is best for you? Let's break it down.

Active investing: Rolling up your sleeves

Active investing is about diving in and doing the work. From flipping a fixer-upper to subdividing land or managing a development project, this approach is all about adding value through effort and expertise. It's a high-risk, high-reward strategy that can accelerate wealth – but it's not for everyone.

Active investing requires significant time, energy, and emotional bandwidth. You'll need skills, a reliable network, and the resilience to handle the literally hundreds of decisions you need to make, plus manage unexpected challenges. And let's not overlook the hidden cost: your time. Many active investors forget to account for the hours they invest, which can diminish the overall returns. While active strategies can produce impressive results, they will come with added time, stress, complexity, and risks.

Passive investing: Quietly building wealth

Passive investing, on the other hand, is the unsung hero of wealth-building. It's about selecting investment-grade properties in proven locations and letting time and compounding do the heavy lifting. Passive investors avoid the headaches of managing renovations, dealing with contractors, or navigating zoning laws. Instead, they focus on building a portfolio that grows steadily and requires minimal hands-on involvement.

This approach resonates with most people because life is already demanding enough. Passive investing offers simplicity, stability, and a clear path to financial freedom. You'll still need to make plenty of important decisions, and there will still be some challenges to manage, but it's about creating a system that quietly works in the background so you can focus on what matters most in your life.

In this book, we advocate for passive investing. Why? Because it's a smarter, simpler way for the majority of people to reach their financial goals. The path to $3,000 per week doesn't require swinging hammers or drawing up subdivision plans. As you'll see in our case studies later in the book, this goal is entirely achievable with as few as two investment properties and without the added complexity of active strategies.

That's not to say active investing doesn't have its place. For those who thrive on the challenge, it can offer a fast track to higher returns – the classic risk versus reward equation. But for most, passive investing provides a sustainable, low-stress solution that aligns with real life. It's a proven approach that delivers freedom without unnecessary complications and often without too great a risk.

Forget the noise of flashy headlines and complicated strategies. Passive investing works because it's intentional, straightforward, and scalable. It builds wealth in a way that complements your life rather than complicating it.

So, we prefer to keep it simple.

Exchange Traded Funds

It would be remiss of us not to talk about a growing trend around ETFs (Exchange Traded Funds). Finfluencers – financial influencers on social media – are shaping how younger generations think about investing. Whether it's on TikTok, Instagram, or YouTube, these personalities are making wealth creation feel accessible and relatable. Their bite-sized advice often focuses on ETFs, shares, and micro-investing platforms, offering an appealing alternative to those who feel the property market is out of reach.

Here's how finfluencers are changing the investment landscape:

- **Making investing accessible:** Finfluencers simplify complex topics, showing how small, consistent contributions to ETFs can grow over time. Their relatable approach often bridges the knowledge gap for first-time investors, helping them feel more confident in taking that first step.

- **Promoting micro-investing:** Platforms that allow fractional ownership of shares have surged in popularity, thanks to finfluencers. The idea of 'invest while you save' appeals to those wanting to feel proactive about their money without needing a large upfront commitment.

- **Reframing property:** Some finfluencers argue that ETFs offer advantages that property can't match: liquidity, diversification, and lower barriers to entry. This messaging resonates with those disillusioned by high house prices or hesitant about taking on significant debt.

For many younger investors, ETFs offer an appealing entry point with their low cost and flexibility. The ability to start small with dollar-cost averaging resonates with those who feel daunted by saving for a property deposit. But this raises an important question: are ETFs a replacement for property, or are they a stepping stone to something more substantial?

While ETFs can be a brilliant tool for building wealth, we feel very strongly about the long-term stability that owning property – at very least, a PPR – provides. A home isn't just an asset; it's a castle. It shields you from rising rents, provides a place to live, and creates a strong foundation for retirement. Just ask someone in retirement who doesn't own their own home how challenging it can be.

However, ETFs can be a considered option for aspiring investors to use to save for a property deposit while keeping pace with inflation and gaining valuable investing experience. They're flexible and accessible, making them a smart starting point. Ultimately, for us, property ownership should remain the

definitive goal. A home delivers what even the most diversified ETF portfolio cannot – a roof over your head, peace of mind, and the ability to live life on your terms.

The rise of ETFs and finfluencers marks a positive shift, making financial literacy more accessible than ever. But for us, the buzz around ETFs shouldn't overshadow the enduring value of property as both a financial and emotional cornerstone. It's about finding balance – leveraging ETFs to build momentum while keeping your eyes on the ultimate prize of owning your own home.

By combining the best of both worlds – starting with ETFs to grow your wealth and transitioning to property ownership – you create a strategy that blends flexibility with long-term security. It's not just about accumulating assets; it's about designing a life where you're in control. For most Australians, that begins with the stability and freedom that come with owning your own home.

Just so we're clear: ETFs are a licensed financial product, so this isn't advice – just our take. Consider this a conversation starter, not a recommendation. Before making any ETF or financial product moves, seek qualified financial advice.

Chapter 11
Lifting the veil on property investing

Property investing can often feel like an insider's game, and for good reason. It's not just about buying, selling, or maybe renovating – it's about accessing a world that most people don't even know exists. Imagine walking through a private door in an exclusive country club. On the surface, everything up until this point seems as expected, but as you step through that door, you realise there's an entirely different game being played inside – a game that operates by a completely different set of rules. Someone greets you as you enter and says, 'Welcome, we've been waiting for you to arrive'. You're taken aback. 'Waiting for me? I didn't even know this room existed!' And that's the thing – until you're on the inside, you don't even realise what you've been missing.

Stepping through that door isn't just about learning who the players are; it's also about understanding the strategies and tactics they use to keep outsiders at a disadvantage. This secret game isn't just about property transactions; it's about hidden networks, exclusive knowledge, and negotiation strategies that favour those who know how the system really works. It's a game where those

on the inside have the tools to win, while those on the outside are often left guessing.

At its core, the property industry is designed to benefit those who understand its intricacies – those who know how the players operate, where the incentives lie, and how to distinguish genuine advice from sales tactics. That's why our podcast tagline is, and always will be, the 'Insider's Guide to Property, Finance, and Money Management'. We want to help you step through that door, lift the veil, and understand the game on a deeper level. We want to arm you with the knowledge and confidence to navigate the industry effectively, avoid common pitfalls, and make decisions from a level playing field.

The first step to getting on the inside is understanding who the players in the game are so you can sidestep the first tripwire you'll encounter: conflicts of interest.

Free or fee advice?

With property advice, there are two models of service:

1. **Free advice**, where professionals are paid a commission or fee by the seller of the property.
2. **Fee-for-service advice**, where you pay a professional to act in your best interests.

The difference is critical because it highlights the biggest conflict of interest in property investing. Free advice may seem appealing on the surface – it doesn't cost you upfront – but it's rarely free of bias. Professionals offering free advice are typically aligned with the self-interest of the seller, as their commission depends on closing the deal. This creates an inherent conflict: the advice they give will prioritise the seller's goals, not yours.

Fee-for-service advice, on the other hand, is aligned with you, the buyer, because you're the one paying for it. This structure removes the conflict of interest, ensuring that the advice you receive is tailored to your needs and not influenced by a self-serving outcome or, even worse, hidden incentives. To navigate this effectively, ask yourself these key questions when dealing with any property professional:

- Who is this person working for?
- Are they advising me or selling me something?

Recognising this distinction is your first step toward navigating the property game like an insider. Knowing the motivations of those you deal with and understanding where their incentives lie is crucial to making informed decisions. True independence in property advice comes at a price – but it's a price worth paying when your financial future is on the line. By learning these strategies, you're not just stepping through that door – you're mastering the game being played on the other side (the insider's game).

Meet the players

To truly understand how the property industry operates, you need to identify the key players shaping it. Let's break down who they are, what they do, and where their loyalties lie.

Free advice-givers

Let's start with the left-hand side of the quadrant (see opposite) – the real estate agent and the project marketer. They operate within the free-advice component of the industry, and you're likely to encounter them. They market and advertise heavily and look flashy and sophisticated, and they'll give you free information in the form of webinars, seminars, brochures, or flyers. They also enable you to buy a property that they're offering for free (i.e. you just pay the price of the property with no additional payment to the agent). This is because their client is the seller of the property.

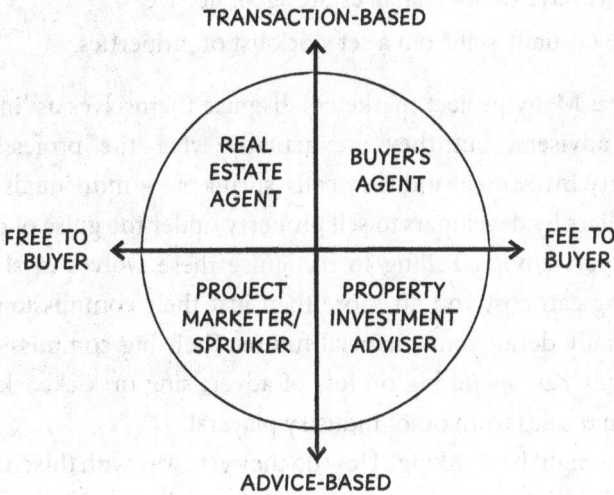

```
                    TRANSACTION-BASED
                            ↑

                    REAL         BUYER'S
                    ESTATE       AGENT
                    AGENT

  FREE TO  ←─────────────────┼─────────────────→  FEE TO
  BUYER                      │                     BUYER

                    PROJECT      PROPERTY
                    MARKETER/    INVESTMENT
                    SPRUIKER     ADVISER

                            ↓
                      ADVICE-BASED
```

THE INDUSTRY PLAYERS

Let's break it down further.

Real estate agents:
- Primarily deal with established properties.
- Work for the seller, not the buyer.
- Their goal is to achieve the highest sale price, as they earn a commission (1% to 3% of the sale price).
- Must hold a valid real estate agent licence.
- If they don't sell, they don't eat.

Project marketers:

- Sell brand-new off-the-plan apartments, house-and-land packages, or townhouse developments.
- Represent the developer, not the buyer.
- Get paid a significant sales commission (5% to 10% of the purchase price).
- Don't have to hold a real estate agent licence.
- They usually sell from a set stock list of properties.

Beware: Many project marketers disguise themselves as 'investment advisers', but they are actually what the professional property investment industry calls 'spruikers' – individuals paid big dollars by developers to sell property under the guise of offering expert advice. Failing to recognise these wolves in sheep's clothing can cost you far more than just their commission – it can totally derail your financial future. Their big commission is why they can spend big on lots of advertising or kickbacks for leads and sales from other industry players!

You might be thinking, 'How do they get away with this?' Good question! It's because direct property isn't a licensed investment product, so it's unregulated – that's how they get around it.

Fee-for-service providers

On the right-hand side of the quadrant, we move into the fee-paying scenarios, of which there are two: the buyer's agent and the property investment adviser. These guys are fee-for-service providers, which means their income is derived from the money they charge their clients. Let's break it down again.

Buyer's agents:

- Represent and work for you, the buyer, to find the best property in the marketplace that aligns with your interests.

- Are paid a flat fee or a percentage (1% to 3%, typically) of the purchase price by you, the client.
- Must hold a valid real estate agent licence.
- Work exclusively in your best interests (i.e. Step 4 of our Five Essential Steps – 'Implement').

Property investment advisers:

- Their client is you, the property investor.
- Offer advisory and property investment planning services tailored to your objectives and based on your financial situation and risk profile.
- Should have a supporting qualification to do the work they perform, such as a Qualified Property Investment Adviser (QPIA) qualification.
- Don't sell from set stock lists.
- Charge a fixed planning fee, often comparable to traditional financial planners, that typically ranges from $3,500 to $6,000 for a full plan and an annual review fee of $1,000 to $2,000 to help manage and review a client's property portfolio.
- Perform and coordinate each of the Five Essential Steps and offer end-to-end professional service.

*

One of the most surprising aspects of the property industry is its low barrier to entry. Unlike doctors or lawyers, who require years of education and rigorous qualifications, anyone can label themselves a 'property expert' without formal training. A sharp suit, a polished pitch, and a rented seminar or online webinar room are often all it takes.

This lack of regulation allows unscrupulous operators to prey on uninformed investors, often pushing high-commission properties under the guise of 'investment opportunities'. That's why understanding the motivations behind free advice is critical – hidden agendas often lurk behind glossy brochures and high-pressure sales pitches.

Getting to the insider's game doesn't mean endorsing their rules – it simply means understanding them and making them work for you. By knowing who the players are, how they get paid, and whose interests they're serving, you can make better decisions.

This isn't about cynicism; it's about clarity. The property game is full of genuine professionals who provide excellent services, but it's also rife with operators who thrive on enthusiastic yet uninformed consumers via confusion, deception, and deceit. The more you know, the less likely you are to fall for the latter.

So, when dealing with any property professional, keep these questions in mind:

- Are they providing tailored advice based on my circumstances?
- How are they getting paid?
- Are they aligned with my goals, or are they incentivised to sell a specific property?
- Who are they working for?
- Are they licensed or qualified?

Now that we've peeled back the curtain on the players and their motivations, it's time to dig deeper into the strategies used to sell property. Developers, in particular, have mastered the art of persuasion with tactics designed to lure buyers into deals that might look great on paper but fall short in practice. In the next section, we'll unpack the developer tactics you'll face – giving you the tools to spot their tricks, sidestep their traps, and take the driver's seat on your property journey.

Buyer beware!

Hopefully, we've made it clear throughout this book that we firmly believe in the value of established property over brand-new developments. The reasons are simple – established properties typically offer stronger growth potential, better locations, and more reliable performance over time. We see far too many investors lured into the flashy promises of new house-and-land or off-the-plan apartment investment stock.

Why does this happen? Developers and their army of spruikers often have enormous marketing budgets, enabling them to create persuasive ads and campaigns filled with hook promises that seem impossible to resist. From rental guarantees to tax depreciation benefits, these messages are carefully designed to appeal to emotions and offer quick-fix solutions. The allure can feel overwhelming, especially for first-time investors or those who haven't had the opportunity to dig deeper into the numbers.

So, let's call them out. Over the next few pages, we've outlined the most common tricks spruikers use to sell developers' properties. Armed with this knowledge, you'll be better prepared to see through the spin, make informed decisions, and avoid costly mistakes. It's not just about being aware of the tricks – it's about recognising how they're designed to influence you, and taking back control of your investment journey.

Spruiker trick #1: Tax and the depreciation allure

Developers often use depreciation as their primary sales tool, promoting the tax savings you'll enjoy by purchasing a brand-new property. While depreciation can indeed offer tax benefits, it doesn't improve the intrinsic value of the property. Depreciation-focused pitches distract buyers from the main game: capital growth. If the property lacks scarcity or owner-occupier appeal, any tax benefits won't make up for poor long-term performance. Instead, you could invest in an established property in a better area and create depreciation benefits through a smart renovation – without sacrificing growth potential.

Spruiker trick #2: Tax and the holding cost illusion

Another common tactic is to downplay the actual cost of holding the property by factoring in depreciation to make the numbers look appealing. The pitch usually goes like this: 'With all the tax benefits, this property will cost you just $50 a week to hold'. While this sounds manageable, these numbers often fail to account for rising interest rates, vacancy periods, or unexpected expenses. In many cases, an established property with better growth prospects and a lower rental yield could offer better value for only slightly higher holding costs.

Spruiker trick #3: The land-is-king myth

'Land is what drives price growth' is a mantra often used to promote house-and-land packages in far-flung suburbs or greenfield estates. While it's true that, ultimately, land value is what appreciates over time, it's not just about the land's size – it's about its location and scarcity. For example, a smaller share of land in a high-demand area closer to the CBD often outperforms a land parcel in an outer suburb with limited scarcity or lifestyle amenities and weaker demand drivers. The higher land component of the purchase price in premium locations generally leads to stronger long-term capital growth, and the same is true in outer locations where more of the value is in land and not the improvements (dwelling), yet typically, the improvements cost more than the land in new estates. Hence, we like established properties in older estates on our city fringes because more of the value is in the land rather than the improvements.

Spruiker trick #4: The rental-guarantee trap

Rental guarantees are often marketed as a safety net, promising a fixed rental income for a set period, typically one or two years. However, the guarantee is usually built into the property's inflated purchase price, meaning you're effectively paying for your own guarantee upfront. Moreover, if the property were truly investment-grade, such guarantees wouldn't be necessary, as demand would already exist. Once the guarantee expires, you may be left with a property that struggles to attract tenants at the promised rate.

Spruiker trick #5: Limited-time offers

Developers frequently use artificial scarcity to create urgency with phrases like 'Offer ends this weekend' or 'Only three units left at this price!' These tactics are designed to pressure buyers into making hasty decisions without fully understanding the deal. Genuine opportunities don't need manufactured deadlines. Take the time to conduct proper due diligence rather than succumbing to high-pressure sales tactics.

Spruiker trick #6: Overpromising future infrastructure

One of the most enticing hooks developers use is promoting nearby infrastructure that is 'coming soon'. From new train stations to schools and shopping centres, these promises are used to justify high property prices and growth predictions. However, many of these projects are delayed, scaled back, or cancelled altogether. Always verify claims of future infrastructure through independent sources and focus on areas with existing demand drivers to reduce risk.

Spruiker trick #7: Unrealistic growth promises

Developers love to make bold or generic claims about future growth, such as 'This area is set to double in value over the next four to seven years!' These predictions are often based on selective or outdated data and fail to account for oversupply risks, changing demographics, or broader market conditions. Always base your decisions on independent research rather than taking growth promises at face value.

Spruiker trick #8: Inflating property values with incentives

Developers often inflate property prices to absorb government incentives or grants, such as first home buyer schemes, the NDIS (National Disability Insurance Scheme), or build-to-rent programs. These schemes are designed to help first home buyers and tenants (and for good reason), but unscrupulous developers use them to make their properties appear more appealing while disguising inflated prices. For example, an NDIS property may promise high rental yields but could come with high management fees, restrictive tenant requirements, significant market limitations, and limited demand for future re-sale. Always calculate whether the numbers stack up independently of the incentives.

Spruiker trick #9: Investing in your SMSF without adequate planning

Developers often target self-managed superannuation fund (SMSF) investors, promoting the idea of buying property within your super to save on taxes and grow wealth. However, this approach is not suitable for everyone. SMSFs generally require higher levels of financial literacy, have limited borrowing capacity, and come with various obligations, while properties within SMSFs often have high associated costs and restrictions on usage (e.g. you cannot live in the property). For investors with lower SMSF balances, the high costs of managing an SMSF can erode returns. Always consult a qualified and experienced SMSF specialist before committing to such a strategy.

Spruiker trick #10: High-yield, low-growth areas

High-yield properties, such as those in mining towns or low-demand regional areas, are frequently marketed as cashflow winners. While high yields may look appealing in the short term, these properties often suffer from limited capital growth potential. When the boom cycle ends, the property's value can drop significantly, leaving investors exposed to losses. Instead, focus on 'balanced' properties (covered in Chapter 6, 'Asset selection') that deliver both reasonable cashflow and strong growth prospects.

Spruiker trick #11: Buy six, sell three

Spruikers often promote the idea of rapidly building a six-property portfolio, then selling three to pay off debt and own the remaining three outright. While this sounds like a smart strategy, it benefits the spruiker far more than the investor – they secure six commissions instead of three. Statistics show that most investors stop at just one property (more on that later), making this an overly aggressive and unnecessarily risky approach. It also ignores the mental load of scaling from no properties to a large portfolio in a short time, which can be overwhelming and difficult to manage.

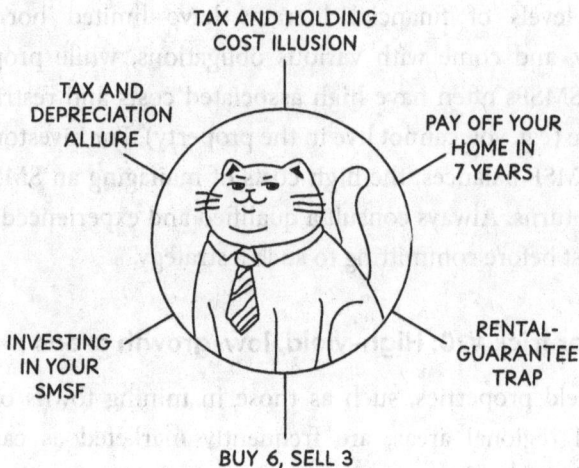

TAX AND HOLDING
COST ILLUSION

TAX AND
DEPRECIATION
ALLURE

PAY OFF YOUR
HOME IN
7 YEARS

INVESTING
IN YOUR
SMSF

RENTAL-
GUARANTEE
TRAP

BUY 6, SELL 3

PROPERTY SPRUIKERS' TRICKS

Spruiker trick #12: Pay off your home in seven years

Many spruikers exploit homeowners' desire to be debt-free, pitching strategies that claim to eliminate mortgages quickly. In reality, these tactics often involve shifting debt into investment loans while pushing overpriced new builds or off-the-plan properties that build a premium into the price only to be returned as a rental guarantee to be 'positive cashflow'. Rather than genuinely reducing debt, these schemes create a false sense of security while benefiting the spruiker. Worse still, some of these strategies may fall into legally grey areas, increasing the risk of scrutiny from regulatory authorities. A better approach is to focus on structured, sustainable debt reduction – buying quality assets and avoiding gimmicks that promise shortcuts but deliver long-term financial consequences.

Spruiker trick #13: FREE webinar/seminar funnel

Free property seminars or webinars often appear educational but are actually hard sells. Spruikers lure attendees with promises of 'insider secrets' before upselling them into expensive mentorship programs, which position them as 'VIP' investors. This so-called exclusivity is just another sales funnel – giving spruikers a curated list of buyers to whom they can push overpriced properties. These events create urgency, limiting attendees' ability to conduct due diligence, often leading to rushed purchases. Genuine education empowers investors to make informed, independent decisions – without pressure, sales tactics, or inflated promises.

*

If you want to hear more about how these tactics play out in real life, check out Episode 538, 'Property Spruikers 2.0: The Latest Tactics Designed to Trap You', where we unpack these schemes in detail and reveal the red flags to watch for.

The four ways you'll pay as a property investor

By now, you've seen how the property game is played and the tricks some players use to sway unsuspecting buyers. But here's the thing: even when you know the rules, there are still ways you can end up paying more than you should. Let's dive into the four most common mistakes investors end up making – and how to avoid them.

1. Buying the wrong asset

The biggest (and costliest) mistake is choosing the wrong property. Many investors assume that because they've lived in a home, they know how to pick a great investment. But residential real estate isn't like other investment markets – it's dominated by emotional owner-occupiers, not rational investors.

Why it matters:

- **Low growth potential:** Poorly chosen properties often underperform, achieving limited capital growth compared to well-selected assets. When compounded over time, the gap can be enormous.

- **Missed opportunities:** Without scarcity or strong owner-occupier appeal, properties struggle to gain value, leaving money on the table.

2. Procrastination

The second way investors pay is through inaction. Waiting for the 'perfect time' to invest, or endlessly researching without making a decision, has a hidden cost that compounds over time and is one of the most expensive mistakes you'll never see coming.

Why it matters:

- **Higher entry costs:** Property markets don't wait, and rising prices can push entry-level investments out of reach.

- **Lost compounding growth:** Every year you delay is a year of missed opportunity for your investment to grow.

3. Paying too much

Overpaying for a property is another trap, particularly for those who lack negotiation experience or fall for the shine of brand-new builds.

Why it matters:

- **Skilled negotiators:** Real estate agents negotiate daily, giving them the upper hand over inexperienced buyers.
- **The illusion of new:** Brand-new properties are often inflated with emotively attractive features, developer margins, marketing fees, and build costs, leaving little room for growth.

4. Professional advice

Finally, some investors believe they can do it all themselves or that 'free' advice is just as good as paid, expert guidance. The reality? Free advice often comes with hidden agendas.

Why it matters:

- **True independence costs:** Fee-for-service professionals, like Qualified Property Investment Advisers and buyer's agents, act in your best interests – not the seller's.
- **Compounding returns:** A well-chosen property that grows even 1% to 2% more per year can create extraordinary long-term wealth.
- **The hidden cost of 'free' advice:** Sales commissions (up to 10%) are often buried in the price of new builds – so you're paying, whether you realise it or not.

*

You get to decide how you pay. Some people avoid upfront costs by skipping expert advice only to realise later that they've paid far more through lost time, poor decisions, or missed opportunities. At first, paying for professional guidance might seem like a big expense, but in the long run, it's the net result that matters – not just the upfront cost.

To step through that private door and stay on the inside, you need more than theory – you need the right team. And that's exactly what we'll cover in the next section, where we'll show you how to assemble your team – the experts who will guide you, protect you, and make sure you're not just playing the game but winning it.

Building your investment dream team

To succeed in property investing, you need a trusted team of skilled professionals to guide you and the right mindset to help you land the plane.

Your team doesn't just provide technical expertise – they help balance your mindset, encouraging action without recklessness. But who exactly do you need on your dream team? Let's explore.

Qualified Property Investment Adviser

A Qualified Property Investment Adviser (QPIA) is your strategic architect, designing a roadmap for your property journey. Their role goes beyond simple advice – they craft your investment strategy, provide tailored recommendations, and plan your portfolio with a long-term focus.

They clearly document your goals and objectives, your risk appetite, and the risks associated with an investment, all within a comprehensive written property investment plan supported by detailed graphs and tables on future spending, cashflow, borrowings, tax, and wealth forecasts with appropriate assumptions as it relates to your retirement targets. Their expertise ensures you remain focused on the ideal blend of potential locations and best-suited, investment-grade properties that align with your desire to retire on $3,000 per week.

They're the trusted cornerstone of your team, turning your vision into actionable steps and outcomes.

Investment-savvy mortgage broker

An experienced mortgage broker doesn't just source loans – they structure your finances strategically to support your property goals. From credit planning to managing loan structures, they ensure your borrowing strategy forms part of your overall plan for now and in the future. If they're doing their job right, they should really be your 'personal' banker.

Buyer's agent

Your buyer's agent acts as your dedicated market area and property selection specialist, responsible for clarifying your brief, identifying, assessing, negotiating, and securing best-suited investment-grade properties that align with your strategy. They're not just an extra set of eyes – they ARE your eyes and ears on the ground. They are playing every day on the 'inside'!

Financial planner

A licensed financial planner takes a holistic approach to your wealth creation and management, covering superannuation/SMSFs, managed funds, shares, and personal insurances. They ensure your property investments are seamlessly integrated into your broader financial, wealth, and retirement strategy, safeguarding your retirement and long-term objectives and financial security. As the architects of your financial defence pillar, they implement crucial risk insurances to protect your wealth. Think of them as building a moat around your property portfolio.

Accountant

A property-savvy accountant is essential for determining the best ownership structure for your investments – be it individual ownership, partnerships, trusts, companies, or SMSFs. As a licensed tax agent, their expertise ensures your tax position is optimised while remaining fully compliant with regulations. By legally maximising deductions, they play a pivotal role in managing both your income and capital gains tax obligations in an effort to enhance your cashflow, allowing your portfolio to perform more effectively and efficiently.

Solicitor

Your solicitor is indispensable for reviewing contracts, handling conveyancing, and safeguarding your assets. They ensure property transfers and guarantees are seamlessly executed while protecting you from any hidden surprises in the purchase process. Their expertise provides peace of mind and solid legal protection for your investments. Thinking more broadly, they will play an important role in your estate planning and wills as your wealth base grows.

Building and pest inspector

A thorough inspection before purchasing a property is essential. A trusted building and pest inspector helps you avoid costly mistakes by identifying structural issues or pest infestations before they become your problem. Their fee is the best insurance to make sure you don't end up paying thousands.

Property manager

A skilled property manager is your on-the-ground partner for maintaining and maximising the performance of your investment. They handle tenant selection, rent collection, property maintenance, and compliance with rental regulations, ensuring your asset remains a hassle-free source of income. By managing day-to-day operations and addressing any issues promptly, they protect your property's value and free you to focus on growing your portfolio. They also coordinate essential safety and compliance checks – such as electrical, plumbing, and gas inspections to meet minimum standards in your state or territory – to safeguard your investment. A good property manager is an investment in peace of mind and long-term success.

*

These professionals ensure you're equipped to make informed, confident decisions at every stage of your investment journey.

Even with the best team, your success depends on your mindset as a long-term investor. Your team not only provides technical expertise but also helps keep your mindset balanced – encouraging action without recklessness.

Chapter 12

Tax and property

This book wouldn't be complete if we didn't talk about tax. We know – it's not the most exciting topic, but it's an essential part of investing in property. On the upside, property investors have a unique opportunity to utilise the tax system in ways that can significantly improve cashflow. For instance, negative gearing allows you to offset property losses against other income, such as salary or wages, often resulting in a tax refund that can help fund your investment journey.

But tax isn't all upside – there are other costs investors need to be aware of, such as stamp duty, capital gains tax, and land tax. These can impact your returns if not managed thoughtfully.

In this chapter, we'll break it all down and simplify it, giving you a clear understanding of what you'll encounter as a property investor. By the end, you'll be informed and better prepared to navigate this critical part of building wealth through property. While tax might not be thrilling, understanding the basics will be an important factor in your success.

Ownership and tax impacts

Navigating the complexities of tax and ownership structures in property investing is no small task. With ever-changing regulations and financial implications that can significantly impact your returns, this topic could fill an entire book on its own.

For this book, we're keeping it simple, summarising the basics so you can understand the core differences in ownership structures and their tax impacts. But if property investing is set to become a serious business for you, it's critical to seek advice from a licensed tax professional (accountant). A well-structured ownership plan, tailored to your situation, can make a world of difference to your long-term success.

Again, this is not intended to be advice, but rather a high-level guide to help you identify key considerations and work with your own legal and accounting team to ensure you're making informed decisions.

Personal/Individual ownership

This is by far the most common and straightforward way to own investment properties – and for good reason. Individual ownership keeps things simple, stripping away the additional tax complexities that come with trusts or companies.

From a day-to-day perspective, rental income and expenses are reported in your personal tax return, just like any other income or deductible expense. If your property makes a profit, that income is added to your taxable earnings for the year. If it makes a loss, that loss can be offset against your other taxable income – a key advantage known as negative gearing (which we'll cover in more detail shortly).

From a capital perspective, when you sell a property, any gain is treated as income in the year of sale. The key benefit? If you hold the property for at least 12 months, you qualify for a 50% capital gains tax (CGT) discount, meaning only half the gain is taxed – one of the biggest advantages of personal ownership.

Pros:

✔ Negative gearing benefits apply (see the next section).

✔ 50% CGT discount if the property is held for 12+ months.

✔ Minimal admin and compliance costs – no need for complex tax lodgements.

✔ Lower land tax costs in most states and territories.

Cons:

✗ Potential for higher taxes on future income and profits as your portfolio grows.

✗ Less asset protection – the property is in your personal name, so it could be at risk if you are sued.

✗ Limited tax flexibility – compared to other structures, fewer options exist to minimise tax or plan for estate transfers.

Bottom line: If you're just getting started, keeping it simple with personal ownership is often the best way forward. It's cost-effective, tax-efficient (thanks to CGT discounts and negative gearing), and doesn't require the ongoing admin burden of a company or trust structure.

Joint ownership

Many investors choose to partner up – whether with a spouse, family member, or friend – to enter the property market sooner and share the financial load. Joint ownership can be structured in two main ways:

1. **Joint tenants:** Each owner holds an equal share in the property, and the rule of survivorship applies – meaning if one owner passes away, their share automatically transfers to the other owner(s). This is common among couples.

2. **Tenants in common:** Ownership can be split into unequal shares (e.g. 60/40 or 70/30), allowing flexibility in how income and expenses are distributed. This is often used by siblings, business partners, or friends investing together.

Pros:

✔ **Easier entry into the market:** Sharing costs and risk can make investing more achievable.

✔ **Access to CGT benefits:** Because you are still buying as individuals, the 50% CGT discount still applies after 12 months.

✔ **Estate planning flexibility:** With tenants in common, each owner can dictate what happens to their share of the property in their will.

Cons:

✗ **Taxed at individual rates:** If one owner earns significantly more than the other, there's less flexibility to distribute income tax-efficiently.

✗ **Joint and several liability:** You are financially tied to your co-owners. If they can't meet their obligations, you may have to cover their share of the debt.

✗ **Big decisions require agreement:** Selling or refinancing needs all co-owners' consent, which can be challenging if goals change over time.

Bottom line: Joint ownership can be a great stepping stone into property investing, particularly for couples or those needing help with affordability. However, going in with friends or extended family requires careful consideration – clear agreements and a shared long-term vision are essential to avoid complications down the track.

Trust ownership

Trusts are less common for those looking to own just one or two investment properties, but they become more relevant for investors scaling larger portfolios or seeking asset protection and tax planning flexibility.

A trust is not a separate legal entity but a legal structure where a trustee holds assets on behalf of beneficiaries. Income generated from the property is distributed to beneficiaries, who then pay tax at their individual rates.

The two main types of property-owning trusts are:

1. **Discretionary trusts (family trusts):** These provide flexibility in how income is distributed among beneficiaries, and are often used for family wealth planning and asset protection.

2. **Unit trusts:** Instead of income being allocated at the trustee's discretion, ownership and income distribution are fixed based on the number of units held by each investor. Unit trusts are often used by business partners or unrelated investors pooling resources.

Pros:

✓ **Potential tax planning benefits:** Discretionary trusts allow income to be distributed to beneficiaries in lower tax brackets.

✓ **Strong asset protection:** As the property is held by the trustee, it is not personally owned, reducing personal liability in legal disputes.

✓ **Estate planning advantages:** Trust structures can provide continuity and control over how assets are passed down to future generations.

Cons:

✗ **No negative gearing benefits:** Losses are trapped in the trust and cannot be offset against personal income, making it less attractive for early-stage investors.

✗ **Higher running and compliance costs:** Trusts require specialist accounting, ongoing administration, and compliance with tax laws and trust deeds.

✗ **Limited CGT benefits:** While some trusts may qualify for capital gains tax discounts, there are more restrictions compared to individual ownership.

Bottom line: Trusts offer protection, estate planning benefits, and tax flexibility, but they come with complexity and higher costs. They tend to work best for investors planning a multi-property strategy or those wanting greater control over asset distribution. However, for most everyday investors, individual ownership is simpler and more cost-effective.

Company ownership

Company ownership is less common for individual property investors, as it introduces tax complexity, compliance costs, and administrative overhead. However, for those building a larger portfolio or seeking strong asset protection, it can be a viable structure.

When a company owns an investment property, rental income and capital gains belong to the company, which then pays tax at the corporate rate. After costs, profits can be distributed to shareholders as dividends, but unlike trusts, there's limited flexibility in how income is distributed.

Pros:

✔ **Flat tax rates:** Companies are taxed at a fixed rate (typically 25% to 30%), which may be lower than individual marginal tax rates, depending on income levels.

✔ **Stronger asset protection:** The company structure provides a legal separation between personal and business assets, reducing direct personal liability.

✔ **No forced distributions:** Unlike trusts, companies can retain profits rather than being required to distribute them annually.

Cons:

✘ **No CGT discount:** Companies do not qualify for the 50% capital gains tax discount available to individuals and some trusts, meaning capital gains are taxed in full.

✘ **Trapped negative gearing losses:** Just as for trusts, any property-related losses stay within the company and cannot offset personal income.

✗ **Higher compliance costs:** Running a company requires annual tax returns, financial statements, ASIC reporting, and additional administrative obligations.

✗ **Limited distribution flexibility:** Unlike trusts, companies cannot distribute income in a discretionary manner to take advantage of lower tax brackets.

Bottom line: While a company structure offers tax consistency and asset protection, the lack of CGT discounts and higher operating costs make it a less attractive choice for most small-scale investors. If property investing is part of a broader business strategy or portfolio expansion, professional tax advice is essential to determine if this structure is appropriate.

Self-managed super funds: A specialised path to property ownership

Being a member of a standard superannuation fund restricts you from buying an investment property outright with your super. This can only be done through a self-managed super fund (SMSF), where the property is held as part of the fund's assets. SMSFs operate under strict rules and regulations, making them a highly specialised ownership structure.

While SMSFs offer attractive tax settings – including concessional tax rates on rental income and capital gains – they also come with significant compliance requirements and higher operating costs.

Pros:

✓ **Lower tax rates:** Rental income is taxed at just 15% while the fund is in accumulation mode, and 10% CGT applies if the property is held for more than 12 months. Once the fund enters the pension phase, the tax rate can drop to 0%.

✓ **Asset protection:** The property is safeguarded from personal financial difficulties, ensuring it remains part of your retirement savings.

Cons:

✗ **Strict borrowing rules:** Limited recourse borrowing arrangements (LRBAs) make financing more expensive, with higher deposit requirements and restrictions on refinancing.

✗ **High running costs:** SMSFs require ongoing administration, financial reporting, audits, and compliance, all of which come with additional costs.

✗ **Restricted use:** The property cannot be lived in or rented by the SMSF member, their family, or any related party.

Bottom line: In our opinion, SMSFs can be a tax-effective way to build wealth for retirement, but they are typically only suitable for experienced investors with a strong understanding of financial management. The complexity, ongoing compliance obligations, and high costs mean they aren't a fit for most everyday investors. Strict rules around borrowing, property use, and superannuation regulations make this an option best suited for financially savvy investors with an appropriate super balance and expert financial advice. Before pursuing this path, it's critical to consult an SMSF specialist to ensure it aligns with your long-term wealth strategy.

*

In summary, ownership matters. Tax implications, financial flexibility, and long-term security all depend on making informed decisions. Our approach – both personally and with our clients – is to start simple and (unless you're planning to become Australia's next property mogul) keep it simple.

As you progress on this journey, your experience will grow, and maybe your appetite will also grow to do more and be more active. That's been our journey too. If that happens, continue to plan carefully and seek the best advice to ensure your strategy keeps working for you.

Understanding negative gearing

Negative gearing is one of those terms that gets thrown around a lot in property circles, but what does it really mean for you as an investor, given it's actually a made-up term? Put simply, it happens when the costs of owning and running an investment property – like mortgage interest, maintenance, and property management fees – are higher than the rental income it generates. This creates an overall income loss, which you can offset against other income, like your salary, which in turn reduces your taxable income. In the early years, when expenses tend to outweigh income, the resulting tax credit can make property investment more manageable. The 'negative' refers to the shortfall, while 'gearing' refers to the borrowing to fund the purchase.

Here's the thing: negative gearing isn't a strategy – it's just a tax outcome. The real strategy lies in choosing high-quality properties that grow in value and eventually generate positive cashflow. Negative gearing might help you with cashflow in the short term, but the ultimate goal is to create a portfolio that supports your financial independence without running at a loss, so that over the longer term, the property is generating passive income, on which you will also one day pay taxes.

If you've ever wondered why negative gearing is so popular, the answer lies in its ability to help you manage cashflow while building long-term wealth. For many Australians, negative gearing is a way to manage the upfront financial burden of property ownership. The ability to offset losses against your income reduces your tax bill, making property investment more accessible for everyday Australians. If this short-term incentive wasn't in play, then two things would probably eventuate. First, fewer investment properties would be available for rent. Second, rents would be significantly higher to help adjust for the higher operating costs of running an investment property as a private rental accommodation business. Think of it as a financial stepping stone that helps you get started on your journey.

Negative gearing is just the beginning. Over time, as your rental income grows and you pay down your debt, your property transitions from negatively geared to neutrally geared (where the rent covers the expenses) and eventually to positively geared (where the rent exceeds the expenses). Positive gearing is the dream destination – it means your properties are generating extra income to support your lifestyle or fund further investments. Again, as your property moves to positively geared, you will start paying taxes on the income you are generating.

The bigger picture

Negative gearing has its place, but property investment is all about the long game. It's about creating wealth through assets that appreciate in value and eventually generate passive income. While negative gearing can ease the early cashflow challenges of property ownership, the focus should always be on building a portfolio that transitions to long-term financial independence.

Of course, negative gearing isn't without risks. It relies on property values increasing over time, which isn't guaranteed. Because it involves out-of-pocket losses, you need a solid buffer and a plan to weather unexpected expenses or changes in the market. Staying informed about potential tax law changes is also crucial, as these could impact the future benefits of negative gearing.

At its core, negative gearing is just a tool – a way to make the early days of property investing easier. The real magic happens when you focus on growing your portfolio and transitioning to a point where your properties pay you back, creating a future of financial independence.

Who are Australia's property investors?

When the media talks about property investors, they typically promote images of wealthy professionals – doctors, lawyers, or high-flying executives. But the reality is far more grounded. Everyday Australians, often from humble professions, make up the majority of the nation's residential property investors. They're teachers, nurses, police officers, and construction workers – not chasing extravagance but quietly striving to self-fund their retirement and secure a lifestyle by design.

Consider these figures about property investors – folks who also happen to be the backbone of our communities. According to 2021/22 data from the Australian Taxation Office (ATO), a significant number of investors come from essential professions:

- School teachers: 81,354
- Nurses and midwives: 61,773
- Protective services workers (police, fire, and defence): 23,198
- Child carers and education aides: 23,039
- Retail workers and managers: 44,332
- Truck, bus, rail, and delivery drivers: 28,230
- Bricklayers, carpenters, plumbers, painters, and tilers: 23,710

These individuals work hard to serve their communities, often in roles that don't come with salaries guaranteeing a comfortable retirement. For them, property investing is a way to bridge the gap – a practical path to supplementing their income while continuing to contribute to society. Their goal isn't to build sprawling empires but to achieve financial peace and create opportunities for their families.

Also according to the ATO, as of the end of 2021/22, most property investors stop at just one property. This reflects the latest available data, which accounts for delays in releasing statistics due to late tax return submissions.

PROPERTY INVESTMENT BY OWNERSHIP

Number of properties owned	2021/22 investors	% of overall investors
1	1,620,663	71.5%
2	428,020	18.9%
3	132,338	5.7%
4	47,633	2.1%
5	19,530	0.9%
6 or more	19,977	0.9%
Total	**2,268,161**	**100.0%**

Source: Australian Taxation Office

Of the 2.26 million property investors in Australia, fewer than 1% own six or more properties. Most Australians invest in property not to build massive portfolios but to create a secure future, often starting with just one property. However, while taking more action than most, stopping at one property often falls short of achieving a self-funded retirement. Financial independence isn't the norm in Australia – far too many retirees rely on the government pension, a safety net designed for basic needs rather than true freedom. By choosing to invest in property and build even a modest portfolio, you're breaking away from the herd, paving your own path to financial freedom, and often challenging the traditional mindsets of your family or social network.

But here's the key takeaway: this book isn't about pushing you into the elite 1% of investors who own six or more properties. Instead, it's about guiding you towards a more achievable goal – owning two to four properties, as demonstrated in the case studies later in this book. For us, that's the sweet spot where the magic happens. With the right strategy and action, owning a small, high-performing portfolio can completely transform your financial future. Property investing isn't reserved for the wealthy or elite – it's accessible to anyone willing to act, learn, and commit to a proven process. The stories and strategies ahead will show you what's possible.

As you read on, you'll uncover case studies modelled on real-life stories of individuals and families who've built secure futures with just two to four properties. These stories prove that financial freedom is achievable – and within reach for those who 'step into the arena'.

Getting your tax refund sooner

What if you could boost your cashflow throughout the year instead of waiting for a big tax refund at the end? That's where a Form 15-15 PAYG withholding variation application comes in. This ATO form allows you to receive your tax refund in smaller, regular amounts throughout the year instead of as a lump sum at tax time. It's a valuable tool for property investors, helping them access increased cashflow more effectively while still benefiting from negative gearing.

When you own an investment property, you may incur expenses like mortgage interest, maintenance, and property management fees. If these costs exceed the rental income, the loss can be offset against other taxable income, such as your salary. Usually, this means waiting until the end of the financial year to claim these deductions and receive your tax refund.

But with the Form 15-15 PAYG withholding variation application, you don't have to wait. By submitting this form to the ATO, in conjunction with working with your employer's payroll team (if applicable), you can adjust the amount of tax withheld from your regular income, giving you access to your tax refund throughout the year. This means more cash in your pocket when you need it, making it easier to manage property-related expenses or reinvest in your portfolio.

If you're finding it hard to manage cashflow while waiting for your tax refund, or you want to take advantage of having this money sitting in your offset or savings account, this might be the solution you didn't know you needed. For property investors, it's particularly useful because it aligns your cashflow with the ongoing costs of property ownership. By using this ATO service, you're improving cashflow and freeing up resources to focus on building your property portfolio and moving closer to your financial goals.

Here's what to keep in mind:

- **Accurate estimates are key:** It's crucial to get your numbers right. Overestimating deductions could leave you with a surprise tax bill and possible additional interest charges from the ATO at the end of the year, so work closely with a property-savvy accountant to ensure accuracy. (The Moorr platform can help you calculate the numbers for free.)

- **Annual process:** Remember, this isn't a set-and-forget solution – you'll need to reapply every year. Think of it as part of your annual financial health check.
- **Not for everyone:** If you love that big end-of-year refund, this might not be your thing. However, for those who prefer consistent cashflow throughout the year, it can make a big difference.
- **Work with professionals:** The process is simpler than you think, especially with the help of a property-savvy accountant who can guide you through the steps and ensure your application is correct.

Remember, the key to successful property investing is making every dollar work harder for you. By using the PAYG withholding variation application, you can unlock cashflow during the year, helping you cover property expenses, reduce financial strain, and reinvest in your future. It's one more tool in your kit to ensure your property journey is not just manageable but truly rewarding.

Stamp duty: A cost you can't ignore

Stamp duty is one of the unavoidable costs property investors face when buying real estate in Australia. It's essentially a tax on the transaction itself, levied by state and territory governments. The amount you pay is calculated based on the purchase price or market value of the property – whichever is higher – and can vary significantly depending on where you're buying.

Each state and territory has its own stamp duty rates. While there are exemptions and concessions for first home buyers, these usually apply to owner-occupiers, not investors. For property investors, stamp duty is a critical one-off cost you need to account for in your budget, as it can significantly impact the upfront costs of purchasing.

Planning for stamp duty from the outset ensures you're not caught off guard during the purchase process. This is why it's so important to consult with your investment-savvy mortgage broker, who can guide you on whether it's possible to include stamp duty in your lending arrangements. As discussed in Chapter 7, 'Borrowing power', incorporating these costs into your loan structure can help maintain your cashflow and keep your investment strategy on track.

Land tax: The cost of property ownership

Land tax in Australia is a state- and territory-based tax applied to the ownership of land, typically excluding your PPR (in most cases). It's a recurring, annual cost that property investors need to factor into their calculations, as it directly affects the profitability of their portfolio. This tax is levied on taxable land, which includes investment properties, vacant land, and holiday homes, and the rates differ across states and territories.

The tax is calculated based on ownership against the combined unimproved value of all taxable properties you own within that state or territory. Each state or territory sets its own thresholds – if the total value of your properties exceeds this threshold, land tax applies. Beyond the threshold, land tax rates are tiered, meaning the higher the value of your taxable properties, the higher the tax rate you'll pay.

Exemptions to land tax exist in certain cases, such as for your primary residence or land used for farming. However, for property investors, this is typically an unavoidable expense and should be considered when planning your property portfolio. Ignoring land tax can lead to surprises that strain cashflow or reduce returns, particularly for those with a high concentration of properties in states with lower thresholds or higher rates.

Again, it's worth highlighting that land tax is cumulative. If you own properties in multiple states, each state calculates its land tax independently based on the properties within its borders. Diversifying your portfolio across states with more favourable thresholds and rates can be an effective strategy to manage land tax obligations, reduce holding costs, and improve passive income returns.

Understanding land tax is a critical piece of the property investment puzzle. Factoring it into your strategy upfront helps you avoid surprises and keeps your portfolio on track. With the right advice and planning, you can confidently navigate land tax as part of your journey toward financial freedom.

Capital gains tax on investment profits

Capital gains tax (CGT) is another crucial consideration for property investors, as it applies to the profit made from selling assets such as property, shares, or businesses. When you sell an investment property for more than you paid for it, the profit – known as the 'capital gain' – is added to your taxable income for that tax year and taxed at your marginal tax rate. This makes understanding and planning for CGT an essential part of your investment strategy.

The good news for long-term investors who purchase in their own names is that if you hold the property for more than

12 months, you're eligible for a 50% CGT discount, meaning only half of the capital gain is taxable. However, if you sell within 12 months, this discount does not apply, potentially increasing your tax liability. On the other hand, your Principal Place of Residence (PPR) – the home you live in – is generally exempt from CGT, offering some relief for owner-occupiers.

For property investors, accurate record-keeping is essential. This includes tracking your purchase price, costs of improvements, and selling expenses, all of which can reduce your capital gain and, subsequently, your CGT liability. Additionally, if you incur a capital loss (e.g. selling an asset for less than its purchase price), this can be used to offset current or future capital gains from other investments, reducing your overall tax burden.

It's also worth remembering that CGT is only payable when you sell an asset. Following the guidance in this book, we strongly advocate a 'buy and hold' strategy for property investing. Ideally, you wouldn't be exposed to CGT, as your investment properties would form part of your long-term wealth-building plan and legacy. By holding onto your properties, you allow them to continue to grow in value and act as a cornerstone of your financial future, and you can eventually pass them on to loved ones through your will.

Reframing the narrative

As we delve deeper into the tax side of property investing, it's worth pausing to reflect on a broader issue: the perception of property investors. Too often, we're portrayed as greedy opportunists or property hoarders, exploiting the system for personal gain. This narrative, while pervasive, fails to capture the reality for the majority of us.

Most property investors are everyday Australians – such as teachers, nurses, and tradespeople to name a few – who take calculated risks to fund their own retirements, provide future financial security for their families, and supply much-needed rental housing. Far from being 'fat cats', they shoulder the financial and emotional risk of factors beyond their control, including interest rate movements, government and regulatory market interference, lending market interference, rising compliance obligations, and insurances and property taxes, to name just a few. Despite these challenges, they strive to achieve a return that justifies the investment and risks involved.

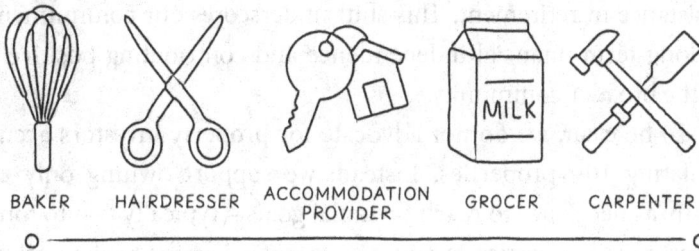

| BAKER | HAIRDRESSER | ACCOMMODATION PROVIDER | GROCER | CARPENTER |

WE ARE ALL SMALL BUSINESS OWNERS

Think of property investors as small business owners, much like entrepreneurs, who allocate money, time, and resources, manage risks, and provide a service – private rental accommodation. Just as small businesses drive local economies, property investors play a crucial role in meeting rental housing demand, providing consumer choice, alleviating pressure on the public housing system, and fostering current and future economic growth by supporting human capital mobility.

For many of us, the pension is not the goal; we view it as a safety net for the more vulnerable in our community. Our aim is to reach a point where our investment properties, combined with other investments and superannuation, provide the lifestyle by design we've worked hard for, taking calculated risks and making sacrifices to achieve financial security for ourselves and our families.

This approach also positively impacts society by ensuring governments don't need to excessively tax citizens to fund greater public housing. It reflects the transition from utilising initial tax benefits, such as negative gearing, to becoming net tax contributors. This includes billions in capital gains taxes paid, and ultimately, as self-funded retirees, not relying on pensions or government assistance in retirement. This shift underscores our commitment to long-term financial independence and contributing positively to the broader community.

To be clear, we do not advocate for property investors accumulating 10+ properties. Instead, we support owning only as many as necessary to reach financial goals – typically two to four investment properties. Again, we *do not* subscribe to the notion that 'whoever dies with the most property wins' – rather, we focus on sustainable, goal-driven investing.

We also understand the interconnected nature of the property market. Any policy changes or market disruptions aimed at property investors can have far-reaching and unintended consequences – not just for us but for renters, builders, and the broader economy. It's essential to view property investment as part of the housing ecosystem, not as a standalone pursuit.

By truthfully framing property investors as aspiring Australians operating small private rental accommodation businesses – individuals taking proactive steps to shape their futures and contribute to their communities – we can help shift the narrative. Property investing isn't solely about personal gain; it's about fostering a more flexible, dynamic, and resilient housing market that creates greater opportunities for a wide range of participants.

This journey isn't without its challenges, and we recognise that collaboration and shared understanding are key. By standing together as property investors, we not only advocate for our own interests but also support a vision of financial independence and a stable housing market for all Australians.

If you're interested in learning more about an association that supports and represents the interests of property investors, we recommend the Property Investors Council of Australia (PICA). We're proud to support and be actively involved with this association. You can find out more at pica.asn.au.

Useful resources

As we've emphasised throughout this book, understanding the tax implications of property investing is critical to long-term success. Taxation can significantly impact your cashflow, borrowing capacity, and overall return on investment, so it's essential to stay informed and factor these costs into your planning.

That said, this chapter is not designed to provide personal tax advice – we strongly recommend seeking guidance from a property-savvy tax accountant. The insights provided here are meant as conversation starters to help you navigate key taxation considerations and ensure you're making informed decisions about your property portfolio.

Given that tax laws and thresholds change regularly, following are key resources to help you stay informed and navigate your tax obligations effectively. You can visit www.thepropertycouch.com.au/playbook for live links to each of the websites listed.

Stamp duty (transfer duty)

Some states offer concessions or exemptions, particularly for first home buyers.

To check the latest stamp duty rates, visit:

- **NSW:** revenue.nsw.gov.au/taxes-duties-levies-royalties/transfer-duty
- **VIC:** sro.vic.gov.au/land-transfer-duty
- **QLD:** qro.qld.gov.au/transfer-duty
- **SA:** revenuesa.sa.gov.au/taxes-and-duties/stamp-duties
- **WA:** www.wa.gov.au/organisation/department-of-finance/transfer-duty
- **TAS:** sro.tas.gov.au/property-transfer-duties
- **ACT:** revenue.act.gov.au/duties/conveyance-duty
- **NT:** treasury.nt.gov.au/dtf/territory-revenue-office/stamp-duty

Land tax

Each state has its own land tax rules, including thresholds, exemptions, and rates. For the most up-to-date information, check the following official websites:

- **NSW:** revenue.nsw.gov.au/taxes-duties-levies-royalties/land-tax
- **VIC:** sro.vic.gov.au/land-tax
- **QLD:** qro.qld.gov.au/land-tax
- **SA:** revenuesa.sa.gov.au/landtax
- **WA:** www.wa.gov.au/organisation/department-of-finance/land-tax

- **TAS:** sro.tas.gov.au/land-tax
- **ACT:** revenue.act.gov.au/land-tax
- **NT:** treasury.nt.gov.au/dtf/territory-revenue-office

Capital gains tax (CGT)

For details on CGT and exemptions, visit ato.gov.au/individuals/capital-gains-tax.

Negative gearing and tax deductions

For eligible deductions, early tax refunds, and negative gearing rules, refer to the ATO guides on rental property deductions, and the PAYG withholding variation application:

- ato.gov.au/forms-and-instructions/rental-properties-2024
- ato.gov.au/forms-and-instructions/payg-withholding-variation-application

Goods and services tax (GST)

GST is generally not applicable to residential property purchases or rental income. However, it may apply if you're developing property for sale or investing in commercial real estate.

For guidance on GST and property transactions, visit ato.gov.au/business/gst/in-detail/your-industry/property.

ATO clearance certificate

From January 2025, all residential properties being sold by an Australian resident for tax purposes need a clearance certificate from the ATO. This certificate is required to avoid having 15% of the sale price withheld by the purchaser at settlement.

Check out ato.gov.au/individuals-and-families/investments-and-assets/capital-gains-tax/foreign-residents-and-capital-gains-tax/foreign-resident-capital-gains-withholding/australian-residents-and-clearance-certificates.

We get it – some of these links are pretty long. Just scan the QR code or head to www.thepropertycouch.com.au/playbook to access all the live links mentioned in this section.

Seeking professional advice

The smartest thing you can do is seek professional tax planning advice. A property-savvy accountant will help you:

- **Optimise your tax strategy** to maximise deductions and minimise liabilities.
- **Structure your investments wisely** to protect your assets and grow your wealth with a future eye on potential tax planning.
- **Strike a balance** between minimising tax and optimising lending and borrowing power options.
- **Stay compliant** with all tax regulations.

For those serious about building long-term wealth through property, a property-savvy accountant should be a key player on your dream team.

Tax is a reality of property investing, but it doesn't have to be a burden. The right knowledge, expert advice, and proactive planning can turn taxation into a tool for wealth creation. So, get on the front foot – get informed, get advice, and use smart tax strategies that work for you.

Chapter 13

Landing the plane

Wealth-building isn't a one-time act; it's a journey with two distinct phases: getting wealthy and staying wealthy. Each phase demands a different mindset, skill set, strategy, and plan of action. Mastering the shift between them is key to long-term financial success.

Getting wealthy: The offensive game

Getting wealthy is about taking calculated risks, seizing opportunities, and leaning into optimism. It's the phase where bold moves create momentum, setting your financial engine in motion. Property investors in this phase might:

- **Leverage** by borrowing money to acquire assets that grow faster than savings alone.
- **Access equity** from the family home.
- **Have a strategic vision** to invest in markets or opportunities with a clear roadmap for sustainable growth, avoiding fads or short-term gains that lack stability.
- **Act decisively** and move quickly when opportunities arise.

This phase rewards boldness and belief in a better future, but optimism without a safety net can lead to overreach. The cautionary proverb? Fortunes built on shaky foundations crumble when conditions change.

Staying wealthy: The defensive game

If getting wealthy is offence, staying wealthy is defence. It's about protecting what you've built, avoiding losses, and ensuring your wealth outlasts you. Staying wealthy demands:

- **Risk aversion:** Shifting from big moves to minimising risks that could wipe out years of gains. Basically, don't be greedy.
- **Humility:** Recognising that luck often plays a role in success and acting accordingly.
- **Preparation for uncertainty:** Expecting the unexpected – interest rate hikes, market downturns, or personal setbacks.

In property investing, this phase focuses on:

- **Retiring debt:** Shifting your focus to reducing any remaining debt.
- **Maintaining buffers:** Keeping sufficient cash or equity reserves to weather market shifts or unforeseen expenses.
- **Prioritising cashflow:** Stopping acquiring new properties and ensuring your income streams cover expenses and sustain your lifestyle, preventing a situation where you're asset-rich but cash-poor.
- **Mitigating risk:** Protecting yourself against setbacks by securing insurance, diversifying your portfolio, and managing leverage conservatively.

The fragility of wealth

Wealth is fragile. History shows fortunes can disappear faster than they're built. Consider those who bought multiple properties during Australia's record-low interest rates of 0.10% cash rate, only to struggle when rates rose 13 times between May 2022 and 2023. Without buffers or risk mitigation, many were forced to sell under pressure and risk their wealth base.

Staying wealthy means acknowledging this fragility and acting accordingly. It's less about relentless growth and getting too greedy and more about ensuring you don't lose too much ground in the inevitable downturn events within an economic cycle. As Morgan Housel aptly notes in his best-selling book, *The Psychology of Money*, 'Compounding only works if you can stay in the game'.

The hardest part of wealth management is knowing when to switch gears. The skills that help you build wealth – sound planning, taking calculated risks, acting decisively, and staying optimistic – aren't the same ones required to preserve it. Staying wealthy necessitates a shift from offence to defence, transitioning from the accumulation phase to the preservation or retirement phase, often referred to as the pension phase.

And yet, offence and defence are two sides of the same coin. The key is balance – staying optimistic while managing to protect your downside, growing your portfolio while managing cashflow, and making bold moves while keeping buffers in place.

For property investors, this balance means building a portfolio that's not just about accumulating assets but also ensuring they work for you long term. It's about creating wealth with stability – an income statement that supports your goals, strategies that prioritise sustainability, and buffers that shield you from volatility.

For those just beginning, this might sound hard to believe, but staying wealthy is harder than getting wealthy. It requires humility, patience, and foresight. But it's also the more rewarding game – one where you shift from building a balance sheet to leaving a legacy through Grade 7 of financial well-being: contribution. By mastering the transition from offence to defence, you're not just securing wealth for today; you're ensuring it endures for generations.

Exit options: Realising your gains in retirement

As you approach retirement, the question becomes: how do you convert the gains from your property investments into a sustainable lifestyle? There are three broad strategies to consider, each with its own merits, challenges, and suitability depending on your circumstances and goals.

Option 1: Use debt to service debt

The idea of using debt to fund your lifestyle in retirement can sound counterintuitive, but for some, it's a viable strategy. The concept revolves around leveraging the increasing value of your property portfolio to borrow funds for living expenses – tax-free, as borrowed money isn't taxable income. This approach relies on the assumption that your portfolio's growth outpaces the cost of borrowing, making the debt manageable while preserving your assets.

Pros:

- Allows you to maintain ownership of your properties, benefiting from continued appreciation and rental income.

- Tax-free access to funds through borrowing.

Cons:

- Increases debt levels, which can be risky if property values decline or interest rates rise.
- Requires disciplined financial management and is heavily reliant on strong portfolio growth.
- Limited accessibility due to tighter lending regulations.

Bryce's early lesson: The seven properties in seven years approach

When I first encountered this strategy through my first mentor back in 1998, it was presented as a game-changing approach. My mentor advocated acquiring seven properties in seven years, with the assumption that property values doubled every seven years. By year eight, the first property's value would have doubled, allowing you to borrow up to 80% of its value to fund your lifestyle. The allure was strong – this was tax-free income. My mentor even suggested renting instead of buying your own home to maximise investment potential – my first exposure to rentvesting, long before it was the mainstream strategy it is today.

This 'seven in seven' strategy thrived in the 1990s, with low-doc and no-doc loans making it feasible for investors to easily access funds. However, as lending standards tightened over the years, this became the domain of high-net-worth individuals with specialised access to banks via the 'back door'. For the average investor, navigating this strategy through the 'front door' of the bank or even via the 'side door' with mortgage brokers has become significantly more challenging.

Option 2: Retire debt

The most conservative and common-sense approach, retiring debt focuses on paying down all loans by the time you retire – or, if your income exceeds your expenses, continuing to pay down debt during retirement. This strategy prioritises financial security by eliminating the need to rely on future growth or additional borrowing to fund your lifestyle. With no debt commitments, your rental income, superannuation, and any other investment returns become your primary sources of funds for living expenses.

As staunch advocates of this method, we like its practicality and alignment with the mindset of most Australians. The psychological comfort of being debt-free resonates strongly with many, offering a sense of security and freedom. Additionally, with lending conditions becoming stricter over time, retiring debt has become an increasingly appealing and achievable goal for many investors.

Pros:

- Eliminates financial stress and reduces risk during retirement.
- Provides a steady income stream without the burden of loan repayments forever.
- Aligns with the conservative mindset of most Australians.

Cons:

- Requires discipline and a healthy and consistent income during working years to pay down debt while building your portfolio.
- Limits the ability to expand your portfolio or reinvest in other opportunities.

Option 3: Sell down/divest

For some investors, selling part or all of their portfolio is the best planned and calculated way to realise their gains and fund their retirement. This strategy is particularly relevant for those who start investing later in life, own underperforming properties, or face life circumstances like divorce or lack of heirs.

Selling can make sense for various reasons, but it should always be part of a considered plan. For example:

- Selling underperforming properties to reinvest in better opportunities.
- Generating a lump sum to pay off remaining debts or cover living expenses.
- Addressing personal circumstances, such as divorce or downsizing in later years.

This strategy provides immediate access to capital but comes with trade-offs, including the potential loss of future growth and tax implications.

Pros:

- Provides immediate liquidity for debt paydown, reinvestment or living expenses in retirement.
- Simplifies financial management by reducing the number of assets.

Cons:

- Triggers capital gains tax liabilities, reducing net proceeds.
- Eliminates the opportunity for future appreciation and rental income.
  - Requires careful planning to ensure long-term sustainability.

Each strategy has its place, and the right choice depends on your unique financial situation, risk tolerance, and retirement goals. Whether you aim to leverage debt, eliminate it entirely, or divest strategically, the key is having a clear, tailored plan. Always consult with your professional dream team to ensure your approach aligns with your broader objectives and delivers the retirement lifestyle you've worked so hard to achieve.

That said, as Warren Buffett famously noted, 'Our favourite holding period is forever'. From our professional perspective and experience, we firmly believe in building a plan (if your finances qualify) centred on Option 2, 'Retire debt' as the cornerstone of a solid retirement plan. This approach aligns with the conservative, debt-free mindset that resonates with most Australians and is the focus of the majority of the case studies included in this book.

By retiring debt, you not only secure your financial position but also create the opportunity to hold your portfolio indefinitely. This also aligns with our belief that the best holding period is forever – allowing you to enjoy the benefits of a well-constructed property portfolio without the need to sell, ensuring it continues to grow, generate income, and support your financial goals for the long term.

For those unable to achieve a debt-free retirement, Option 3, 'Sell down/divest' is our next preferred option, offering a clear and practical pathway to financial freedom.

Finally, while Option 1, 'Use debt to service debt' might seem attractive in theory, we do not advocate this approach. The risks and lending limitations associated with increasing debt levels in retirement far outweigh the potential benefits for the vast majority of investors. Our conservative philosophy prioritises security, stability, and long-term financial well-being over speculative strategies.

By choosing a pathway forward now, grounded in proven principles and guided by clear goals and objectives, you can confidently move forward. As you reach certain milestones, you should review and take stock. When you eventually get closer to the retirement date, the decision about how you manage your remaining debt will become much clearer. And knowing you started today – or even yesterday – will be deeply fulfilling when you take that moment to reflect.

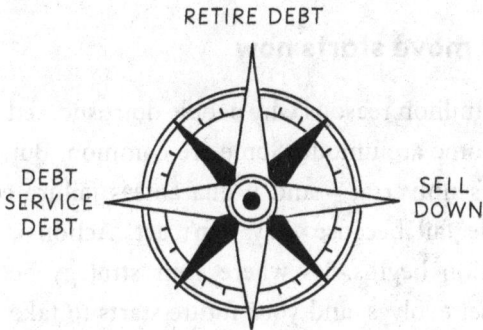

RETIRE DEBT

DEBT
SERVICE
DEBT

SELL
DOWN

WHICH PATH WOULD YOU CHOOSE?

Part III – Wrap

Your next move starts now

There are a million reasons why people don't succeed at property investing. Some are unique. Some are common. But, there's one reason that's universal – and it guarantees failure every single time: people fail because they don't act. Action is where the transformation begins. It's where your strategy becomes real, your mindset evolves, and your future starts to take shape – on your terms.

We know it's not always easy. The fears, the limiting beliefs, the hidden myths we inherit about money are real. We've had to overcome them too. That's why we spent time naming them, unpacking them, and helping you see them for what they are: barriers that can be broken.

Now that you've seen the inside of the property investing game – how the industry really works, who the players are, and how to navigate it with clarity and confidence – you're ready. This journey doesn't require perfection. It just requires momentum.

We also lifted the lid on two very different investing paths – active and passive. While one might feel flashier or faster, time and again the other has proven to be the smarter and more sustainable option for most everyday Australians. Why? Because life's already busy enough. Passive investing works *with* you – not against you – quietly compounding wealth in the background so you can focus on what matters most.

We even shone a light on tax – yes, it's boring, but it's essential. Understanding tax isn't just a box to tick – it's a lever to pull. When you know how to use it wisely, it can accelerate your results in ways most investors miss.

Finally, we explored what comes next – what it looks like to land the plane. Whether you plan to retire the debt, sell down, or use debt to service lifestyle expenses, having a clear exit strategy is just as important as how you begin.

So, here's the good news: your story is still being written. You don't need to have all the answers today. You just need to act. Take one step. Then another. Then another. That's how every investor who reaches an income of $3,000 a week gets there – by putting one foot in front of the other, by showing up, and moving forward, even when it's uncomfortable.

Now, in the next part, you'll see what that looks like in the real world. We've included case studies of people just like you who decided to act. These are people who built a small but mighty portfolio – two, three, maybe four investment properties – and completely changed their financial future. These people chose their number and backed themselves to go get it.

So, let's keep climbing. It's time to see what action looks like in motion.

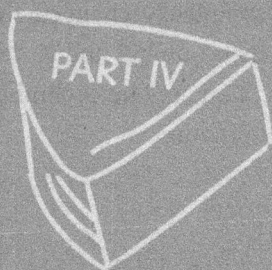

PART IV
Bringing the $3,000-a-week Goal to Life

Congratulations! You've made it to the most exciting part of this journey. This is where the rubber meets the road, and we bring everything together to show you how to achieve $3,000 a week in passive income through property investing. Whether your goal is to retire early, gain financial freedom, or simply have the choice to work on your own terms, this chapter will give you the blueprint to make it happen.

Let's be clear about what $3,000 a week in passive income means. This isn't just a number – it's effectively a weekly income allocation AFTER tax that allows you to live your best life in today's dollar terms. After covering all investment portfolio costs, including property maintenance, management, taxes, and lending expenses, this is an allocated $3,000 weekly allowance to fund your lifestyle by design. Importantly, it's indexed to account for the rising cost of living – because, let's face it, a coffee today won't cost the same in five or ten years' time. In short, this strategy ensures that $3,000 a week in today's dollars will give you confidence your lifestyle goals will remain achievable well into the future.

Why case studies matter

Over the years, we've worked with thousands of clients, and these case studies represent the most common profiles of people we help every day. They are designed to show you that no matter your starting point, financial challenges, or goals, there can be a 'planned' pathway to success. Whether you're a young professional, a couple with kids, or someone nearing retirement, these examples offer a playbook you can adapt to your own situation.

The beauty of these case studies is that they demonstrate how ordinary Australians can achieve extraordinary financial outcomes through optimised and well-planned sequencing of household finances and wise property investing. You don't need to be a millionaire to start. In fact, most of our clients begin with modest means, leveraging the right strategies to build wealth over time. By ensuring their properties 'wash their own face' – that is, they are self-funding, generate enough rent to both cover their own expenses and generate passive income for the investor – these clients create a portfolio that not only sustains itself but also delivers surplus income for living.

This approach is about more than just financial security – it's about the freedom to choose how you spend your time, pursue your passions, and create a lifestyle you truly love. We hope these case studies will inspire and guide you to take the next steps confidently, turning your property investing dreams into reality.

What makes these scenarios different?

These case studies aren't theoretical or pie-in-the-sky ideas. They're grounded in decades of professional experience, robust data, and sophisticated modelling. They have been developed using our professional advisory expertise, our uniquely talented team, and our cloud-based Property Wealth Planning Simulator built into the client services area of our Moorr platform.

The genesis of our property modelling simulator was sparked by the question Ben and his wife, Jane, asked themselves back in the early 2000s: 'How many of these properties do we actually need to hit our passive income goal?' Determined to find the answer and to navigate the complexities of multiple property investments, including cashflows, offset accounts, taxation impacts, multiple loan splits, and growth and yield forecasts – the concept of the property modelling simulator took shape.

Today, our property modelling simulator and services stand as a powerful resource, specifically designed for folks seeking to build and manage multiple property portfolios to achieve a self-funded retirement income. It's the very same tool our team use to develop tailored plans for thousands of clients, which is why we're confident in the examples we're sharing. This tool's effectiveness forms the backbone of the case studies you're about to explore.

Our proprietary property modelling simulator has helped us craft more than $10.45 billion (yes, with a 'B') in planned property purchases for our clients. It also played a key role in earning Ben the Property Investment Adviser of the Year award in 2014 and 2015, when he was actively directly working with clients, and helped our team secure the inaugural Property Investment Advisory Business of the Year award in 2018.

Real people, real scenarios

You're about to meet a variety of investor profiles, each reflecting common situations and goals:

- **Couple with a young family:** Unlocking the equity in their home and putting it to work.

- **Couple with teenage kids:** Making up for lost time, as they're starting a little later in their life cycle.

- **DINKs (double income, no kids):** Leveraging surplus cashflow to fast-track financial independence.

- **Empty nesters:** Also in the 'making up for lost time' category, but with a tailored approach for this stage of life.

- **Single female professional:** Balancing career aspirations with smart, strategic property investments.

- **Divorcee:** Navigating the challenges of raising a family on a single income while building a secure financial future.

- **Rentvestor:** Renting where they want to live while investing in areas that offer stronger financial returns.

These scenarios aren't intended to be one-size-fits-all solutions. Instead, they reflect real-world situations designed to inspire and guide you. Even if your circumstances don't align perfectly with one of these profiles, the principles and strategies outlined can be adapted to suit your unique situation, often by drawing from two or more options. Furthermore, while these case studies purely focus on generating passive income, other real-world scenario modelling we do includes upsizing or downsizing the family home, renovating, turning an existing home into an investment property, etc., which highlights the importance and power of planning and modelling your future needs and wants.

To fully appreciate the insights within these case studies, it's essential to understand the moving parts involved in modelling accurate cashflow and wealth creation outcomes (see diagram below). Using our simulator ('sim'), we can integrate assumptions, forecasts, and projections to simulate real-world scenarios like the ones we just highlighted above with remarkable precision. We're excited to share the framework and assumptions that underpin this system, so if you attempt to model your own plans, you'll know exactly which variables and factors to consider.

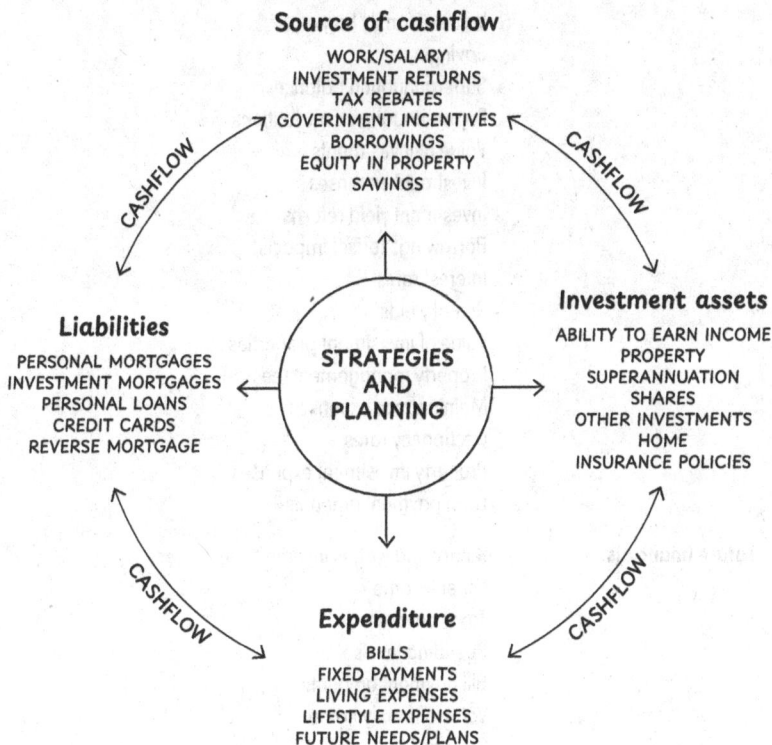

Source of cashflow
WORK/SALARY
INVESTMENT RETURNS
TAX REBATES
GOVERNMENT INCENTIVES
BORROWINGS
EQUITY IN PROPERTY
SAVINGS

CASHFLOW

CASHFLOW

Liabilities
PERSONAL MORTGAGES
INVESTMENT MORTGAGES
PERSONAL LOANS
CREDIT CARDS
REVERSE MORTGAGE

STRATEGIES AND PLANNING

Investment assets
ABILITY TO EARN INCOME
PROPERTY
SUPERANNUATION
SHARES
OTHER INVESTMENTS
HOME
INSURANCE POLICIES

CASHFLOW

CASHFLOW

Expenditure
BILLS
FIXED PAYMENTS
LIVING EXPENSES
LIFESTYLE EXPENSES
FUTURE NEEDS/PLANS

CASHFLOW CYCLE IN PROPERTY WEALTH PLANNING

In the table below we show 'variables' and 'assumptions' to consider when modelling sophisticated money and wealth outcomes over many decades.

MODELLING VARIABLES AND ASSUMPTIONS

Category	Variables and assumptions
Current financials	Salary and wages income Other income Taxation rates Spending levels Bill payment amounts Value of family home Savings Superannuation balances Superannuation contributions Value of investments Investment expenses Investment yield returns Borrowings (offset impacts) Interest rates Rental yields Value of investment properties Property management fees Maintenance expenses Occupancy rates Property investment expenses Loan payment amounts
Future financials	Salary and wages income Other income Taxation rates Spending levels Bill payment amounts Value of family home Savings Superannuation balances Superannuation contributions

Category	Variables and assumptions
Future financials (cont.)	Investment growth rates
	Investment expenses
	Investment yield returns
	Borrowings (offset impacts)
	Interest rates
	Rental yields
	Property value growth rates
	Property management fees
	Maintenance expenses
	Occupancy rates
	Property investment expenses
	Loan payment amounts
	Property purchase expenses
	New loan balances
	Land tax commitments
One-off events	Expected one-off lump sum incomes
	Expected one-off expenditures
Tax and income impacts	PAYG tax scales and impacts
	ATO income-variation impacts
	Superannuation tax impacts
	Defined benefit tax treatments and impacts
Variations and adjustments	Future spending variations
	Short-term income variations
	Long-term income variations
	Short-term expense variations
	Long-term expense variations
Performance monitoring	Constant income monitoring
	Constant expenditure monitoring
	Regular investment performance reviews
	Regular investment performance adjustments
Provisioning	Regular provisioning – income adjustment
	Regular provisioning – expenditure adjustment

Category	Variables and assumptions
Adjustments	Regular adjustment variables percentage Regular review of assumptions percentages
Other considerations	Your discipline to make it happen

When you think about it, this framework of variables and assumptions is exactly as it should be – comprehensive! As we've mentioned, property investing is like running a business, and every successful business needs a solid plan to achieve its goals. All thriving businesses create detailed financial projections – just as BHP wouldn't develop a mine without a rigorous financial and feasibility assessment. That's their secret to success – they plan.

Use the same approach and ensure you have a game plan before embarking on your journey to achieve your $3,000-a-week passive income.

What are the assumptions?

To help you understand the level of detail that goes into these models – without making you break into a cold sweat – we've distilled the key general assumptions into clear headline takeaways for each case study:

- **Income growth:** All income is forecast to grow at 2.5% per annum.
- **Expenditure growth:** All expenditure is forecast to grow at 2.5% per annum.
- **Superannuation Guarantee (SG):** Employer SG contributions are 12% of gross wages.

- **Bank savings interest:** Savings in the bank earn interest at 2.5% per annum.
- **Borrowings – interest rates:** All existing and new lending is assumed to incur 6.5% interest costs.
- **Superannuation returns:** Superannuation returns are assumed at 5.5% per annum.
- **Property acquisition costs:** Set at 6% of the purchase price.
- **Taxation rates:** Tax rates are current as of 2024–25 settings, indexing at 2.5% per annum.
- **Property holding costs:** Ongoing costs for maintaining the property in good letting order are 1.5% of initial purchase costs, increasing at 2.5% per annum.
- **Property management fees:** Assumed at 7.7%.
- **Occupancy rates:** Set at 96%, assuming the property is vacant for two weeks each year.
- **Depreciation:** No depreciation benefits have been included for existing or proposed purchases.

By now, it should be no surprise that property is our key vehicle for generating $3,000 a week in passive income. That doesn't mean we're against shares, traditional superannuation, or business investments – in fact, our firm provides advisers across all of these asset classes. However, as we've shown throughout this book, our skill sets and qualifications are deeply rooted in property investment.

While it's impossible to predict the exact location of every investment property in our scenarios over the next decade, we know these opportunities exist in today's market, and we're confident these scenarios will remain viable well into the future.

Regardless of your starting point, following a proven process and strategy can lead to the incredible outcome of becoming a self-funded retiree over time.

So, let's get started. Let's discover how everyday aspiring Australians are transforming their property dreams into reality – and how you can too.

Case study 1

Richard and Kate – Couple with young kids

Richard and Kate, now 37 and 35, met through mutual friends in their mid-20s. Over the next couple of years, as their relationship grew, they realised they wanted to spend the rest of their lives together. Rather than rushing into marriage, they made a strategic decision to buy a home first and then focus on starting a family.

In early 2014, they secured their first property for $640,000, pooling their savings to make it happen. As their family plans took shape, they renovated – opening up the living area and adding an alfresco deck, making it the perfect family home.

Fast forward to today: their home has grown in value to $922,000, with a remaining mortgage of $520,000. Over the years, they've worked hard to pay it down, though progress slowed when Kate took time off work to raise their two young children.

Now, with both kids in primary school, Kate is returning to work part-time, giving their household a welcome boost in both cashflow and borrowing power.

Lately, they've found themselves at a crossroad. They've been diligently paying down their mortgage for years – but is that really the smartest way to build wealth? They're starting to wonder: should they be doing something more?

Their biggest concern is ensuring they have enough assets to retire comfortably without becoming a future financial burden on their kids.

For Richard and Kate, financial security isn't just about retirement, however – it's about creating a legacy. With housing affordability becoming an increasing challenge, they want to be able to help their children as they grow into adulthood. If they take the right steps now, they could set themselves up not just for a worry-free retirement but to provide the kind of generational support that could make a real difference in their children's lives.

Long-term goals

Richard and Kate's goal is clear: to build enough wealth to generate $3,000 per week in retirement without stress, debt, or property holding costs.

Right now, flexibility is key. Kate's part-time work allows them to create the balanced lifestyle they want for their family – where time with their kids is not sacrificed in the pursuit of financial goals.

But the real question is: can they have both financial security and a lifestyle they love? Can they maintain this flexibility while still setting themselves up for a secure future? Is it possible to continue their current lifestyle without delaying or jeopardising their long-term financial security?

Their challenge is clear: striking the right balance between now and later – between being present for their young family today and securing their financial freedom tomorrow. Let's look at their starting position: income, expenses, cashflow, assets, liabilities and future expenses.

Starting position for Richard and Kate

Income

Income type	Richard	Kate	Combined
Salary	$155,000	$56,000	
Dividends	$900	$0	
Tax and Medicare	-$42,139	-$8,548	
Total net income	**$113,761**	**$47,452**	**$161,213**

Expenses

Expense type	Amount	Frequency	Total annual
Loan repayments	$3,350	Monthly	$40,200
Spending	$68,760	Yearly	$68,760
Total annual expenses			**$108,960**

Current cashflow position

	Monthly	Annually
Total income	$13,434	$161,213
Total expenses	-$9,080	-$108,960
Cashflow surplus/deficit	$4,354	$52,253

Assets

Asset type	Class	Description	Value
Owner-occupier	Securable	Family home	$922,000
Other investment	Securable	Shares	$22,000

Asset type	Class	Description	Value
Total securable assets			$944,000
Superannuation	Non-securable	Accumulation account	$264,200
Cash			$84,500
Total non-securable assets			$348,700
Total assets			**$1,292,700**

Liabilities

Description	Class	Amount	Rate	Payment	Frequency	Terms
Home loan – basic variable	Secured	$520,000	6.5%	$3,300	Monthly	P&I
Total secured liabilities		$520,000				
Credit card	Unsecured	$500	19%	$50	Monthly	P&I
Total unsecured liabilities		$500				
Total liabilities		**$520,500**				

Modelled future expenses

Reason	Amount	Frequency	Start	End
Buyer's advocacy service	$14,950	Once-off	Jun 2025	–
Buyer's advocacy service	$14,950	Once-off	May 2028	–
Special family holiday	$15,000	Once-off	Jul 2028	–
Renovation #1	$60,000	Once-off	Sep 2028	–
Increase in education fees (high school)	$5,000	Yearly	Feb 2030	Feb 2036
Replacement car	$35,000	Once-off	Jun 2031	–

Reason	Amount	Frequency	Start	End
Increase in education fees (high school)	$5,000	Yearly	Jan 2032	Jan 2038
Special family holiday	$15,000	Once-off	Jul 2032	–
Replacement car	$20,000	Once-off	Jun 2033	–

The strategy

With a strong household income and growing home equity, Richard and Kate are in a prime position to act now rather than waiting and missing key opportunities. Their strategy is clear:

- **Use property and superannuation:** This will create a self-sustaining retirement income.
- **Secure two investment properties in the next four to five years:** This maximises the time in the market and compounding returns.
- **Focus on reducing debt after building their portfolio:** This will ensure long-term financial security as they approach retirement.
- **Retire at 60:** That's in 2048 for Richard and 2050 for Kate. Upon retirement they will have a self-sustaining $3,000 a week income – providing them with financial security.

This approach lets them grow wealth without overextending and sacrificing today's lifestyle – setting them up for financial freedom on their terms.

Strategy targets

Property type	Target value	Target date	Target growth	Target yield
Investment property 1	$850,000	Jun 2025	7.00%	$3.00%
Investment property 2	$704,545	May 2028	5.50%	4.50%

Investment Property 1: Laying the foundation

Their first investment property is a crucial foundation for long-term success. With time on their side, they're leveraging compounding growth to build wealth, anticipating significant value appreciation over the next decade.

		Area/location strategies	Property selection strategies
Purchase price	$850,000		
Purchase date	Jun 2025	Proven performer	Piggy-backer
Ownership structure	Joint	Rare earth	Scarce diamond
		City fling	Reliable and durable
Capital growth p.a.	7.00%		Shoulder rider
Rental yield p.a.	3.00%		

Key benefits of Investment Property 1 include:

- **Growth potential:** A well-chosen property in a high-demand location positioned for strong long-term capital growth.
- **Rental income:** As demand increases, so will rental returns – creating a stable and growing income stream.

Starting loan details

Total lending balance	Monthly repayments	Annual repayments
$901,000	$4,880	$58,560

	Loan #1 for investment property 1	Loan #2 for investment property 1
Total lending balance	$680,000	$221,000
Loan date	Jun 2025	Jun 2025
Interest rate	6.5%	6.5%
Repayment type	Interest only	Interest only
Security	Investment property 1	Family home

Who pays the cost?

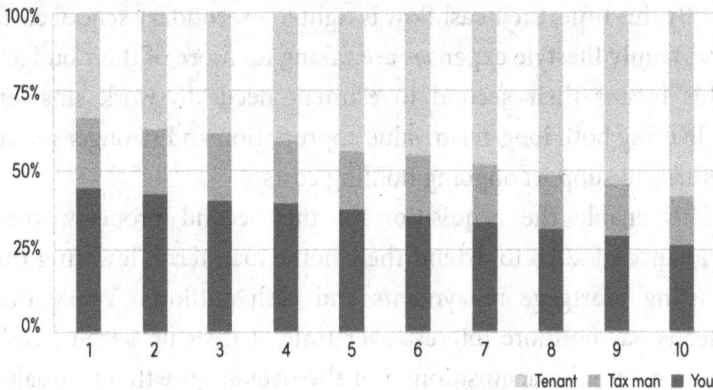

Tenant / Tax man / You

With their first property in place, the next step is strategic: acquiring a second investment that balances stronger cashflow with continued growth.

Investment Property 2: Balancing growth and cashflow

		Area/location strategies	Property selection strategies
Purchase price	$704,545		
Purchase date	May 2028	Changing places	Reliable and
Ownership structure	Joint	City fling	durable
		No vacancies	Shoulder rider
Capital growth p.a.	5.50%	Wave rider	Ugly duckling
Rental yield p.a.	4.50%		

This investment property's projected value accounts for expected market growth, ensuring a realistic future purchase price. This approach ensures the estimate aligns with what Richard and Kate will likely pay when the time comes to buy.

By this time, their cashflow is tighter – secondary school costs and family lifestyle expenses are taking up more of their budget. This means their second investment needs to work smarter, delivering both long-term value appreciation and stronger rental returns to support ongoing holding costs.

To enable the acquisition of this second property, they refinance in 2028 to extend their home loan term, lowering the existing mortgage repayments and cash outflows. While this means paying more interest over time, it frees up surplus cash to complete the acquisition, and the overall growth and wealth outcome dwarfs the downside interest costs.

Here's how their second investment property is structured to achieve this balance:

- **Higher yield focus:** Unlike their first property, this investment is chosen for its stronger rental return, helping to offset holding costs from day one.
- **Strategic portfolio growth:** While capital growth remains important, this asset is selected for its ability to contribute to cashflow sooner.
- **Balanced return:** The combination of Property 1's capital growth and Property 2's higher yield ensures a well-rounded portfolio that supports their financial goals both now and into retirement.

With both properties working together, Richard and Kate have set themselves up for long-term financial success.

Starting loan details

Total lending balance	Monthly repayments	Annual repayments
$746,818	$4,045	$48,540

	Loan #1 for investment property 2	Loan #2 for investment property 2
Loan amount	$563,636	$183,182
Loan date	May 2028	May 2028
Interest rate	6.5%	6.5%
Repayment type	Interest only	Interest only
Security	Investment property 2	Family home

Who pays the cost?

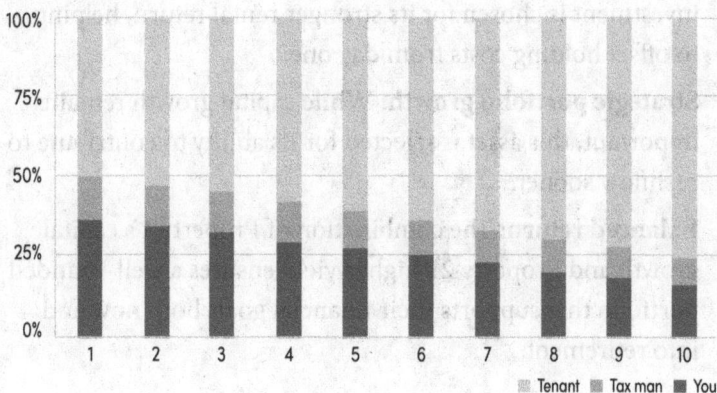

However, strategy alone isn't enough. Next, we look at how cash-flow management plays a key role in making this plan sustainable.

The cashflow story

A property portfolio is only as strong as the cashflow that keeps it running. Richard and Kate's strategy ensures they always have a financial buffer – keeping them in control, even as they grow their investments.

The next graph highlights that even after purchasing their second investment property in May 2028, Richard and Kate stay in a positive cashflow position. Their household income of $21,336.67 covers all expenses ($20,495.31), leaving a monthly surplus of $841.36.

Over time, these surpluses increase, reinforcing their ability to sustain their investment strategy without financial strain.

Monthly income and expenditure

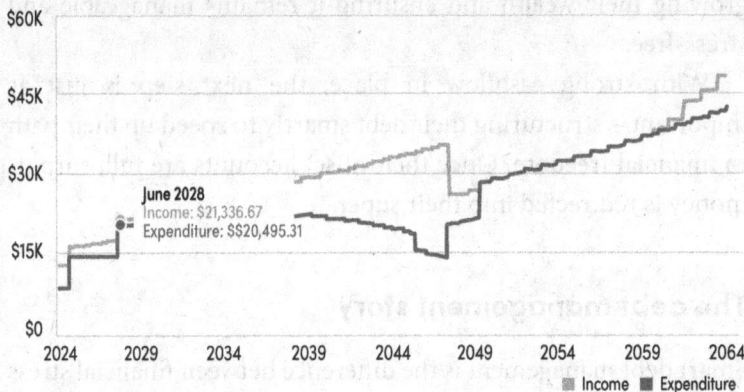

June 2028
Income: $21,336.67
Expenditure: $$20,495.31

$60K
$45K
$30K
$15K
$0
2024 2029 2034 2039 2044 2049 2054 2059 2064

■ Income ■ Expenditure

The graph below illustrates how their household liquidity remains strong at every stage. Even during investment periods, their cash buffer never drops below $77,781 – giving them the financial breathing room to handle unexpected expenses or rental vacancies. This safety net is crucial, ensuring their plan stays on track without unnecessary stress.

Household cash position

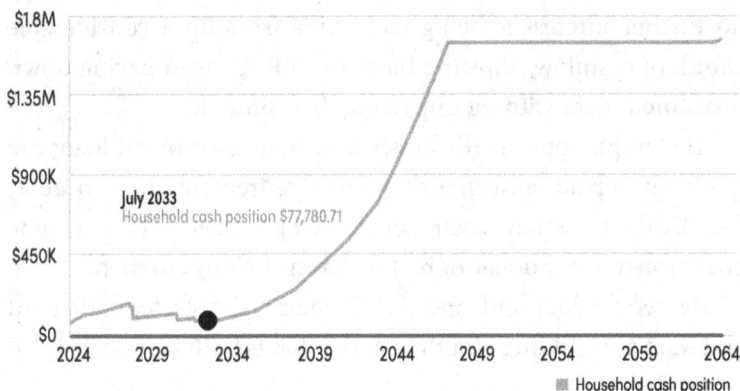

$1.8M
$1.35M
$900K
$450K
$0

July 2033
Household cash position $77,780.71

2024 2029 2034 2039 2044 2049 2054 2059 2064

▧ Household cash position

By carefully structuring their investments, Richard and Kate are growing their wealth and ensuring it remains manageable and stress-free.

With strong cashflow in place, the next step is just as important – structuring their debt smartly to speed up their path to financial freedom. Once their offset accounts are full, surplus money is redirected into their super.

The debt management story

Smart debt management is the difference between financial stress and long-term confidence. Richard and Kate are using productive debt strategically – leveraging it to grow wealth while following a clear plan to pay it down.

In the early years of the accumulation phase, Richard and Kate rely on 'productive debt' – borrowing to acquire high-quality properties that grow in value over time. Their loan-to-value ratio (LVR) steadily declines as their assets appreciate, making their debt more manageable each year.

By Year 13, a major milestone is reached – their home loan balance is covered by the funds in their offset account, meaning no further interest is being paid. This frees up a considerable chunk of cashflow, allowing them to shift focus to paying down investment debt without impacting their lifestyle.

The graph opposite illustrates how their investment loans are gradually repaid, ensuring they enter retirement close to debt-free. By the time they reach their $3,000 per week passive income goal, nearly every dollar of rental income belongs to them.

By sequencing and optimising their debt strategy, Richard and Kate are building wealth in a way that is both sustainable and controlled.

With their debt under control, it's time to shift focus to the real game-changer – how rental income creates true financial independence.

Projected debt reduction

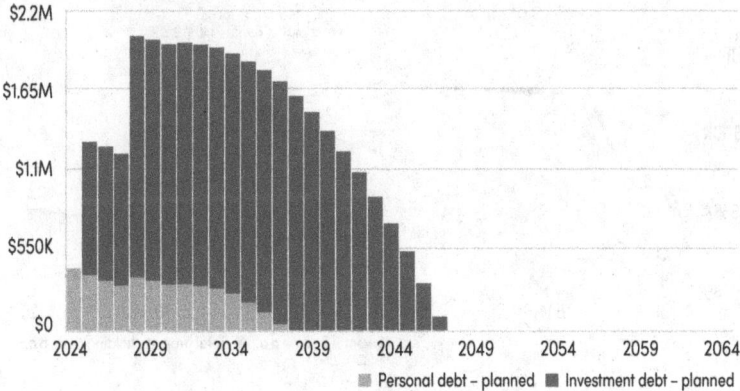

Legend: Personal debt – planned | Investment debt – planned

The passive rental income story

The real magic of property investing happens when the portfolio shifts from 'growth mode' to 'income mode' – when rental income covers all costs and starts delivering true financial freedom.

By Year 16, Richard and Kate hit another crucial milestone – break-even. At this point, rental income covers all expenses, from mortgage repayments to property management, maintenance, and holding costs. This means they no longer need to tip in extra cash to sustain their investments.

Once their properties become self-sustaining, every extra dollar of rental income becomes a wealth-building tool. They reinvest this surplus to pay off loans faster, creating a snowball effect where their debt shrinks while their passive income grows.

This accelerates their financial freedom and strengthens their position heading into retirement.

Projected rental income

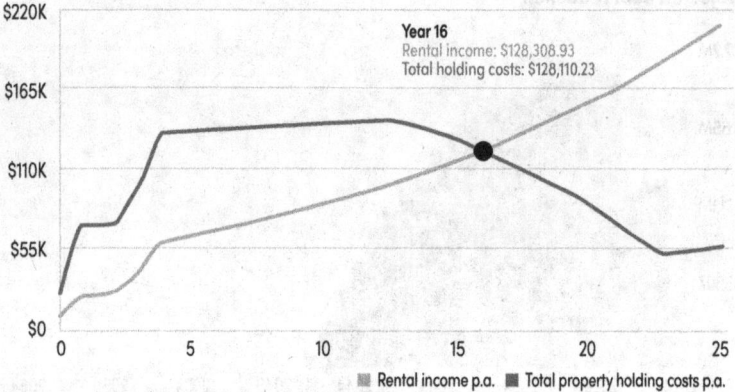

Year 16
Rental income: $128,308.93
Total holding costs: $128,110.23

Rental income p.a. ■ Total property holding costs p.a.

Even using conservative assumptions – like a steady 6.5% interest rate, two weeks of vacancy per year, and conservative holding costs – Richard and Kate's portfolio is on track. In reality, break-even could happen even sooner, further strengthening their financial outlook.

With their portfolio fully self-sustaining, let's see what this means for their long-term wealth and retirement lifestyle.

Wealth projection overview

Smart decisions and forward planning have set Richard and Kate up – not just for a financially secure retirement but to leave a lasting legacy for their children.

By securing the right properties, keeping a financial buffer, and letting time and market growth do the work, they've built a self-sustaining portfolio. Their investments now generate passive income, which will give them full financial freedom in retirement.

Timeframe financial snapshot

By retirement, Richard and Kate's investments are projected to grow to a combined $8.62 million – $6.48 million in investment property and $2.14 million in superannuation.

In today's dollars, their investment capital base (excluding the family home) is projected to be worth $4.57 million by 2048 – providing a secure and comfortable retirement without financial stress.

By May 2048, Richard will have fully retired, meaning his working income will stop, and Kate will retire two years later in January 2050. From this date, their passive income will take over for both of them.

Property portfolio wealth projection model

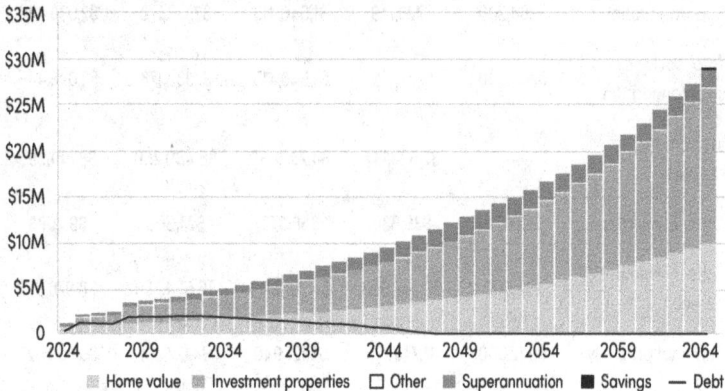

Home value Investment properties □ Other Superannuation Savings — Debt

From May 2048, their working income is replaced with a personal income allocation of $3,000 per week. Their investment portfolio is projected to generate 61% of this, with the remaining 39% comfortably covered by superannuation earnings.

With their home fully paid off and investment loans nearly gone, every dollar of rental income now works for them – not the bank. This means they step into retirement with complete financial freedom and peace of mind.

Most importantly, their plan is flexible. Whether Kate wants to return to full-time work, they want to retire earlier, help their children financially, or adjust their lifestyle as priorities shift, their wealth gives them choices. This isn't just about reaching a number; it's about removing financial stress and designing a life on their terms.

And that's what true financial peace looks like.

Wealth projection overview

	Now (2024)	10 years (2034)	20 years (2044)	Retirement (2050)	30 years (2054)
Superannuation	$264,200	$723,149	$1,540,413	$2,138,178	$2,038,446
Total savings and superannuation	$264,200	$723,149	$1,540,413	$2,138,178	$2,038,446
Investment property	–	$2,534,147	$4,733,437	$6,480,266	$8,881,593
Other investments	$22,000	$35,836	$58,373	$74,500	$95,083
Total investment assets	$22,000	$2,569,983	$4,791,809	$6,554,766	$8,976,676
Personal property	$922,000	$1,743,275	$3,121,940	$4,177,861	$5,590,920
Total assets	$1,208,200	$5,036,406	$9,454,163	$12,870,804	$16,606,042
Total debts	-$436,000	-$1,907,981	-$744,035	–	–

Richard and Kate – Couple with young kids

	Now (2024)	10 years (2034)	20 years (2044)	Retirement (2050)	30 years (2054)
Net worth	$772,200	$3,128,426	$8,710,127	$12,870,804	$16,606,042
Nest egg	-$149,800	$1,385,150	$5,588,187	$8,692,944	$11,015,122
Nest egg (present value)	-$149,800	$1,082,077	$3,410,308	$4,574,529	$5,251,379

Case study 2

Harvey and Ingrid – Midlife investors with teenage kids

For Harvey and Ingrid, family has always been at the centre of their world. Growing up in large families themselves, they always imagined a bustling home filled with kids, laughter, and shared experiences. Now in their mid-40s, with three teenage children (17, 15, and 13), life has been a blur of school runs, sports games, and career commitments – leaving little time to think beyond the day-to-day.

Harvey, turning 45 this year, and Ingrid, 44, have worked hard to provide for their family. But as they step into this new phase – where the kids are becoming more independent – they're realising how quickly time is passing. If they don't act now, another five or ten years could slip by, and they'll have lost valuable time in which compounding growth could have worked in their favour.

They have just 10 to 15 years of full-time work left, and these are their peak earning years. They want to take advantage of their strong monthly cashflow surplus before retirement. They've sacrificed long international holidays to raise their family, but travel is a must-do in their active years post-retirement – including at least one big trip with their children before they start their own adult lives.

Beyond just lifestyle goals, Harvey and Ingrid also want to help their kids financially – whether it's assisting with their first car or contributing toward future wedding costs. With all this in mind, they've run the numbers and know that $3,000 per week in retirement will allow them to live comfortably – but they need to plan, then act, to make it happen.

Long-term goals

This year will be different. Harvey and Ingrid have realised that their peak earning years are upon them, and they need to take full advantage while they still have strong surplus cashflow.

That means hitting a clear financial target: retiring at 65 with $3,000 per week in passive income, giving them full flexibility. But they also want a built-in backup plan – if they decide to retire earlier, they want the option to step back at 60 on $2,200 per week or work part-time to land somewhere in between.

Beyond their own security, they're planning for the experiences that matter most, with at least one full-family trip before their kids move on to independent lives. They've also set aside funds to support their children, including assistance with first cars, potential wedding contributions, and general guidance as they step into adulthood.

To achieve all of this, they need a strategy that makes the most of their peak earning years while ensuring they don't sacrifice their current lifestyle. Their path forward is about creating a future that reflects their values and priorities as well as financial security. Here's their starting position.

Starting position for Harvey and Ingrid

Income

Income type	Harvey	Ingrid	Combined
Salary	$160,000	$115,000	
Dividends	$0	$500	
Tax and Medicare	-$43,738	-$27,748	
Total net income	$116,262	$87,752	$204,014

Expenses

Expense type	Amount	Frequency	Total annual
Loan repayments	$4,287	Monthly	$51,444
Spending	$91,500	Yearly	$91,500
Total annual expenses			$142,944

Current cashflow position

	Monthly	Annually
Total income	$17,001	$204,014
Total expenses	-$11,912	-$142,944
Cashflow surplus/deficit	$5,089	$61,070

Assets

Asset type	Class	Description	Value
Owner-occupier	Securable	Family home	$1,180,000
Other investment	Securable	Shares	$10,000
Total securable assets			$1,190,000
Superannuation	Non-securable	Accumulation account	$386,000
Cash			$198,000
Total non-securable assets			$584,000
Total assets			**$1,774,000**

Liabilities

Description	Class	Amount	Rate	Payment	Frequency	Terms
Home loan – basic variable	Secured	$715,000	6.0%	$4,287	Monthly	P&I
Total secured liabilities		$715,000				
Total unsecured liabilities		$0				
Total liabilities		**$715,000**				

Modelled future expenses

Reason	Amount	Frequency	Start	End
Wedding anniversary special holiday	$20,000	Once-off	Feb 2025	–
Buyer's advocacy service	$14,950	Once-off	Feb 2025	–
Replacement car	$40,000	Once-off	May 2025	–
Help to buy Child 1 first car	$10,000	Once-off	Jan 2027	–
Home renovations	$80,000	Once-off	Jan 2028	–

Reason	Amount	Frequency	Start	End
First child leaves home	-$450	Monthly	Jan 2028	Jan 2046
Buyer's advocacy service	$14,950	Once-off	Sep 2028	–
Help to buy Child 2 first car	$10,000	Once-off	Jan 2030	–
Second child leaves home	-$450	Monthly	Jan 2030	Jan 2046
Replacement car	$20,000	Once-off	Jun 2030	–
Help to buy Child 3 first car	$10,000	Once-off	Jan 2032	–
Third child leaves home	-$450	Monthly	Jan 2032	Jan 2046
Special family holiday	$25,000	Once-off	Jul 2032	–
Replacement car	$45,000	Once-off	Jun 2035	–
Wedding gift	$10,000	Once-off	Nov 2036	–
Wedding gift	$10,000	Once-off	Nov 2038	–
Replacement car	$20,000	Once-off	Jun 2040	–
Wedding gift	$10,000	Once-off	Nov 2040	–

The strategy

With a strong household income, growing home equity, and two decades until retirement, Harvey and Ingrid are in a prime position to make their money work for them. Their approach balances strategic property investment with debt reduction, ensuring they build long-term wealth while maintaining financial flexibility. Their plan is clear:

- **Leverage their strong financial position:** A combination of healthy surplus cashflow and home equity allows them to take action now.

- **Buy two investment properties, 3.5 years apart:** This staggered approach helps manage debt exposure while maximising time in the market.

- **Prioritise growth and cashflow balance:** The first property is growth-focused (7%), while the second balances growth (6.25%) with a stronger yield (3.75%) to support cashflow leading into retirement.

- **Shift focus to debt reduction:** Once both properties are secured, they'll pay off their home loan first, then reduce investment debt before retirement.

- **Retire at 65:** With $3,000 per week in passive income, they have full flexibility to enjoy their next chapter.

This strategy ensures that Harvey and Ingrid are making the most of their peak earning years – building an asset base that will deliver financial security, lifestyle freedom, and the ability to support their family in the years ahead.

Strategy targets

Property type	Target value	Target date	Target growth	Target yield
Investment property 1	$900,000	Feb 2025	7.00%	$3.00%
Investment property 2	$839,624	Sep 2028	6.25%	3.75%

Investment property 1: Building capital growth

		Area/location strategies	Property selection strategies
Purchase price	$900,000		
Purchase date	Feb 2025	Proven performer Rare earth Million-dollar strip	Reliable and durable Piggy-backer Scarce diamond
Ownership structure	Joint		
Capital growth p.a.	7.00%		
Rental yield p.a.	3.00%		

Harvey and Ingrid's first investment property is all about maximising growth while they're in their highest earning years. With time in the market still on their side, this property is positioned for long-term capital appreciation, laying the foundation for their portfolio.

Key investment metrics:

- **Purchase price:** $900,000 (adjusted for future pricing based on expected growth trends).
- **Capital growth target:** 7% per annum – selected in a high-demand location with strong long-term fundamentals.
- **Rental yield target:** 3% – a moderate yield to ensure holding costs are manageable while prioritising growth.

Starting loan details

Total lending balance	Monthly repayments	Annual repayments
$954,000	$5,168	$62,016

	Loan #1 for investment property 1	Loan #2 for investment property 1
Total lending balance	$720,000	$234,000
Loan date	Feb 2025	Feb 2025
Interest rate	6.5%	6.5%
Repayment type	Interest only	Interest only
Security	Investment property 1	Family home

Who pays the cost?

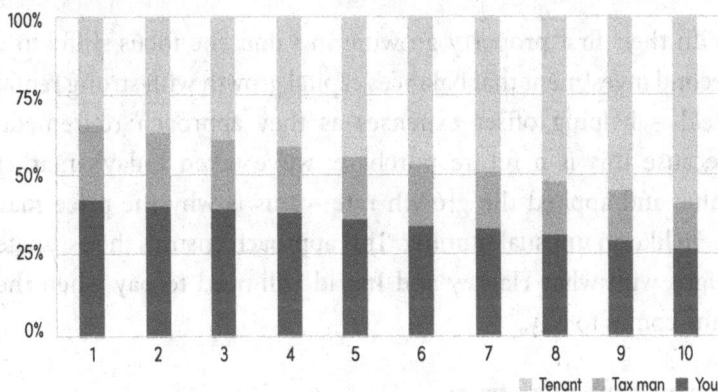

This property forms the backbone of their investment strategy, ensuring they benefit from compounding returns over the next decade.

Investment Property 2: Balancing growth and cashflow

		Area/location strategies	Property selection strategies
Purchase price	$839,624		
Purchase date	Sep 2028	Rare earth	Reliable and durable
		Proven performer	Shoulder rider
Ownership structure	Joint	City fling	Ugly duckling
		Wave rider	Size matters
Capital growth p.a.	6.25%		
Rental yield p.a.	3.75%		

With their first property growing in value, the focus shifts to a second investment that balances capital growth with strong rental yield – helping offset expenses as they approach retirement. Because this is a future purchase, we've taken today's market value and applied the growth rate – this is why the price may seem like an unusual number. This approach ensures the estimate aligns with what Harvey and Ingrid will need to pay when the time comes to buy.

Key investment metrics:

- **Purchase timing:** 3.5 years after the first property – allowing their finances to stabilise before acquiring the next asset.
- **Capital growth target:** 6.25% per annum – still prioritising appreciation, but with more cashflow balance.
- **Rental yield target:** 3.75% – higher than the first property to reduce out-of-pocket contributions.

Starting loan details

Total lending balance	Monthly repayments	Annual repayments
$890,001	$4,820	$57,840

	Loan #1 for investment property 2	Loan #2 for investment property 2
Loan amount	$671,699	$218,302
Loan date	Sep 2028	Sep 2028
Interest rate	6.5%	6.5%
Repayment type	Interest only	Interest only
Security	Investment property 2	Family home

Who pays the cost?

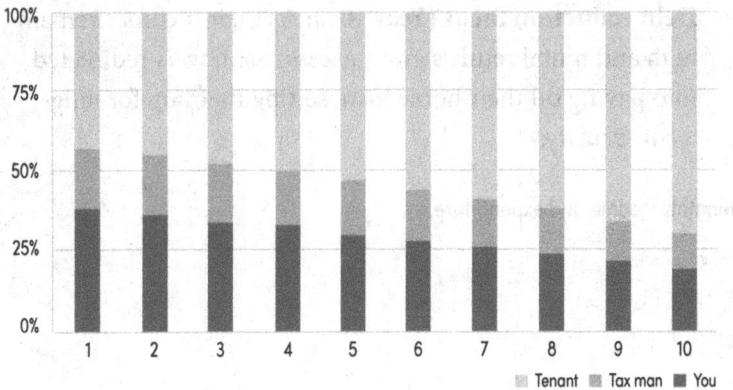

Tenant　Tax man　You

This second investment property plays a critical role in reducing the need for additional personal cash injections, ensuring their portfolio remains financially sustainable while they work toward debt reduction.

The cashflow story

A well-structured investment plan is about acquiring properties and ensuring cashflow remains sustainable at every stage of the journey. Harvey and Ingrid's financial model is designed to keep their household in a comfortable surplus, allowing them to invest with confidence while maintaining financial security for their family. This is how their cashflow evolves over time:

- **Investment Property 1 purchase (Year 1):** Their first property increases holding costs, but with their strong household income, cashflow remains positive.

- **Investment Property 2 purchase (Year 3.5):** A second acquisition adjusts their income and expense balance, but their plan ensures they remain in surplus, with an additional cash buffer built into their model.

- **Debt reduction focus (Year 10+):** As their incomes remain high and rental returns grow, excess cashflow is redirected into paying off their home loan, setting them up for long-term security.

Monthly income and expenditure

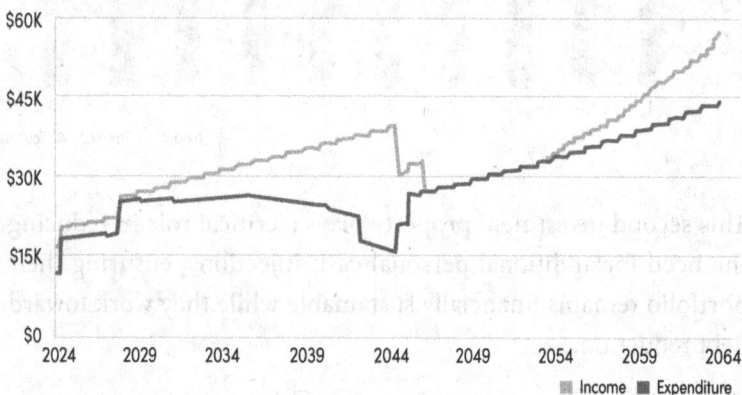

■ Income ■ Expenditure

Unlike more aggressive investors, Harvey and Ingrid are moderate risk-takers – they value security while growing their wealth. Their plan ensures their household savings never fall below $147,000, giving them the confidence to navigate any unexpected financial surprises without derailing their investment strategy.

Household cash position

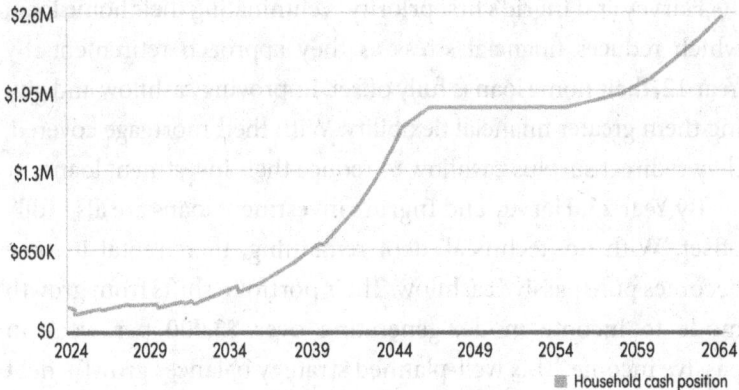

By the time they reach their retirement target, their cashflow shifts from being active-income reliant to passive-income generating. Their portfolio reaches break-even as rental income grows, and just over 10 years post-retirement, their investments are producing income well above their $3,000 per week target. This gives them additional financial flexibility to travel, support their family, or retire even earlier if they choose.

The debt management story

Smart debt management isn't just about borrowing but knowing when and how to pay it down to maximise financial security. Harvey and Ingrid's strategy allows them to leverage productive debt while reducing financial risk over time, ultimately setting them up for a stress-free retirement.

During their wealth-building phase, their debt peaks after purchasing a second investment property. With both assets in place and compounding in value, they focus on growth rather than aggressively repaying debt, allowing time in the market to work in their favour.

Harvey and Ingrid's first priority is eliminating their home loan, which reduces financial stress as they approach retirement. By Year 12, their home loan is fully offset, improving cashflow and giving them greater financial flexibility. With their mortgage covered, they redirect surplus cashflow to reduce their investment loans.

By Year 23, Harvey and Ingrid's investment loans are also fully offset. With no 'technical' debt remaining, their rental income becomes pure passive cashflow. Their portfolio shifts from growth mode to income mode, generating over $3,000 per week in passive income. This well-planned strategy balances growth, debt reduction, and long-term financial security, ensuring Harvey and Ingrid enjoy a comfortable and worry-free retirement.

Projected debt reduction

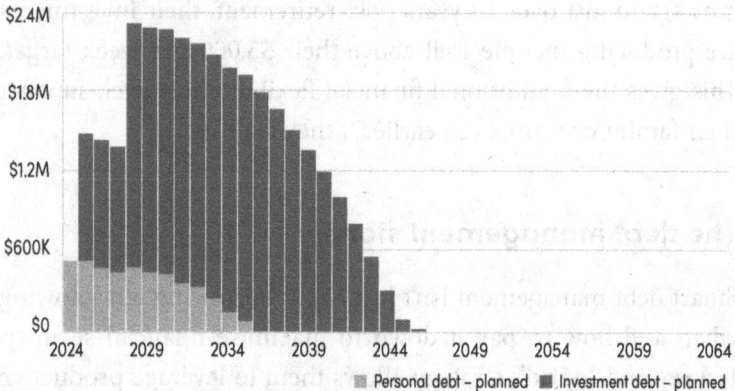

Personal debt – planned ■ Investment debt – planned

By sequencing their debt reduction strategy this way, Harvey and Ingrid can get the best of both worlds – leveraging debt to build wealth early, while ensuring they enter retirement with no financial burdens.

The passive rental income story

The true power of property investing is realised when rental income shifts from covering costs to generating true financial freedom. Harvey and Ingrid's portfolio is designed to not just break even but produce strong passive cashflow, supporting their retirement goals.

In the early years, rental income covers some of the holding costs, though mortgage repayments remain the largest expense. As time passes, rental income gradually increases alongside property values, reducing the need for out-of-pocket contributions.

By Year 16, their rental income fully covers all expenses, including mortgages, property management, maintenance, and other holding costs. At this point, their portfolio is self-sustaining and no longer requires contributions from their personal income.

As they continue to pay down their investment loans, their portfolio shifts from breaking even to generating surplus cashflow. By Year 20, their properties produce over $3,000 per week in net passive income, giving them full financial independence. Even with conservative assumptions – such as 6.5% interest rates, two weeks of vacancy per year, and rising expenses – their rental income remains strong, ensuring they won't need to rely solely on their superannuation.

With this strategy in place, Harvey and Ingrid's rental income becomes key to a financially secure and flexible retirement, free from financial stress.

Projected rental income

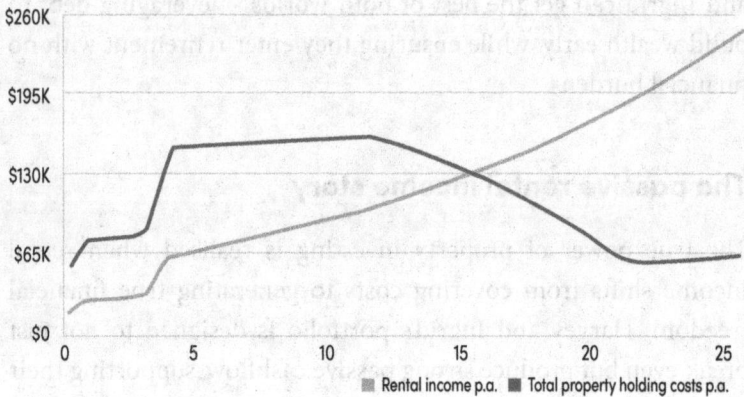

Legend: Rental income p.a. ■ Total property holding costs p.a.

Wealth projection overview

Harvey and Ingrid's story proves that it's never too late to take control of your financial future. By leveraging their strong incomes and home equity, they've built a sustainable wealth strategy that balances security, flexibility, and long-term financial freedom.

Timeframe financial snapshot

By retirement, Harvey and Ingrid's investment properties and superannuation will be worth a combined $8 million.

In today's dollars, their investment capital base (excluding their family home) will hold a value of $4.6 million, ensuring they can retire with confidence.

Property portfolio wealth projection model

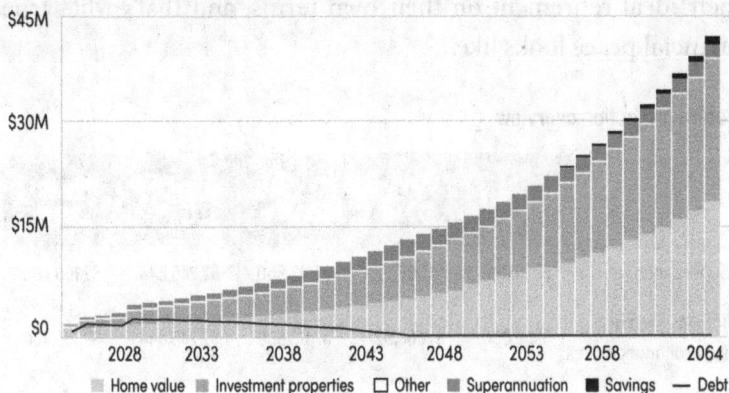

Legend: Home value · Investment properties · Other · Superannuation · Savings · — Debt

From May 2048, Harvey and Ingrid's working income is replaced with a personal income allocation of $3,000 per week, with 56% coming from their property portfolio and 44% from superannuation.

Their strategy isn't just about hitting a number but having options. While their plan is designed for retirement at 65 with $3,000 per week, they have built-in flexibility to adjust if needed and choose between:

- **Option 1:** Retire at 60 with $2,200 per week – a comfortable income, allowing them to step away earlier.

- **Option 2:** Work part-time for a few years – balancing lifestyle and income, landing somewhere between $2,200 and $3,000 per week.

- **Option 3:** Continue full-time until age 65 – maximising their wealth and passive income for an even more secure future.

Their plan gives them financial security and the ability to design their ideal retirement on their own terms, and that's what true financial peace looks like.

Wealth projection overview

	Now (2024)	10 years (2034)	20 years (2044)	Retirement (2046)	30 years (2054)
Superannuation	$386,000	$1,008,927	$2,113,580	$2,245,844	$2,109,460
Total savings and superannuation	$386,000	$1,008,927	$2,113,580	$2,245,844	$2,109,460
Investment property	–	$2,862,590	$5,469,743	$5,836,013	$10,463,871
Other investments	$10,000	$17,908	$32,071	$33,996	$57,435
Total investment assets	$10,000	$2,880,498	$5,501,814	$5,870,009	$10,521,306
Personal property	$1,180,000	$2,457,316	$4,833,913	$5,172,287	$9,509,038
Total assets	$1,576,000	$6,346,741	$12,449,307	$13,288,140	$22,139,804
Total debts	-$517,000	-$1,988,139	-$307,556	-$69,310	–
Net worth	$1,059,000	$4,358,602	$12,141,752	$13,218,829	$22,139,804
Nest egg	-$121,000	$1,901,286	$7,307,839	$8,046,543	$12,630,766
Nest egg (present value)	-$121,000	$1,485,281	$4,459,762	$4,673,952	$6,021,625

Case study 3

Brian and Claire –
DINKs

Brian and Claire, both in their mid-30s, have made a conscious decision not to have children, allowing them to focus on their careers, lifestyle, and financial future. Unlike some who fall into the DINKs (dual income, no kids) category due to circumstances outside of their control, e.g. health challenges, their choice is intentional – one that grants them more freedom, time, and financial flexibility.

They are both deeply fulfilled by their work, pursuing purpose-driven careers that align with their values. While their salaries aren't among the highest, their dual income and lack of dependants provide them with a strong financial base and the ability to invest in experiences rather than expenses.

Their great passion? Travelling to exotic, remote, off-the-beaten-path destinations, immersing themselves in different cultures, and collecting unforgettable experiences. They also love entertaining family and friends and enjoy being the 'best uncle and auntie ever' to their niece and two nephews.

Lately, they've started to think more strategically about how they can sustain this lifestyle into retirement, or even whether they can retire early. They recognise that their time freedom today is tied to their full-time work, and if they want the same flexibility without having to work in the future, they need to start building assets that generate passive income.

With no children to factor into their financial planning, they have a unique advantage – a surplus cashflow that can be redirected toward wealth creation rather than the typical expenses of raising a family.

Long-term goals

Brian and Claire fully understand the time freedom their decision not to have children has afforded them, and want to leverage their ability to balance today's experiences with future security.

For them, the challenge is getting the balance right – enjoying their lifestyle now while ensuring their wealth base grows to sustain them when they choose to stop working. They know their current freedom exists because of their full-time income, but they don't want to be dependent on work to maintain it in the future.

Their goal is clear: build an asset base that generates $3,000 per week in passive income, allowing them to retire no later than age 60 while continuing to travel, experience life, and maintain the lifestyle they love.

They see property as a key vehicle for achieving this. The idea of acquiring a portfolio of residential properties and running a small private rental accommodation business over the next few decades aligns with their financial goals and personal interests.

Most importantly, they want complete financial independence. Unlike many retirees who rely on selling assets to fund their lifestyle, they aim to create a sustainable income stream so they can keep their assets and control their wealth indefinitely.

Starting position for Brian and Claire

Income

Income type	Brian	Claire	Combined
Salary	$110,000	$130,000	
Tax and Medicare	–$25,988	–$32,388	
Total net income	$84,012	$97,612	$181,624

Expenses

Expense type	Amount	Frequency	Total annual
Loan repayments	$3,226	Monthly	$38,712
Spending	$62,850	Yearly	$62,850
Total annual expenses			$101,562

Current cashflow position

	Monthly	Annually
Total income	$15,135	$181,624
Total expenses	–$8,464	–$101,562
Cashflow surplus/deficit	$6,672	$80,062

Assets

Asset type	Class	Description	Value
Owner-occupier	Securable	Family home	$850,000
Superannuation	Non-securable	Accumulation account	$206,750
Cash			$80,000
Total assets			**$1,136,750**

Liabilities

Description	Class	Amount	Rate	Payment	Frequency	Terms
Home loan – basic variable	Secured	$538,000	6.0%	$3,226	Monthly	P&I
Credit card	Unsecured	$0	19%	$0	Monthly	P&I
Total liabilities		**$538,000**				

Modelled future expenses

Reason	Amount	Frequency	Start	End
Buyer's advocacy service	$14,950	Once-off	May 2025	–
Pay down home loan	$60,000	Once-off	May 2025	–
Allocation to new yearly hobbies	$10,000	Yearly	Dec 2025	Jan 2051
Special holiday	$25,000	Once-off	Jan 2026	–
Buyer's advocacy service	$14,950	Once-off	May 2028	–
Car replacement	$30,000	Once-off	Jun 2028	–
Buyer's advocacy service	$14,950	Once-off	May 2033	–
Car replacement	$30,000	Once-off	Jun 2038	–

The strategy

Before getting serious about their financial future, Brian and Claire's healthy monthly surplus was mostly directed toward lifestyle spending. While they enjoyed the benefits of their dual income, they also made significant progress in paying down their mortgage and building a comfortable financial buffer.

Now, they're ready to put their surplus income to work, using a disciplined property investment strategy to create a sustainable passive income stream by the time they retire at 60.

Their investment plan is shaped by three key factors:

1. **Building equity and deposit funds:** Without children, their borrowing power is strong, but their investment speed will depend on how quickly they can accumulate equity and savings for deposits.

2. **Acquiring three investment properties:** Unlike previous case studies that focused on two properties, Brian and Claire plan to scale up their portfolio with a third investment to maximise growth.

3. **Prioritising capital growth:** Their investment timeline allows them to focus on capital growth first, meaning they can afford to hold properties that may be negatively geared in the early years before transitioning to a yield-balanced portfolio closer to retirement.

Their plan is to:

- Secure three investment properties over the next decade, each selected for strong long-term capital growth potential.
- Stage the acquisitions to ensure manageable cashflow, with each property purchased based on equity growth and surplus savings accumulation.

- Gradually transition from capital growth to cashflow as they approach retirement, ensuring their portfolio fully funds their lifestyle by 60.
- Cover their home loan first, via the offset funds, then focus on investment debt reduction in the final years before retirement.

By structuring their portfolio this way, Brian and Claire can continue enjoying their lifestyle today while systematically building financial freedom for the future.

Strategy targets

Property type	Target value	Target date	Target growth	Target yield
Investment property 1	$800,000	May 2025	7.00%	$3.00%
Investment property 2	$845,565	May 2028	6.50%	3.50%
Investment property 3	$844,078	May 2033	5.50%	4.50%

Investment Property 1: Laying the foundation

		Area/location strategies	Property selection strategies
Purchase price	$800,000		
Purchase date	May 2025	Proven performer Rare earth Wave rider Changing places	Reliable and durable Shoulder rider Scarce diamond
Ownership structure	Joint		
Capital growth p.a.	7.00%		
Rental yield p.a.	3.00%		

Brian and Claire's first investment property is the critical first step in their long-term plan. With strong surplus cashflow and a solid equity position, they have the financial flexibility to prioritise capital growth over rental yield.

Key investment metrics:

- **Investment focus:** Long-term capital growth
- **Target growth rate:** 7% per annum
- **Target rental yield:** 3% per annum
- **Financial strategy:**
  - Comfortable covering initial shortfalls as the property appreciates in value.
  - Property located in a high-growth metro or regional centre with strong demand.
  - Focus on maximising equity growth to leverage into future acquisitions.

With time on their side, Brian and Claire's first property is designed to compound in value, building momentum for the next stage of their portfolio.

Starting loan details

Total lending balance	Monthly repayments	Annual repayments
$848,000	$4,594	$55,128

	Loan #1 for investment property 1	Loan #2 for investment property 1
Loan amount	$640,000	$208,000
Loan date	May 2025	May 2025
Interest rate	6.5%	6.5%
Repayment type	Interest only	Interest only
Security	Investment property 1	Family home

Who pays the cost?

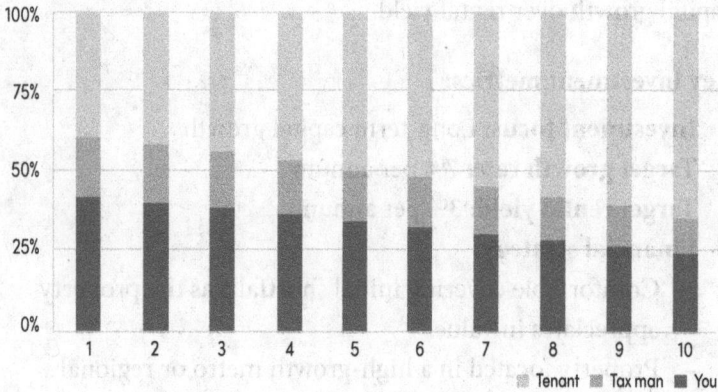

Once this foundation is in place, their focus will shift to Investment Property 2, continuing their structured approach.

Investment Property 2: Continuing the growth strategy

		Area/location strategies	Property selection strategies
Purchase price	$845,565		
Purchase date	May 2028	City fling	Reliable and durable
Ownership structure	Joint	Wave rider	Ugly duckling
		Rare earth	Piggy-backer
Capital growth p.a.	6.50%	Proven performer	
Rental yield p.a.	3.50%		

With their first investment property gaining momentum, Brian and Claire are now ready to leverage their growing equity and surplus savings into their second investment. As this is a future purchase, we've taken today's market value and applied the growth rate – which is why the purchase price may seem like an unusual number. This approach ensures the estimate aligns with what Brian and Claire will need to pay when the time comes to buy.

While their primary focus is still capital growth, they begin to slightly adjust their approach – balancing appreciation potential with a modestly higher rental yield to help manage cashflow.

Key investment metrics:

- **Investment focus:** Continued capital growth with improved cashflow
- **Target growth rate:** 6.5% per annum
- **Target rental yield:** 3.5% per annum
- **Financial strategy:**
  - Funded through equity from the portfolio and savings surplus.
  - Purchased in a diversified market to avoid overexposure to a single location.
  - Property selection considers the future transition to a stronger cashflow.

Starting loan details

Total lending balance	Monthly repayments	Annual repayments
$896,299	$4,855	$58,260

	Loan #1 for investment property 2	Loan #2 for investment property 2
Loan amount	$676,452	$219,847
Loan date	May 2028	May 2028
Interest rate	6.5%	6.5%
Repayment type	Interest only	Interest only
Security	Investment property 2	Family home

Who pays the cost?

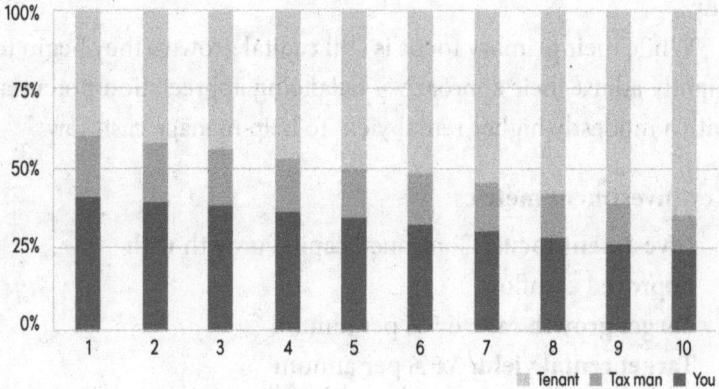

At this stage, cashflow is still manageable, but Brian and Claire are aware that their third investment will need to prioritise rental income to bring the portfolio into balance.

With two strong capital growth properties in place, their next move will be Investment Property 3, ensuring their portfolio generates sustainable income heading into retirement.

Investment Property 3: Completing the portfolio

		Area/location strategies	Property selection strategies
Purchase price	$844,078		
Purchase date	May 2033		
Ownership structure	Joint	Wave rider Changing places Non-aspirers	Scarce diamond Piggy-backer
Capital growth p.a.	5.50%		
Rental yield p.a.	4.50%		

With two high-growth properties compounding in value, Brian and Claire's third and final investment purchase is about balancing the portfolio – shifting towards stronger rental yield while still maintaining reasonable capital growth.

At this stage, their cashflow considerations become more important. While they could afford to take on another purely growth-focused asset, they recognise the importance of increasing passive income as they approach retirement.

Key investment metrics:

- **Investment focus:** Balanced approach – moderate growth with stronger yield
- **Target growth rate:** 5.5% per annum
- **Target rental yield:** 4.5% per annum
- **Financial strategy:**
  - Positioned in a market with both growth potential and strong rental demand.
  - Provides higher rental returns to help offset holding costs of previous investments.
  - Serves as a transition point from capital growth to cashflow optimisation.

Starting loan details

Total lending balance	Monthly repayments	Annual repayments
$894,722	$4,847	$58,164

	Loan #1 for investment property 3	Loan #2 for investment property 3
Loan amount	$675,262	$219,460
Loan date	May 2033	May 2033
Interest rate	6.5%	6.5%
Repayment type	Interest only	Interest only
Security	Investment property 3	Family home

Who pays the cost?

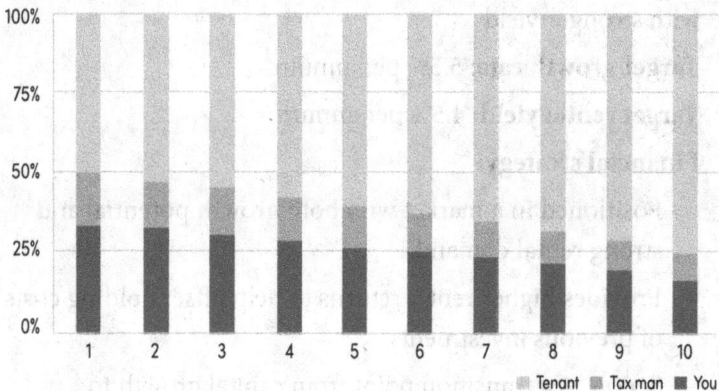

By structuring their acquisitions this way, Brian and Claire ensure their portfolio delivers both appreciation and income – positioning them for a self-funded retirement at 60.

With their portfolio now fully established, the next critical piece of the puzzle is cashflow management – ensuring their strategy remains sustainable and scalable in the years ahead.

The cashflow story

With three investment properties in place, Brian and Claire's portfolio operates in a comfortable cashflow position, thanks to their strong surplus income and lack of dependants. The financial freedom of not raising children allows them to accelerate their wealth-building while still enjoying their lifestyle.

The cashflow model shows that even after purchasing all three properties, their portfolio remains financially sustainable, with:

- **A steady surplus:** Their rental income increases year on year, while their high incomes ensure they are never stretched financially.

- **Planned affordability:** Each property acquisition is staged strategically, ensuring they never overextend themselves.

- **A growing financial buffer:** Their savings and investment strategy never drops below a comfortable level, keeping them well-positioned for any unexpected expenses.

Monthly income and expenditure

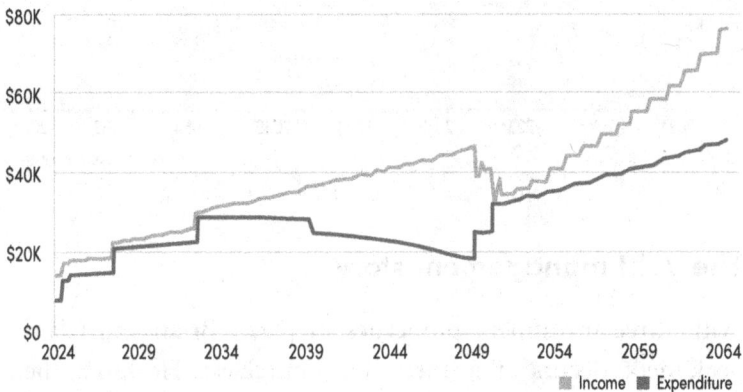

The cashflow projections highlight several key points. Initially, Investment Properties 1 and 2 require out-of-pocket contributions; however, as their rental income grows, these costs gradually reduce. Investment Property 3 plays a pivotal role in shifting the portfolio towards cashflow balance, ensuring Brian and Claire's overall financial position remains strong. By Year 16, the portfolio's rental income is expected to fully cover all costs, marking a crucial break-even point where the properties become self-sustaining. Once offset buckets are full, surplus funds are allocated to super. This structured approach allows Brian and Claire to maintain their desired lifestyle today while systematically building financial freedom for the future.

Household cash position

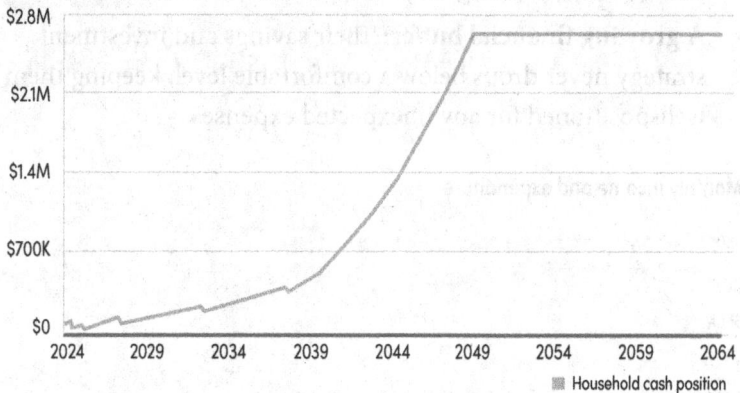

Household cash position

The debt management story

With three investment properties in place, Brian and Claire's peak debt occurs after their third purchase. However, their dual income and surplus cashflow ensure they can manage this comfortably while following a structured repayment strategy.

Their debt reduction approach is phased:

- First priority: build funds against their home loan in offset, freeing up disposable income and reducing financial pressure.
- Next, systematically pay down their investment loans, ensuring they remain on track for a fully self-funded retirement at 60.
- By retirement, their investment debt is completely offset, meaning every dollar of rental income belongs to them – not the bank.

With no remaining debt at retirement, Brian and Claire's portfolio will be in full passive income mode, funding their ideal lifestyle with complete financial freedom.

Projected debt reduction

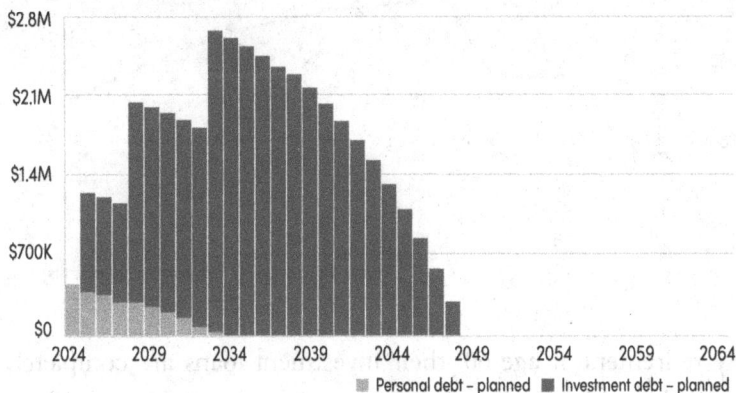

The passive rental income story

The power of Brian and Claire's investment strategy becomes evident when their portfolio transitions from growth mode to income mode – where rental income fully covers all costs and begins generating true financial independence.

By Year 16, their portfolio reaches break-even, meaning rental income now covers all property-related expenses, including mortgage repayments, property management fees, maintenance, and holding costs. From this point, their surplus rental income steadily increases, allowing them to accelerate debt reduction and strengthen their financial position.

Projected rental income

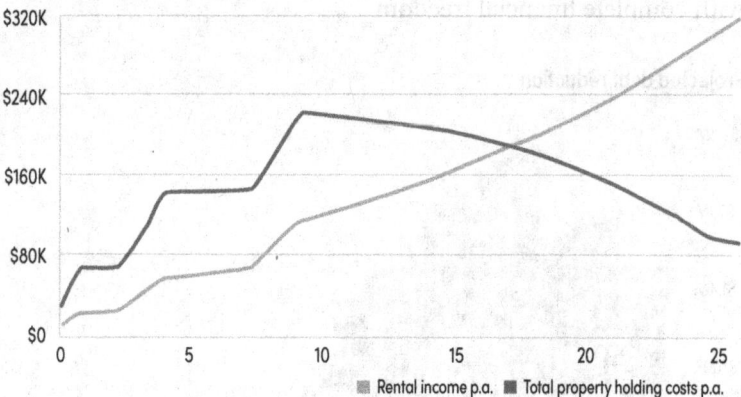

By retirement at age 60, their investment loans are completely repayable with offset funds, ensuring that all rental income flows directly to them. With a sustainable passive income stream of $3,000 per week, they can continue living life on their terms – travelling, entertaining, and enjoying financial security without ever needing to sell down assets.

Their strategy not only funds their retirement but also provides ongoing financial flexibility, ensuring they maintain full control over their wealth for decades to come.

Wealth projection overview

Through smart financial decisions and disciplined execution, Brian and Claire have successfully built a self-sustaining property portfolio that provides them with complete financial independence by age 60. By following their structured investment plan, they have built a portfolio that has grown in value while delivering sustainable rental income. Their strategic approach has ensured they reached their target of $3,000 per week in passive income, fully funding their lifestyle without relying on employment income. Of that $3,000, 63% will come from their investment portfolio and 37% from super.

Timeframe financial snapshot

A key milestone in their journey was clearing all investment debt before retirement, ensuring every dollar of rental income belongs to them. This achievement has secured their financial future, allowing them to maintain ownership of all their properties without the need to sell assets to fund their lifestyle.

With the average cost of raising a child in Australia sitting at around $12,800 per year ($230,400 over 18 years), Brian and Claire's alternative pathway – redirecting these funds toward living today and investing for tomorrow – has played a significant role in fast-tracking their financial success.

Property portfolio wealth projection model

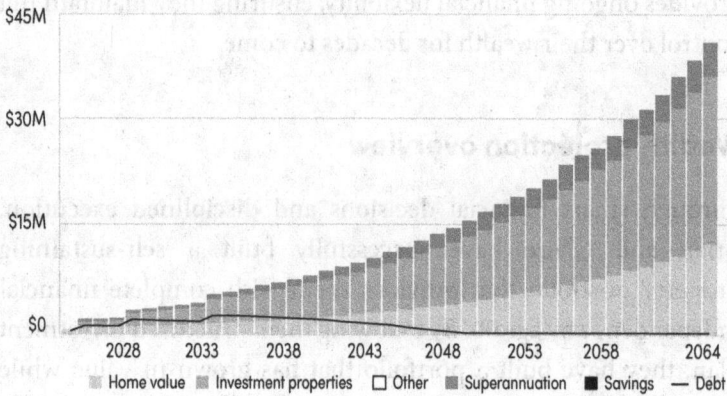

Legend: ■ Home value ■ Investment properties □ Other ■ Superannuation ■ Savings — Debt

Unlike many retirees who need to sell down assets to fund their lifestyle, Brian and Claire's portfolio allows them to maintain ownership of all properties, providing both security and future wealth-building opportunities.

With their financial foundation set, they have the flexibility and freedom to enjoy decades of travel, experiences, and financial peace of mind – all without ever having to work again. And that's what true financial peace looks like.

Wealth projection overview

	Now (2024)	10 years (2034)	20 years (2044)	Retirement (2051)	30 years (2054)
Superannuation	$206,750	$673,031	$1,513,730	$2,579,185	$2,805,123
Total savings and superannuation	$206,750	$673,031	$1,513,730	$2,579,185	$2,805,123
Investment property	–	$3,595,068	$6,730,339	$9,818,701	$12,637,145

Brian and Claire – DINKs

	Now (2024)	10 years (2034)	20 years (2044)	Retirement (2051)	30 years (2054)
Other investments	–	–	–	–	–
Total investment assets	–	$3,595,068	$6,730,339	$9,818,701	$12,637,145
Personal property	$850,000	$1,672,079	$3,289,232	$4,936,250	$6,470,417
Total assets	$1,056,750	$5,940,178	$11,533,301	$17,334,136	$21,912,685
Total debts	-$458,000	-$2,606,988	-$1,324,320	–	–
Net worth	$598,750	$3,333,190	$10,208,981	$17,334,136	$21,912,685
Nest egg	-$251,250	$1,661,111	$6,919,749	$12,397,886	$15,442,268
Nest egg (present value)	-$251,250	$1,297,657	$4,222,922	$6,365,071	$7,361,988

Case study 4

Gary and Nancy – Empty nesters

Gary, 51, and Nancy, 49, are entering a new phase of life. Just a year ago, their home was a lively hub of activity – busy weekdays filled with work and school and weekends spent juggling social and family commitments. But now, their two young adult children have left home to live independently, and for the first time in decades, life feels a little quieter.

While adjusting to this new rhythm, one thing is certain – life is comfortable. Like many in their late 40s and early 50s, they are approaching their peak earning years. Gary's high-responsibility role provides strong financial stability, while Nancy has returned to full-time work now that she no longer manages the daily demands of raising kids. With fewer financial commitments, they're enjoying a strong monthly surplus, allowing them to save more, travel, and enjoy life without financial pressure.

However, as they look toward retirement, one major challenge remains. Their household surplus is still generated by active work, not passive income. If they want to maintain their lifestyle when they stop working, they need to act now to build an income stream that will sustain them long after their careers are over.

Long-term goals

With retirement now on the horizon, Gary and Nancy know they have a limited window of time to build a sustainable income stream before they stop working. With their children now financially independent, this is their prime opportunity to convert today's surplus into long-term financial security.

Their goal is clear: achieve $3,000 per week in passive income, ensuring they can continue enjoying their lifestyle in retirement without financial stress.

Their retirement timeline remains flexible, but they aim to step away from full-time work between 60 and 65. Over the next decade, they will maximise their income while they're still working – ensuring that when they do retire, they have a financially secure and stress-free future.

Starting position for Gary and Nancy

Income

Income type	Gary	Nancy	Combined
Salary	$178,000	$83,000	
Dividends	$750	$750	
Tax and Medicare	-$51,051	-$17,588	
Total net income	**$127,700**	**$66,162**	**$193,862**

Expenses

Expense type	Amount	Frequency	Total annual
Loan repayments	$1,508	Monthly	$18,100
Spending	$67,840	Yearly	$67,840
Total annual expenses			**$85,940**

Current cashflow position

	Monthly	Annually
Total income	$16,155	$193,862
Total expenses	-$7,074	-$84,892
Cashflow surplus/deficit	$9,081	$108,970

Assets

Asset type	Class	Description	Value
Owner-occupier	Securable	Family home	$1,200,000
Other investment	Securable	Shares	$30,000
Total securable assets			$1,230,000
Superannuation	Non-securable	Accumulation account	$346,000
Motor vehicle	Non-securable	Family car	$19,000
Cash			$48,000
Total non-securable assets			$413,000
Total assets			**$1,643,000**

Liabilities

Description	Class	Amount	Rate	Payment	Frequency	Terms
Home loan – basic variable	Secured	$54,000	6.0%	$1,421	Monthly	P&I
Total secured liabilities		$54,000				
Credit card	Unsecured	$900	19%	$75	Monthly	P&I
Total unsecured liabilities		$900				
Total liabilities		**$54,900**				

Modelled future expenses

Reason	Amount	Frequency	Start	End
Buyer's advocacy service	$14,950	Once-off	Mar 2025	–
Renovation #1	$150,000	Once-off	Jun 2026	–
Buyer's advocacy service	$14,950	Once-off	Jun 2027	–
Increase in annual holiday budget	$10,000	Yearly	Jan 2028	Jan 2041
25th wedding anniversary	$15,000	Once-off	Sep 2029	–
Replacement of car	$25,000	Once-off	Jun 2032	–
Wedding gift to only daughter	$20,000	Once-off	Mar 2034	–
Replacement of car	$25,000	Once-off	Jun 2037	–

The strategy

With strong monthly surpluses and ample home equity, Gary and Nancy are in a prime position to act now – but unlike younger investors, time is not on their side. They don't have multiple decades for capital growth to work in the background, meaning their strategy needs to be deliberate, structured, and focused on both growth and income generation.

Their investment plan includes:

- **Acquiring two investment properties strategically staged two years apart:** This will maximise available surplus while keeping risk manageable.

- **Prioritising a balance between growth and yield:** This ensures properties begin generating cashflow sooner to support their retirement plan.

- **Using their home loan offset account:** This will trap surplus cash and reduce interest costs, accelerating their debt reduction strategy.

- **Retiring between age 60 and 65 with a fully repaid portfolio:** This will generate their $3,000 per week lifestyle goal.

By acting now and sequencing their investment approach, they will transition from work-reliant income to a self-sustaining financial future without compromising their current lifestyle.

Strategy targets

Property type	Target value	Target date	Target growth	Target yield
Investment property 1	$750,000	Mar 2025	6.00%	$4.00%
Investment property 2	$633,000	Jun 2027	5.50%	4.50%

Investment Property 1: Building capital growth

		Area/location strategies	Property selection strategies
Purchase price	$750,000		
Purchase date	Mar 2025	Proven performer	Shoulder rider
Ownership structure	Joint	Changing places City fling	Size matters Reliable and durable
Capital growth p.a.	6.00%	No vacancies	Ugly duckling
Rental yield p.a.	4.00%		

For their first investment property, capital growth remains the primary focus, but with a strong secondary emphasis on yield to accelerate cashflow.

Key investment metrics:

- **Target growth rate:** 6% per annum
- **Target rental yield:** 4% per annum
- **Time to positive cashflow:** Year 5
- **Strategy:**
  - Home loan paid off before purchase, allowing rental income and surplus cashflow to be parked in an offset account.
  - This reduces interest costs significantly, allowing this property to turn cashflow positive much sooner than in previous case studies.

Starting loan details

Total lending balance	Monthly repayments	Annual repayments
$795,000	$4,140	$49,680

	Loan #1 for investment property 1	Loan #2 for investment property 1
Total lending balance	$600,000	$195,000
Loan date	Mar 2025	Mar 2025
Interest rate	6.5%	6.5%
Repayment type	Interest only	Interest only
Security	Investment property 1	Family home

Who pays the cost?

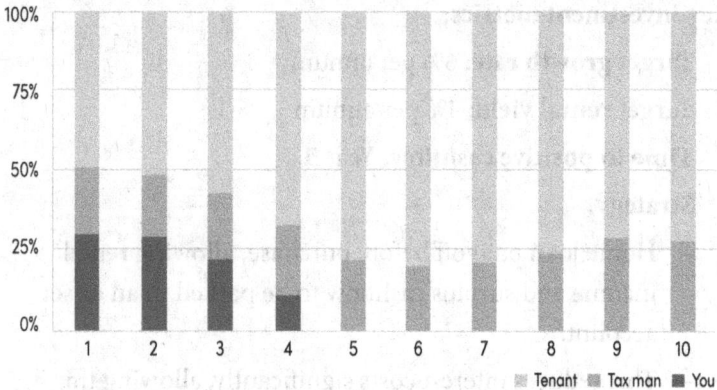

By Year 5, this property begins generating passive income, providing Gary and Nancy with early financial returns while continuing to appreciate in value.

With this foundation in place, Investment Property 2 will further strengthen their cashflow position.

Investment Property 2: Strengthening cashflow

		Area/location strategies	Property selection strategies
Purchase price	$633,000		
Purchase date	Jun 2027	Changing places	Reliable and durable
Ownership structure	Joint	Wave rider	Shoulder rider
		No vacancies	Ugly duckling
Capital growth p.a.	5.50%	Non-aspirers	Size matters
Rental yield p.a.	4.50%		

With their first investment property focused on capital growth, Gary and Nancy's second investment property shifts towards cashflow generation while still maintaining long-term value appreciation. This ensures their portfolio remains financially sustainable as they approach retirement. As this is a future purchase, we've taken today's market value and applied the growth rate – this is why the purchase price may seem like an unusual number. This approach ensures the estimate aligns with what Gary and Nancy will likely pay when the time comes to buy.

Key investment metrics:

- **Target growth rate:** 5.5% per annum
- **Target rental yield:** 4.5% per annum
- **Time to positive cashflow:** Year 9
- **Strategy:**
  - Purchased two years after the first property to stagger debt exposure and manage financial risk.
  - Higher rental yield helps offset expenses earlier, reducing the need for out-of-pocket contributions.

- As offset accounts linked to the first property reach capacity, surplus cash is redirected to this property, lowering interest costs and accelerating the path to positive cashflow.

Starting loan details

Total lending balance	Monthly repayments	Annual repayments
$670,980	$3,634	$43,608

	Loan #1 for investment property 2	Loan #2 for investment property 2
Total lending balance	$506,400	$164,580
Loan date	Jun 2027	Jun 2027
Interest rate	6.5%	6.5%
Repayment type	Interest only	Interest only
Security	Investment property 2	Family home

Who pays the cost?

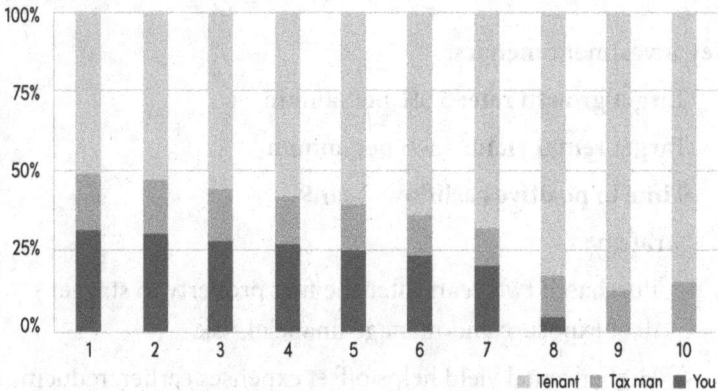

By Year 9, this property also becomes positively geared, further increasing their passive income and setting them up for a stronger financial position in retirement.

The cashflow story

Gary and Nancy's strong household surplus plays a crucial role in keeping their investment plan on track. Even after securing both properties, they continue to maintain a comfortable financial buffer, ensuring their portfolio remains resilient against market fluctuations.

The first investment property remains slightly cashflow negative in the early years, but with their high monthly surplus and offset strategy, the gap closes quickly.

The second property, with its higher rental yield, helps accelerate the overall cashflow position. By Year 9, both investments have become self-sustaining, requiring no additional contributions. Key cashflow milestones that support this outcome include:

- A strong surplus remains after both purchases, allowing flexibility in strategy.
- Offset accounts reduce interest costs, helping each property become cashflow positive sooner.
- By Year 9, both properties are positively geared, meaning rental income fully covers expenses.
- With conservative assumptions, they could bring forward the second purchase by a year if they feel confident in the first property's performance.
- Any surplus funds beyond what's needed in the offset to cover outstanding loans are automatically redirected into superannuation.

Monthly income and expenditure

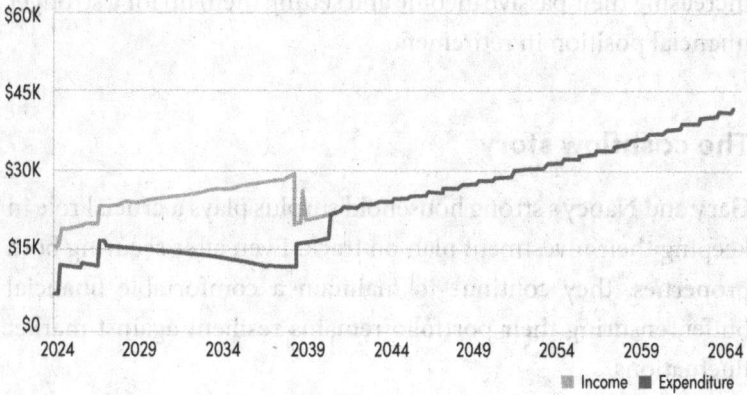

Income ■ Expenditure

Household cash position

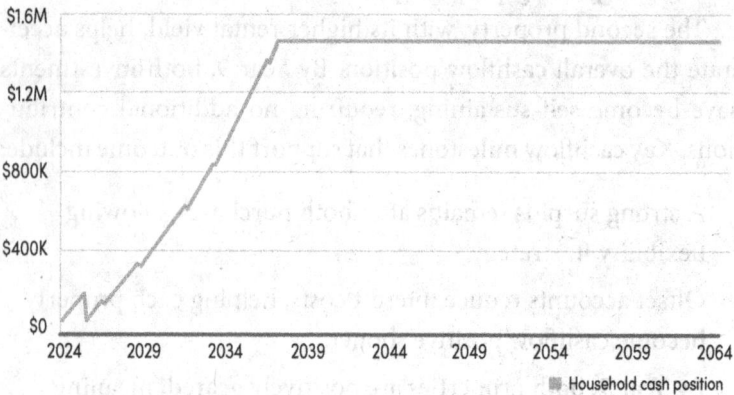

■ Household cash position

The debt management story

Gary and Nancy's strong financial position and high surplus cashflow allow them to take a structured approach to debt management, ensuring their investments remain low-risk and financially sustainable.

Their debt strategy follows a three-phase approach:

1. **Accumulation phase (Years 1–6):**
   - Peak debt occurs after acquiring the second property, but their high household surplus and offset accounts keep repayments manageable.
   - During this period, they focus on directing excess cashflow into their offset accounts, lowering interest costs.

2. **Debt reduction phase (Years 7–12):**
   - With both investment properties becoming cashflow positive by Year 9, excess rental income is now redirected toward accelerating debt repayment, via adding funds to their offset accounts.
   - Debt reduction accelerates as increased income flows into offset accounts.

3. **Pre-retirement phase (Years 13–15):**
   - By their early 60s, investment property loans are significantly reduced, ensuring they step into retirement with minimal financial obligations.
   - At this stage, their properties are generating a strong passive income stream, reinforcing their financial independence.

Projected debt reduction

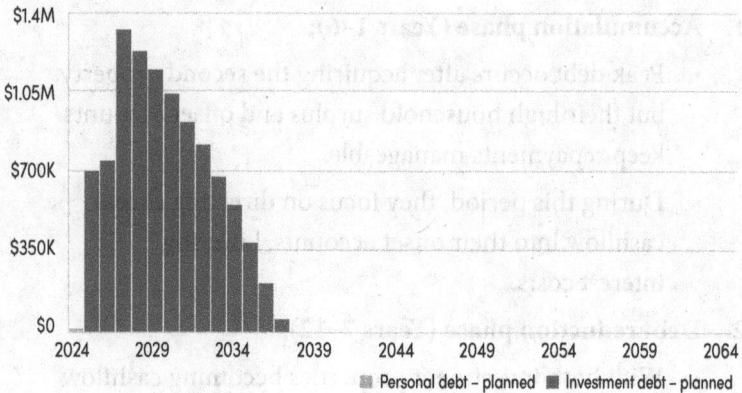

Bar chart with y-axis labeled $0, $350K, $700K, $1.05M, $1.4M and x-axis years 2024, 2029, 2034, 2039, 2044, 2049, 2054, 2059, 2064.

Legend: ■ Personal debt – planned   ■ Investment debt – planned

The passive rental income story

Gary and Nancy's transition from earning an active income to living off passive income follows a well-structured timeline designed to provide financial security in retirement. Their investment strategy gradually shifts from growth mode to income mode, ensuring they can retire comfortably at 65.

By Year 5, their first investment property turns cashflow positive, with surplus rental income helping to reduce interest costs. By Year 9, their second property becomes self-sustaining, meaning its rental income fully covers holding costs.

This structured approach ensures Gary and Nancy enter retirement financially secure, with their assets working entirely for them. With passive income exceeding expenses, they can travel, enjoy life, and even provide financial support to their children if needed – all without money stress.

Projected rental income

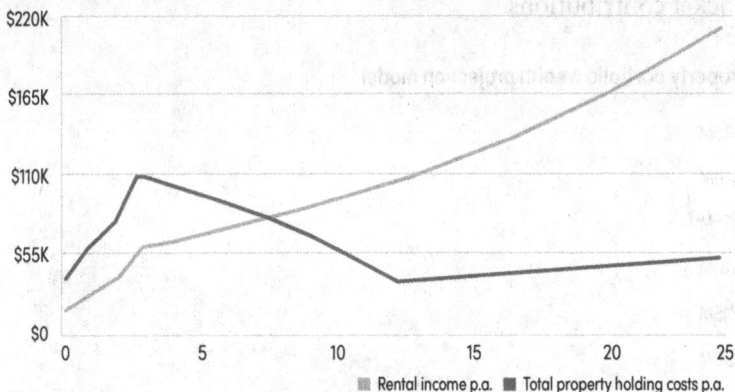

Rental income p.a. ■ Total property holding costs p.a.

Wealth projection overview

Is it too late to start investing in your 50s? Gary and Nancy's story proves the answer is no – so long as you have a clear plan and take action. Even in their early 50s, they have been able to build a self-sustaining property portfolio that will fund their retirement without financial stress.

For those considering investing later in life, starting in your 60s might also be an option – but only if you're contributing cash/savings and avoiding the higher leverage levels illustrated in this example. The key is structuring investments to minimise risk while maximising cashflow.

Timeframe financial snapshot

Gary and Nancy's investment journey followed a clear timeline, with key milestones ensuring their financial security. By Year 15, their portfolio was fully self-sustaining, providing $3,000 per week in passive income and eliminating the need for out-of-pocket contributions.

Property portfolio wealth projection model

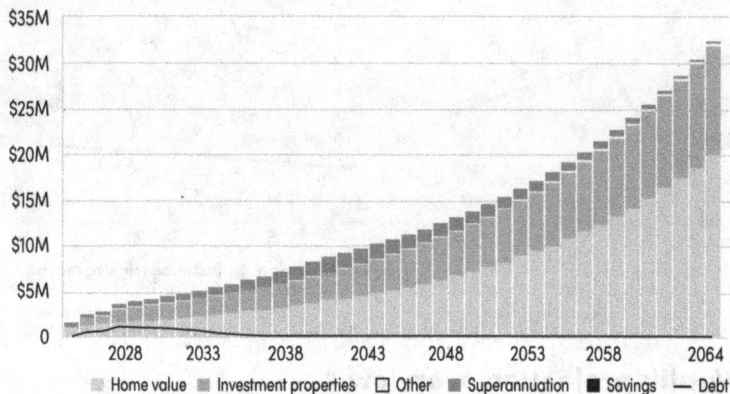

At retirement, Gary and Nancy's financial security is supported by multiple income sources:

- **Wealth at retirement:** $5,445,783 million across their property portfolio and superannuation.
- **Passive income:** $3,000 per week from rental income, fully covering their retirement lifestyle.
- **Debt-free:** Investment loans are cleared before retirement, meaning their properties now generate full passive income.

Their MoneySMARTS system played a critical role in making this possible. By trapping surplus cashflow and injecting it into offset accounts, they reduced interest costs and accelerated their path to financial freedom.

Now, with their financial future secured, they have the freedom to travel, enjoy life, and even provide financial support to their adult children if they choose – all without the worry of running out of money. And that's what true financial peace looks like.

Wealth projection overview

	Now (2024)	10 years (2034)	Retirement (2041)	20 years (2044)	30 years (2054)
Superannuation	$346,000	$957,064	$1,770,245	$1,603,704	$958,283
Total savings and superannuation	$346,000	$957,064	$1,770,245	$1,603,704	$958,283
Investment property	–	$2,187,921	$3,067,074	$3,842,079	$6,750,497
Other investments	$30,000	$53,725	$76,211	$96,214	$172,305
Total investment assets	$30,000	$2,241,647	$3,143,284	$3,938,293	$6,922,802
Personal property	$1,200,000	$2,630,917	$3,948,297	$5,175,411	$10,180,818
Total assets	$1,576,000	$5,829,627	$8,861,825	$10,717,408	$18,061,902
Total debts	-$6,900	-$551,014	–	–	–
Net worth	$1,569,100	$5,278,613	$8,861,825	$10,717,408	$18,061,902
Nest egg	$369,100	$2,647,697	$4,913,529	$5,541,997	$7,881,085
Nest egg (present value)	$369,100	$2,068,376	$3,229,147	$3,382,120	$3,757,249

Case study 5

Sarah –
Single professional
wanting a home

Sarah, 32, is a single professional determined to take control of her financial future. While her income is modest now, she has strong career prospects and understands the importance of building wealth early. She doesn't want to wait for life events – such as meeting a partner or starting a family – to dictate her financial progress. Instead, she's committed to making smart money moves now.

Sarah has been diligently saving for a home deposit after witnessing rising property prices and rental increases. While she enjoys her independence and lifestyle, she recognises that long-term stability starts with homeownership. She's motivated to secure her own place sooner rather than later – giving her both financial security and a foothold in the property market.

At the same time, she wants to strike a balance. Being young and single, she values experiences, travel, and enjoying life today. Her challenge is ensuring that her financial decisions don't compromise her current lifestyle while still setting her up for the future.

Long-term goals

Sarah's long-term vision is clear: she wants financial independence, homeownership, and a secure retirement without feeling like she has to sacrifice everything along the way.

Her first priority is to exit the rental market and own her own home. Once she achieves this, she will shift her focus to wealth creation, using her property to build equity and eventually invest in real estate to generate long-term passive income.

She understands that being on a single income presents challenges, but it also means full control over her financial future. Her ultimate goal is to retire comfortably by age 60 with a self-sustaining investment portfolio and a strong superannuation balance, allowing her to enjoy financial freedom without relying on employment income.

Starting position for Sarah

Income

Income type	Sarah
Salary	$90,000
Tax and Medicare	-$19,588
Total net income	**$70,412**

Expenses

Expense type	Amount	Frequency	Total annual
Rent	$1,950	Monthly	$23,400
Spending	$2,045	Monthly	$24,540
Total annual expenses			**$47,940**

Current cashflow position

	Monthly	Annually
Total income	$5,868	$70,412
Total expenses	-$3,995	-$47,940
Cashflow surplus/deficit	$1,873	$22,472

Assets

Asset type	Class	Description	Value
Superannuation	Non-securable	Accumulation account	$68,000
Motor vehicle	Non-securable	Medium	$20,000
Cash			$80,000
Total non-securable assets			$168,000
Total assets			**$168,000**

Modelled future expenses and income

Reason	Amount	Frequency	Start	End
Mortage insurance for Loan #1 for new family home	$6,500	Once-off	Oct 2025	–

Reason	Amount	Frequency	Start	End
Promotion #1	$15,000	Yearly	Jan 2027	Jan 2054
Promotion #2	$15,000	Yearly	Jan 2029	Jan 2054
Buyer's advocacy service	$14,950	Once-off	Nov 2029	–
Mortage insurance for Loan #1 for investment property 1	$6,000	Once-off	Nov 2029	–
Increase holiday spending	$5,000	Yearly	Dec 2031	Jan 2054
Replacement car	$20,000	Once-off	Sep 2035	–

The strategy

Sarah's first priority is homeownership – giving her stability while ensuring she's not left behind as property prices continue to rise. With her deposit nearly ready, she is in a strong position to purchase a small townhouse that suits her lifestyle and financial goals.

Once she secures her home, her next focus is rebuilding her cash reserves and equity position. This will allow her to leverage into an investment property in the years ahead while maintaining financial flexibility.

Sarah's strategy follows a two-stage approach:

1. **Secure homeownership:** Exiting the rental market while ensuring the loan is manageable on a single income.

2. **Build towards investing:** Using disciplined savings and equity growth to fund an investment property without overextending financially.

By following this structured approach, Sarah ensures she can own a home now while still positioning herself for long-term wealth creation through property investment.

Strategy targets

Property type	Target value	Target date	Target growth	Target yield
Residence – new family home	$620,000	Oct 2025	7.00%	–
Investment property 1	$670,048	Nov 2029	5.0%	4.00%

Investment Property 1: Laying the foundation

		Area/location strategies	Property selection strategies
Purchase price	$670,048		
Purchase date	Nov 2029	Changing places	Piggy-backer
Ownership structure	Sole ownership	Wave rider	Reliable and durable
Capital growth p.a.	5.00%	Proven performer	Shoulder rider
Rental yield p.a.	4.00%	No vacancies	

With retirement still decades away, Sarah's first investment property is chosen for long-term capital growth, with a reasonable rental yield to help offset holding costs.

Key investment metrics:
- **Target growth rate:** 5% per annum
- **Target rental yield:** 4% per annum
- **Out-of-pocket cost:** $358 per week (reducing each year)

- **Investment strategy:**
  - The property is located in a high-growth metro or regional centre with strong demand.
  - Yield covers the majority of holding costs, with Sarah making a manageable contribution.
  - The property will be negatively geared initially, with tax deductions improving affordability.
  - Over time, rental growth and salary increases will ease cashflow pressure, reducing the gap.

This approach ensures Sarah can secure an appreciating asset early while keeping out-of-pocket costs manageable on a single income. With a disciplined approach, she remains well-positioned to progress toward financial independence.

Starting loan details

Total lending balance	Monthly repayments	Annual repayments
$717,909	$3,888	$46,664

	Loan #1 for investment property 1	Loan #2 for investment property 1
Total lending balance	$597,300	$120,609
Loan date	Nov 2029	Nov 2029
Interest rate	6.5%	6.5%
Repayment type	Interest only	Interest only
Security	Investment property 1	New family home

Who pays the cost?

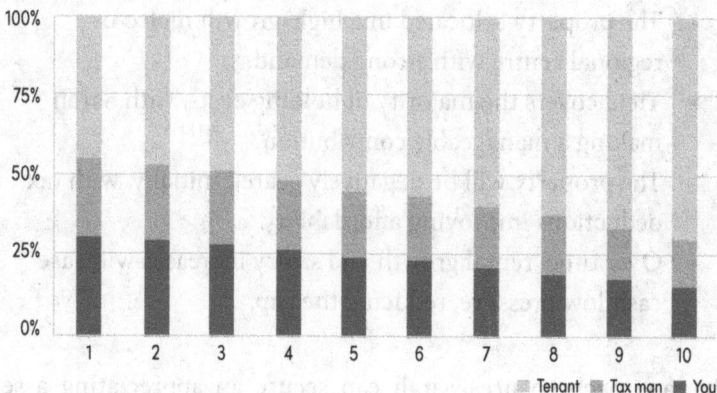

The cashflow story

Sarah's cashflow story is a balance between strategic discipline and financial flexibility. Her single-income status means she needs to carefully manage affordability, but her well-structured approach ensures her financial position remains strong. Key cashflow milestones that support this outcome include:

· **Pre-home purchase:**
  – The strong cashflow position is due to controlled expenses and steady income growth.
  – Savings accumulate efficiently, funding a large deposit for her home.

· **Post-home purchase:**
  – Sarah's cashflow temporarily tightens as she transitions from renting to homeownership.
  – A disciplined approach to spending ensures she remains financially comfortable.

- **Investment property purchase (2029):**
  - Rental income and tax benefits offset holding costs, keeping her cashflow manageable.
  - Expected salary increases over the next 3–5 years provide additional financial breathing room.
- **Long-term cashflow outlook:**
  - Surplus cashflow rebuilds over time, strengthening Sarah's financial position.
  - By focusing on debt reduction, she ensures long-term financial stability.

Even with the upfront commitment of homeownership, Sarah's steady income growth and careful expense management ensure she maintains a strong financial buffer, allowing her to stay on track with her investment goals.

Monthly income and expenditure

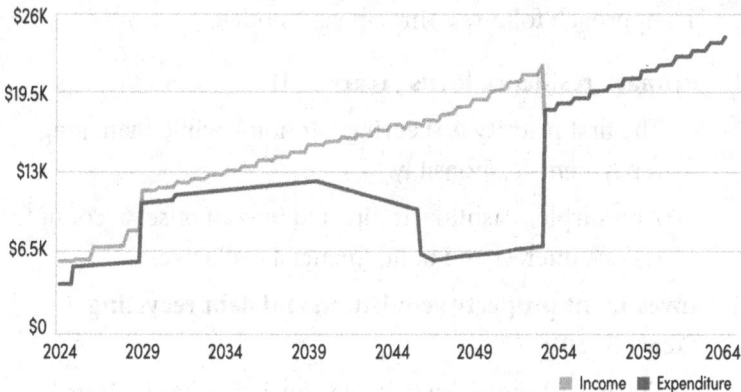

Household cash position

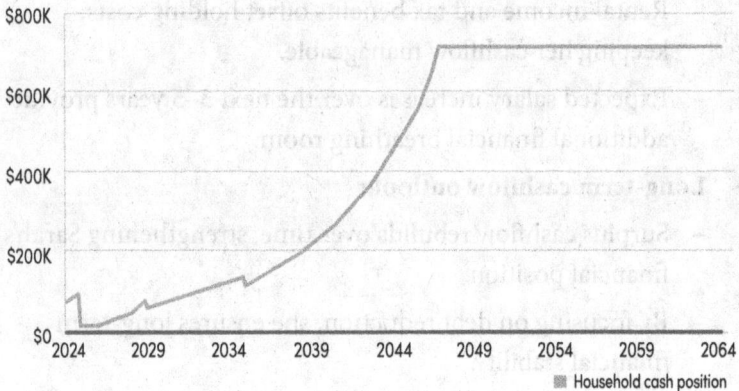

Household cash position

The debt management story

Sarah's debt strategy is carefully structured to prioritise financial flexibility while ensuring her investment plan remains sustainable on a single income.

Her approach follows a three-phase model:

1. **Primary residence focus (Years 1–4):**
   - The first priority is securing her home while managing repayments responsibly.
   - Any surplus cashflow is directed into an offset account to reduce interest and build financial resilience.

2. **Investment property acquisition and debt recycling (Years 5–10):**
   - Once her home loan is stable and equity has built up, Sarah refinances to release capital for her investment purchase.

- She maintains an interest-only loan on the investment property while focusing on paying down the non-deductible home loan.

3. **Final debt reduction phase (Years 11–20+):**

- After her home loan is fully repaid, surplus cashflow is redirected toward paying off the investment loan.

- By retirement, she achieves full ownership of both her home and investment property, ensuring a strong passive income position.

This structured approach allows Sarah to balance financial security with strategic wealth-building while keeping the door open for future opportunities – whether that means investing further or combining finances should her circumstances change.

Projected debt reduction

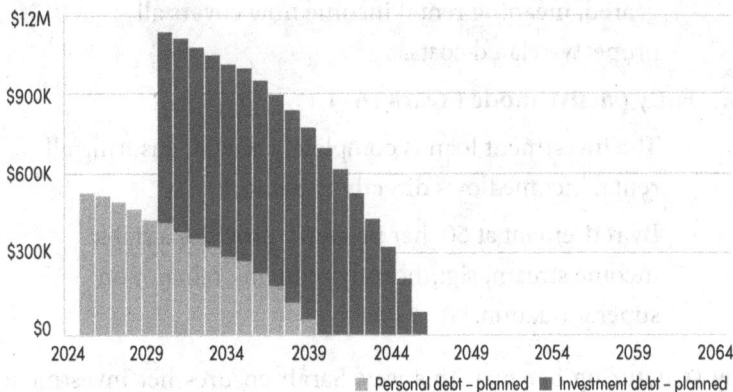

Legend: Personal debt – planned, Investment debt – planned

The passive rental income story

Sarah's pathway to financial independence follows a disciplined transition from securing her home to building a sustainable passive income.

Her passive income strategy follows three key phases:

1. **Investment growth phase (Years 1–10)**
   - The investment property is initially negatively geared, meaning rental income doesn't yet cover all costs.
   - However, steady rental increases and tax benefits keep the out-of-pocket expense manageable.

2. **Break-even and cashflow shift (Years 11–15)**
   - With her primary residence loan fully offset, surplus cashflow is redirected to her investment loan.
   - The investment property transitions to positively geared, meaning rental income now covers all property-related costs.

3. **Fully passive mode (Years 16+)**
   - The investment loan is completely repaid, ensuring all rental income flows directly to Sarah.
   - By retirement at 60, her property provides a stable income stream, significantly reducing reliance on superannuation.

By structuring her plan this way, Sarah ensures her investment property not only grows in value over time but also becomes a key driver of financial security in retirement.

Projected rental income

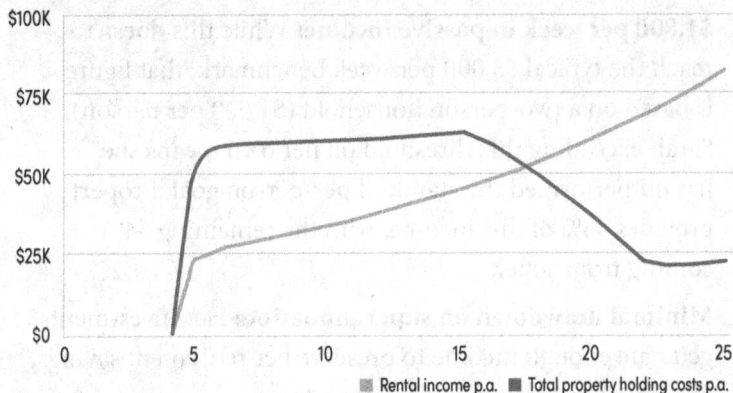

Legend: ▪ Rental income p.a.   ▪ Total property holding costs p.a.

Wealth projection overview

Sarah's story highlights what is possible with a single income and a clear plan. By balancing lifestyle and financial security, she has successfully built a future that gives her both freedom and security.

Her key achievements by retirement at 60 include:

- **A fully paid-off home:** Eliminating mortgage costs ensures Sarah has complete financial stability.
- **A strong investment property:** Now debt-free and generating a stable passive income to fund her retirement.
- **A well-built superannuation balance:** Providing additional financial security and optionality.

Timeframe financial snapshot

By the time Sarah retires at 60, her financial position will allow her to enjoy a stable and sustainable lifestyle.

Key highlights include:

- **$1,800 per week in passive income:** While this doesn't reach the typical $3,000 per week benchmark, that figure is based on a two-person household ($1,500 per person). Sarah exceeding this threshold on her own means she has outperformed the standard per-person goal. Property provides 46% of this income, with the remaining 54% coming from super.

- **Minimal drawdown on superannuation:** Her investments generate enough income to preserve her retirement savings, ensuring long-term financial confidence.

Property portfolio wealth projection model

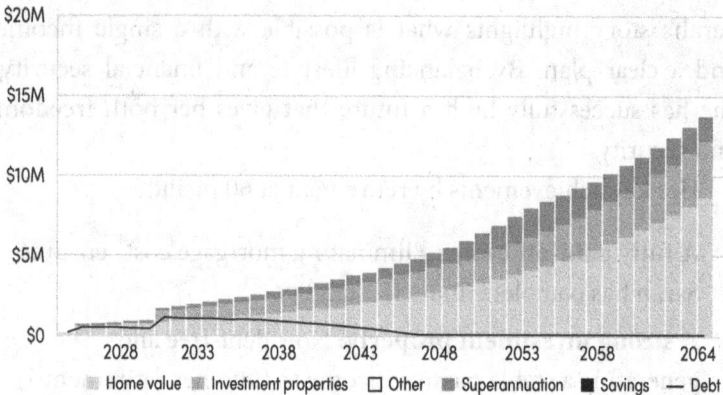

Home value   Investment properties   ☐ Other   ■ Superannuation   ■ Savings   — Debt

Sarah's passive income stream comes from two key sources:

1. Her debt-free investment property generates stable rental income.
2. Her well-built superannuation balance provides additional financial security and flexibility.

Sarah's strategic approach has ensured that she can retire stress-free, live comfortably, and even have the flexibility to increase her spending or adjust her plans if needed.

This isn't just about hitting a number – it's about having the financial confidence to design life on her terms. And that's what true financial peace looks like.

Wealth projection overview

	Now (2024)	10 years (2034)	20 years (2044)	Retirement (2054)	40 years (2064)
Savings	$80,000	–	–	–	–
Superannuation	$68,000	$265,593	$643,776	$1,813,029	$1,525,169
Total savings and superannuation	$148,000	$265,593	$643,776	$1,813,029	$1,525,169
Investment property	–	$814,447	$1,326,649	$2,160,971	$3,519,994
Other investments	–	–	–	–	–
Total investment assets	–	$814,447	$1,326,649	$2,160,971	$3,519,994
Personal property	–	$1,139,845	$2,242,247	$4,122,280	$8,676,789
Total assets	$148,000	$2,219,885	$4,212,672	$8,096,280	$13,721,952
Total debts	–	-$1,014,360	-$324,443	–	–
Net worth	$148,000	$1,205,524	$3,888,229	$8,096,280	$13,721,952
Nest egg	$148,000	$65,680	$1,645,982	$3,974,000	$5,045,164
Nest egg (present value)	$148,000	$51,309	$1,004,495	$1,894,575	$1,878,973

Case study 6

Olivia – Divorcee

At 43, Olivia is navigating a new chapter in life after finalising her divorce. While this period has brought significant changes and uncertainty, she has taken a crucial step toward stability – using her settlement funds to purchase a townhouse for herself and her daughter, Trudi. With a secure home now in place, Olivia's focus has shifted to rebuilding her financial future and ensuring long-term security as a single parent.

Having previously lived on a dual income, she is adjusting to a new financial reality – one that requires careful planning to maintain her lifestyle and secure her retirement. Olivia is determined to take control of her finances, build wealth, and create a future in which she remains financially independent while also providing for her daughter.

Long-term goals

Right now, Olivia's focus is on financial stability – ensuring she can comfortably provide for her daughter while adjusting to managing a household on a single income. While she doesn't seek an extravagant retirement, she wants the reassurance that she can maintain her independence and won't become a financial burden on Trudi in later years.

Olivia's goal is twofold:

1. **A secure and self-sufficient retirement:** She wants to build a financial foundation that allows her to retire between 60 and 65 without stress, ensuring she has at least $1,500 per week in spending money. While this is lower than the $3,000 per week benchmark referenced in other case studies, that figure is based on a two-person household ($1,500 per person). On a per-person basis, Olivia is achieving financial security at the same level as dual-income couples.

2. **A legacy for her daughter:** Recognising the challenges young people face in property ownership, she hopes to pass down assets to give Trudi a financial head start in adulthood.

By focusing on a simple yet effective investment strategy, Olivia aims to achieve peace of mind, knowing she will always have financial security – both for herself and for her daughter's future.

Starting position for Olivia

Income

Income type	Olivia
Salary	$95,000
Tax and Medicare	-$21,188
Total net income	**$73,812**

Expenses

Expense type	Amount	Frequency	Total annual
Loan repayments	$1,290	Monthly	$15,480
Spending	$42,860	Yearly	$42,860
Total annual expenses			**$58,340**

Current cashflow position

	Monthly	Annually
Total income	$6,151	$73,812
Total expenses	-$4,862	-$58,340
Cashflow surplus/deficit	$1,289	$15,472

Assets

Asset type	Class	Description	Value
Owner-occupier	Securable	Family home	$650,000
Total securable assets			$650,000
Superannuation	Non-securable	Accumulation account	$147,000
Motor vehicle	Non-securable	Family car	$27,000
Cash			$68,000
Total non-securable assets			$242,000
Total assets			**$892,000**

Liabilities

Description	Class	Amount	Rate	Payment	Frequency	Terms
Home loan – basic variable	Secured	$215,000	6.0%	$1,290	Monthly	P&I
Total secured liabilities		$215,000				
Total liabilities		**$215,000**				

Modelled future expenses

Reason	Amount	Frequency	Start	End
Increase income	$10,000	Yearly	Jan 2025	May 2047
Buyer's advocacy service	$14,950	Once-off	Jun 2025	–
Gift toward Trudi's first car	$10,000	Once-off	Jun 2026	–
Increase income	$10,000	Yearly	Jan 2028	May 2047
Cosmetic renovation	$40,000	Once-off	May 2029	–
Special 50th holiday gift to self	$15,000	Once-off	Jun 2031	–
Replacement car	$20,000	Once-off	Jun 2032	–
Trudi leaves home	–$450	Monthly	Jan 2033	May 2047
Wedding gift for Trudi	$20,000	Once-off	Nov 2039	–
Semi-retire	–$50,000	Yearly	Jan 2042	May 2047

The strategy

With a single income and a dependent child, Olivia's financial approach must be both conservative and effective. The priority is ensuring financial security without overextending debt, allowing her to comfortably manage her commitments now while setting herself up for a stable future.

Her investment strategy is structured as follows:

1. **Maximise stability first:**
   - Olivia has already secured a home for herself and her daughter, purchasing within her means to ensure manageable repayments.
   - With only a small mortgage, she has a strong equity position, which she can leverage for her investment plan.

2. **Invest cautiously but strategically:**
   - Rather than building a multi-property portfolio, Olivia will focus on acquiring one high-quality investment property, balancing capital growth (5.5%) and rental yield (4.5%) to ensure affordability.
   - The projections show this approach keeps her out-of-pocket contribution at a manageable $346 per week, reducing over time.

3. **Prioritise debt management:**
   - The plan ensures her home mortgage is repaid first before aggressively paying down the investment debt.
   - Debt repayments are structured so that she is debt-free before retirement, allowing her rental income to fully support her lifestyle.

4. **Create financial flexibility for retirement:**
   - By age 60, her investment property will have transitioned to a fully self-sustaining asset, providing a passive income stream.
   - This, combined with her superannuation balance, will allow her to retire with $1,500 per week in spending money – equivalent to the benchmark of $3,000 per couple.

This plan ensures Olivia maintains financial security without taking unnecessary risks, giving her peace of mind that both she and her daughter will be well-supported in the years ahead.

Strategy targets

Property type	Target value	Target date	Target growth	Target yield
Investment property 1	$580,000	Jun 2025	5.50%	$4.50%

Investment Property 1: Laying the foundation

		Area/location strategies	Property selection strategies
Purchase price	$580,000		
Purchase date	Jun 2025	Proven performer	Reliable and durable
Ownership structure	Sole ownership	City fling	Shoulder rider
Capital growth p.a.	5.50%	Changing places	Size matters
Rental yield p.a.	4.50%	Wave rider	Piggy-backer

For Olivia, investing in one quality property is the best strategy – balancing capital growth and rental yield while ensuring affordability on a single income. Given her focus on financial security rather than rapid expansion, we target a property with strong fundamentals that will provide stable, long-term returns.

Key investment metrics:
- **Target growth rate:** 5.5% per annum
- **Target rental yield:** 4.5% per annum
- **Out-of-pocket cost:** $346 per week (reducing each year)

- **Loan structure:**
  - 80% loan-to-value ratio (LVR) on the investment property.
  - Uses $150,800 in equity from her home to reduce borrowing requirements.
- **Investment strategy:**
  - Olivia's strategy is balanced between growth and yield, ensuring the investments remain affordable and financially sustainable.
  - Her property is positioned in a high-demand rental market to minimise vacancy risk and maintain stable rental income.
  - A cash buffer is consistently maintained, providing Olivia with financial flexibility to manage unexpected expenses or market fluctuations.

Starting loan details

Total lending balance	Monthly repayments	Annual repayments
$614,800	$3,330	$39,960

	Loan #1 for investment property 1	Loan #2 for investment property 1
Total lending balance	$464,000	$150,800
Loan date	Jun 2025	Jun 2025
Interest rate	6.5%	6.5%
Repayment type	Interest only	Interest only
Security	Investment property 1	Family home

Who pays the cost?

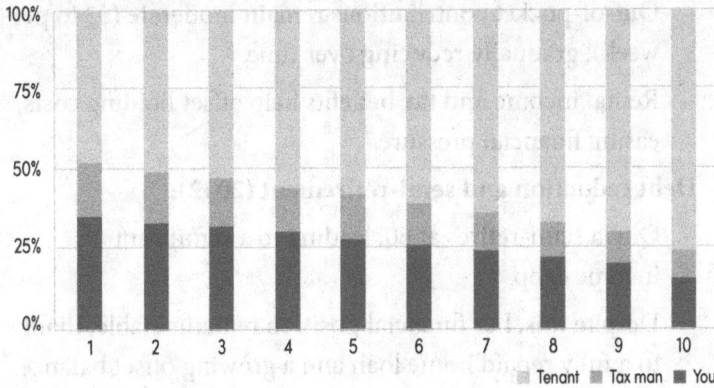

By securing a single, high-quality investment property, Olivia can grow her wealth without taking on excessive financial strain. The property's rental income and tax benefits keep costs manageable, allowing her to comfortably hold the asset long-term.

The cashflow story

Olivia's cashflow remains tight but manageable, aligning with her conservative financial approach. Given her single-income status and focus on financial security, the strategy is designed to ensure long-term stability rather than aggressive expansion.

Key cashflow milestones that support this outcome include:

· **Pre-investment purchase:**
  – Strong cashflow position with disciplined spending and consistent savings growth.
  – The cash buffer remains intact, providing financial flexibility.

- **Post-investment property purchase:**
  - Out-of-pocket contributions remain moderate ($346 per week), gradually reducing over time.
  - Rental income and tax benefits help offset holding costs, easing financial pressure.
- **Debt reduction and semi-retirement (2042):**
  - Olivia semi-retires at 60, leading to a significant income drop.
  - Despite this, her financial position remains stable, thanks to a fully repaid home loan and a growing offset balance.
- **Retirement at 65:**
  - Investment property loan is fully repaid, allowing rental income to transition into a passive income stream.
  - Strong superannuation and investment income ensure a secure retirement.

Monthly income and expenditure

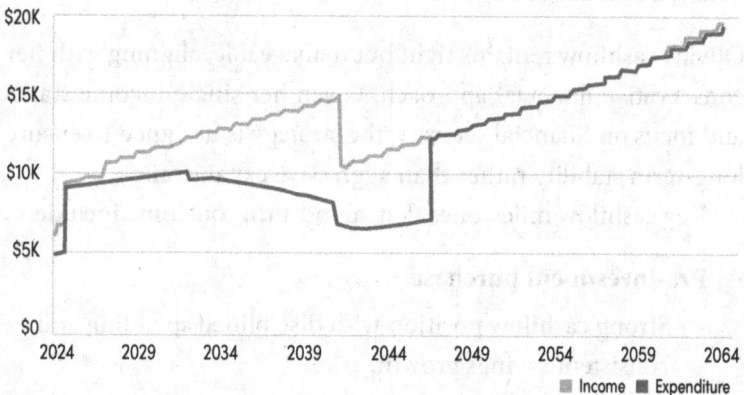

By prioritising cash buffers and focusing on one quality investment property, Olivia ensures she remains financially comfortable, even in a lower-income phase later in life. The long-term accumulation of cash in her offset account plays a crucial role in securing her financial future. Once the offset account is full, surplus money is redirected to super; the chart below reflects this.

Household cash position

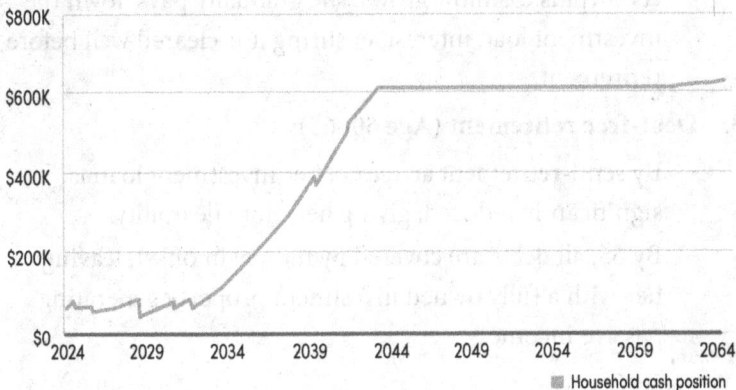

Household cash position

The debt management story

Olivia's debt strategy is focused on stability and sustainability, ensuring she can manage her obligations comfortably on a single income while still securing a stronger financial future.

Her approach has three phases:

1. **Home loan reduction (Years 1–10):**
   - Priority is placed on repaying her non-deductible home loan as quickly as possible.
   - Strong cash discipline allows her to accelerate repayments while maintaining a financial buffer.

- By Year 10, her home loan will be fully offset, significantly reducing her financial commitments.

2. **Investment loan management (Years 11–20+):**

   - With her home loan repaid, Olivia shifts focus to offsetting and reducing the investment loan.
   - She maintains an interest-only structure in the early years, using her offset to minimise interest costs.
   - As surplus cashflow grows, she gradually pays down the investment loan interest, ensuring it is cleared well before retirement.

3. **Debt-free retirement (Age 60–65):**

   - By semi-retirement at age 60, her investment loan is significantly reduced, giving her more flexibility.
   - By 65, all debts are covered by money in offset, leaving her with a fully owned investment property generating passive income.

Projected debt reduction

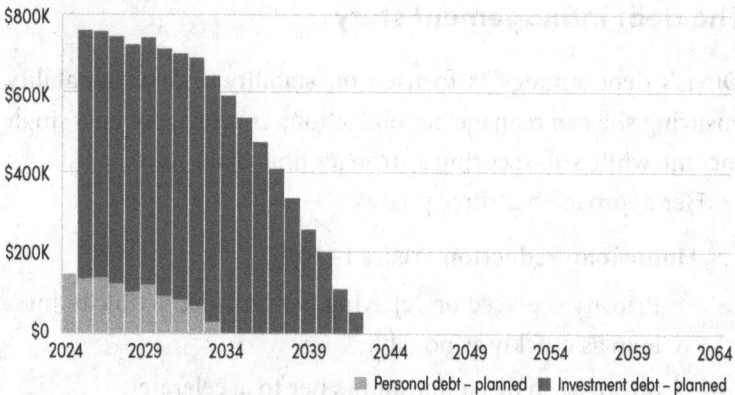

Personal debt – planned   Investment debt – planned

This structured approach ensures Olivia enters retirement completely debt-free, with her investment property fully paid off and delivering a stable rental income. By prioritising non-deductible debt first, she maximises financial efficiency and secures long-term stability without unnecessary financial stress.

The passive rental income story

Olivia's investment strategy is designed to gradually shift from capital growth to income generation, ensuring she has a stable passive income stream by the time she reaches retirement.

Her passive income strategy follows three key phases:

1. **Early investment years (Years 1–10)**
   - Initially, Olivia's investment property is negatively geared, meaning rental income does not yet cover all costs.
   - Tax benefits and rental growth help offset expenses, keeping out-of-pocket costs at a manageable $346 per week.

2. **Break-even and cashflow transition (Years 11–15)**
   - With her home loan fully repaid, Olivia shifts her focus to reducing her investment debt.
   - The property moves towards positively geared status, meaning rental income now covers all expenses.
   - Extra surplus funds are directed toward the loan via the offset account, accelerating debt offsetting.

3. **Fully passive mode (Years 16+)**
   - By semi-retirement at 60, Olivia's rental income is generating a strong surplus.

- By 65, the investment loan is completely cleared, ensuring 100% of rental income flows to her as passive income.

By following this structured approach, Olivia secures a self-sustaining retirement income. Her investment property now serves as a financial safety net, reducing her reliance on superannuation and allowing her to retire comfortably with $1,500 per week – equivalent to the per-person benchmark in previous case studies.

Projected rental income

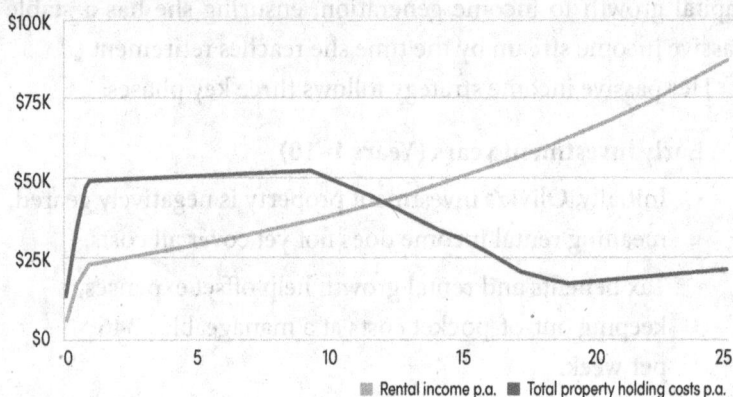

Rental income p.a.   Total property holding costs p.a.

Wealth projection overview

Olivia's story demonstrates that even with a single income and one investment property, financial independence is achievable. By prioritising stability, strategic cashflow management, and disciplined savings, she has successfully built a plan that allows her to retire comfortably without financial stress.

Her key outcomes by retirement (age 60–65) include:

- **A fully paid-off home:** Olivia has no mortgage repayments, ensuring full financial security in retirement.

- **A debt-free investment property:** Generating a stable passive income stream, reducing her reliance on superannuation.
- **A strong cash buffer:** By maintaining surplus cash in her offset account, she ensures financial flexibility and security.

Timeframe financial snapshot

By the time Olivia reaches retirement age, her decisions will have positioned her for success. Key financial outcomes include:

- **$1,500 per week in passive income:** While this is lower than the $3,000 benchmark for couples, it achieves the per-person equivalent of $1,500, demonstrating her financial success as a single-income investor. Of this, 47% comes from her property portfolio, and 53% from her super.
- **Minimal drawdown on superannuation:** Olivia's investment property income allows her to preserve her retirement savings, ensuring long-term financial confidence.

Olivia's financial stability in retirement is underpinned by:

- Income from her debt-free investment property providing a reliable passive income stream.
- A well-maintained cash buffer in her offset account, ensuring liquidity and flexibility to manage unexpected expenses.

By acting early, staying disciplined, and focusing on a well-balanced investment, Olivia has secured a stress-free retirement. Her financial plan allows her to enjoy a modest but comfortable lifestyle, maintain control over her assets, and even provide for her daughter's future.

Property portfolio wealth projection model

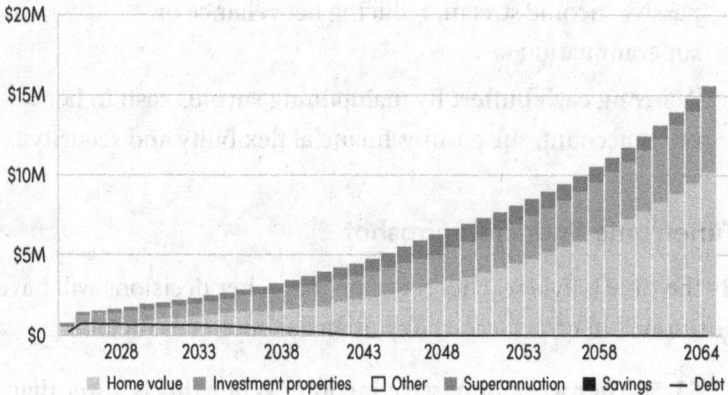

Her story highlights that a single, well-chosen investment property – paired with smart financial planning – can be enough to transform a retirement outlook. And that's what true financial peace looks like.

Wealth projection overview

	Now (2024)	10 years (2034)	20 years (2044)	Retirement (2047)	30 years (2054)
Superannuation	$147,000	$393,387	$871,353	$1,188,576	$1,018,374
Total savings and superannuation	$147,000	$393,387	$871,353	$1,188,576	$1,018,374
Investment property	–	$939,075	$1,604,075	$1,785,376	$2,739,992
Other investments	–	–	–	-	–
Total investment assets	–	$939,075	$1,604,075	$1,785,376	$2,739,992
Personal property	$650,000	$1,342,020	$2,639,956	$3,022,485	$5,193,192

Olivia – Divorcee

	Now (2024)	10 years (2034)	20 years (2044)	Retirement (2047)	30 years (2054)
Total assets	$797,000	$2,674,481	$5,115,384	$5,996,437	$8,951,558
Total debts	-$147,000	-$592,658	–	–	–
Net worth	$650,000	$2,081,823	$5,115,384	$5,996,437	$8,951,558
Nest egg	–	$739,804	$2,475,428	$2,973,952	$3,758,366
Nest egg (present value)	–	$577,933	$1,510,682	$1,685,330	$1,791,773

Case study 7

Adam – Rentvestor

At just 25, Adam is already taking control of his financial future. While he's still early in his career, he isn't waiting for salary promotions to drive his income growth. Instead, he has taken the initiative – launching a side hustle 18 months ago, now generating an additional $15,000 per year.

Adam prefers rentvesting over traditional homeownership – leveraging property investment while maintaining flexibility to live where he chooses. With the ability to work remotely, he enjoys the freedom of renting while directing his savings toward wealth creation. His focus is clear: build financial independence early so he has options later.

Long-term goals

Adam is driven by financial independence but also enjoys his work and sees himself continuing his career in some form until age 60. However, he wants options – not financial obligations dictating his decisions.

His strategy is clear: continue renting for flexibility while using his income to build a strong property portfolio. By investing early and strategically, he can enjoy lifestyle freedom now without sacrificing his future.

Adam has set an ambitious goal of $2,000 per week in retirement income. This is high for a single-income earner, exceeding the $1,500 per person benchmark used in dual-income case studies – proving that his financial plan is set to deliver a strong, independent future.

Starting position for Adam

Income

Income type	Adam
Salary	$65,000
Self-employed income	$15,000
Tax and Medicare	-$16,388
Total net income	**$63,612**

Expenses

Expense type	Amount	Frequency	Total annual
Rent	$400	Weekly	$20,800
Spending	$20,484	Yearly	$20,484
Total annual expenses			**$41,284**

Current cashflow position

	Monthly	Annually
Total income	$5,301	$63,612
Total expenses	-$3,440	-$41,284
Cashflow surplus/deficit	$1,861	$22,328

Assets

Asset type	Class	Description	Value
Superannuation	Non-securable	Accumulation account	$27,000
Motor vehicle	Non-securable	Car	$20,000
Cash			$75,000
Total non-securable assets			$122,000
Total assets			**$122,000**

Liabilities

Description	Class	Amount	Rate	Payment	Frequency	Terms
Credit card	Unsecured	$0	19%	$0	Monthly	P&I
Total liabilities		**$0**				

Modelled future expenses

Reason	Amount	Frequency	Start	End
Reduce spending for deposit	-$500	Monthly	Dec 2024	Jan 2027
Promotion	$20,000	Yearly	Jan 2026	Jan 2060
Buyer's advocacy service	$14,950	Once-off	Oct 2026	–
Mortage insurance for loan for investment property 1	$7,724	Once-off	Oct 2026	–
Promotion	$20,000	Yearly	Jan 2030	Jan 2060
Buyer's advocacy service	$14,950	Once-off	Jun 2031	–
Car purchase	$20,000	Once-off	Jun 2032	–
Car purchase	$20,000	Once-off	Jun 2042	–
Car purchase	$20,000	Once-off	Jun 2052	–
Semi-retire	-$60,000	Yearly	Jan 2055	Jan 2060

The strategy

Adam's first challenge is building a deposit for his first property. Instead of waiting years to save a full 20%, he is using lenders mortgage insurance (LMI) to enter the market sooner – ensuring he benefits from property growth rather than chasing rising prices.

His strategy follows a two-stage approach:

1. **Build and buy fast:**
   - Reducing discretionary spending by $500 per month to accelerate savings and paying off credit card monthly.
   - Aiming to purchase his first investment property by 2026, using 88% LVR with LMI to minimise time out of the market.
   - Securing a high-growth asset, allowing time to work in his favour before retirement.

2. **Scale smartly and build momentum:**
   - Leveraging equity growth and savings to acquire a second investment property in four to five years once in the market.
   - Aiming for $200,000 in combined savings/equity before the second purchase.
   - Ensuring the second investment property has a higher yield to balance his portfolio's cashflow.

By leveraging his time advantage and ability to take calculated risks, Adam is positioning himself to build wealth faster while maintaining flexibility in his lifestyle.

Strategy targets

Property type	Target value	Target date	Target growth	Target yield
Investment property 1	$639,000	Oct 2026	6.50%	$3.50%
Investment property 2	$758,364	Jun 2031	5.50%	4.50%

Investment Property 1: Laying the foundation

		Area/location strategies	Property selection strategies
Purchase price	$639,000		
Purchase date	Oct 2026		Scarce diamond
Ownership structure	Sole ownership	No vacancies	Reliable and durable
		Non-aspirers	Shoulder rider
Capital growth p.a.	6.50%	Boom towners	Slice and dice
Rental yield p.a.	3.50%		

With decades of working life ahead of him, Adam's first investment property is focused on capital growth – leveraging time and compounding to build wealth before retirement. Given his strong financial discipline and lack of personal debt, this first purchase is positioned to maximise appreciation over the long term. As this is a future purchase, we've taken today's market value and applied the growth rate, which is why the price may seem like an unusual number. This approach ensures the estimate aligns with what Adam will likely pay when the time comes to buy.

Key investment metrics:

· **Target growth rate:** 6.5% per annum

- **Target rental yield:** 3.5% per annum
- **Loan structure:**
  - 88% loan-to-value ratio (LVR)
  - Principal and interest (P&I) repayments (if it provides a slight interest rate reduction)
- **Investment strategy:**
  - Focuses on targeting high-growth metro or regional locations with strong rental demand to maximise potential returns.
  - While yield is considered, the primary focus is on capital appreciation over time to build long-term wealth.
  - To ensure financial stability, Adam keeps holding costs manageable, supported by his surplus cashflow and available tax deductions.

Starting loan details

Total lending balance	Monthly repayments	Annual repayments
$570,546.06	$3,606.24	$43,274.88

	Loan for investment property 1
Total lending balance	$570,546
Loan date	Oct 2026
Interest rate	6.5%
Repayment type	P&I
Security	Investment property 1

Who pays the cost?

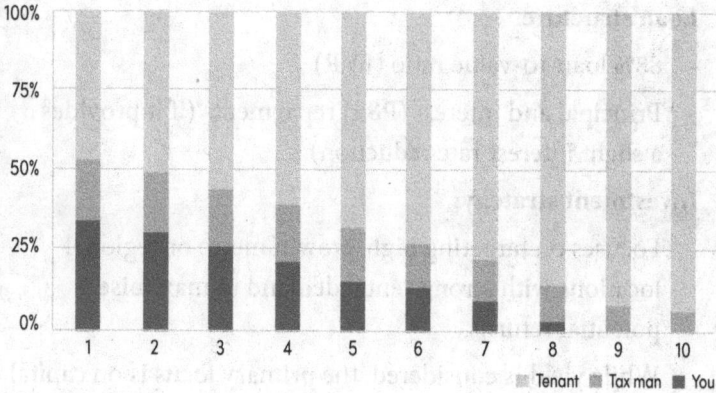

This structured approach ensures Adam gets into the market early, allowing time and compounding to do the heavy lifting. With disciplined savings and a focus on financial efficiency, this property sets the foundation for future acquisitions while maintaining flexibility.

Investment Property 2: Strengthening the portfolio

		Area/location strategies	Property selection strategies
Purchase price	$758,364		
Purchase date	Jun 2031	Wave rider	Reliable and durable
Ownership structure	Sole ownership	Changing places No vacancies	Scarce diamond Ugly duckling
Capital growth p.a.	5.50%	Non-aspirers	Shoulder rider
Rental yield p.a.	4.50%		

With his first investment property gaining momentum, Adam's second purchase is about balancing growth with yield to maintain affordability while continuing to build wealth. By this stage, his financial position has strengthened, allowing him to strategically add another property without overextending.

Key investment metrics:

- **Target growth rate:** 5.5% per annum
- **Target rental yield:** 4.5% per annum
- **Loan structure:**
  - 80% LVR
  - Interest-only period to optimise cashflow
- **Investment strategy:**
  - Adam's investment strategy follows a balanced approach, ensuring that rental yield is sufficient to support holding costs.
  - His properties are located in a diversified market, reducing exposure to risks associated with a single region.
  - By generating rental income, Adam effectively offsets debt while maintaining stability across his investment portfolio.

Starting loan details

Total lending balance	Monthly repayments	Annual repayments
$803,865.35	$4,354.27	$52,251.24

	Loan #1 for investment property 2	Loan #2 for investment property 2
Total lending balance	$606,691	$197,175
Loan date	Jun 2031	Jun 2031
Interest rate	6.5%	6.5%
Repayment type	Interest only	Interest only
Security	Investment property 2	Investment property 1

Who pays the cost?

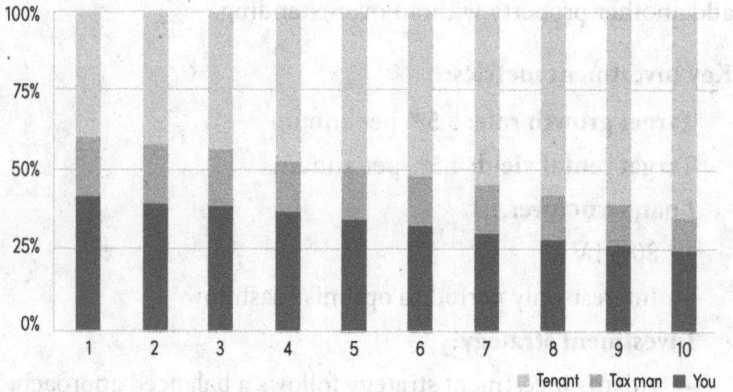

By introducing a higher-yielding asset at this stage, Adam ensures his portfolio remains financially sustainable while continuing to benefit from long-term capital appreciation.

The cashflow story

Adam's cashflow remains positive throughout, though it tightens after each property purchase – something he is comfortable with given his long investment timeline and willingness to make temporary sacrifices. His strong earning potential, disciplined spending, and side income all play key roles in keeping his financial position stable.

Key cashflow milestones that support this outcome include:

1. **Before the first property purchase (2026):**
   - Adam is focused on aggressively saving for a deposit while maintaining his flexibility as a renter.
   - He wants to reduce his discretionary spending by $500 per month to build his deposit faster.
   - Household cash remains strong, providing a comfortable buffer.

2. **After first investment purchase (2026–2031):**

   - Cash reserves drop to $15,000 after purchase – a temporary but expected position.

   - The investment property requires moderate out-of-pocket contributions but remains affordable.

   - Rental expenses increase 5% per year, but his side hustle helps offset these costs.

   - Strong income growth over this period helps rebuild his financial buffer, via funds in offset accounts.

3. **After second investment purchase (2031–2040):**

   - A more balanced asset ensures cashflow remains manageable despite increased debt.

   - First property's rental growth starts to ease financial pressure.

   - Investment loans remain on interest-only initially to maintain affordability.

   - Cashflow remains tight but controlled, reflecting Adam's willingness to play the long game.

4. **Semi-retirement at 55 (2050):**

   - Adam has the option to slow down or step back from full-time work if he chooses.

   - By this stage, rental income is covering all holding costs, improving his surplus.

   - He can either continue working or begin debt paydown acceleration.

5. **Full retirement at 60 (2058):**

   - With both properties fully paid off, rental income becomes a pure passive income stream.

- With no debt and additional superannuation contributions, Adam comfortably achieves his $2,000 per week retirement spending goal.

Adam's early start and disciplined approach ensure that, even with the challenges of rentvesting, his strategy allows him to reach financial freedom on his terms.

Monthly income and expenditure

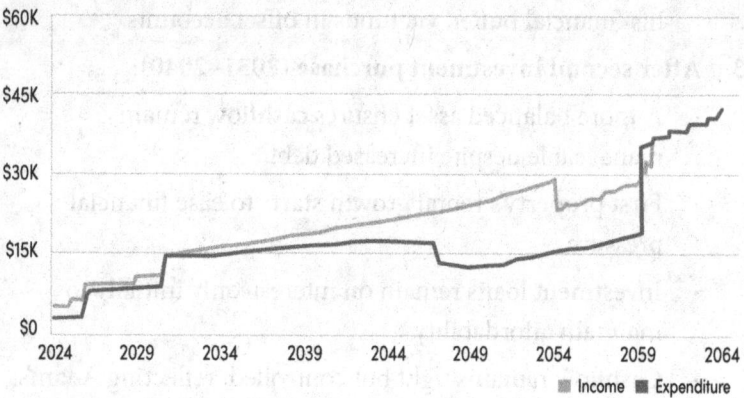

■ Income ■ Expenditure

Household cash position

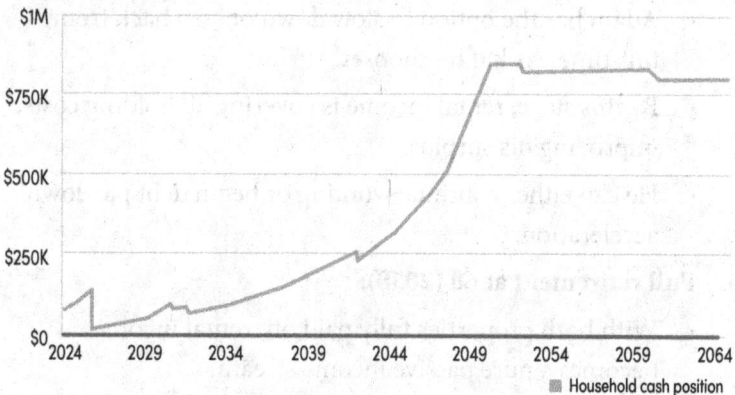

■ Household cash position

The debt management story

Adam's debt strategy follows a structured approach, leveraging his strong financial discipline to balance investment growth with responsible debt reduction. His plan to use his offset accounts ensures that he systematically repays his investment loans while maintaining financial flexibility.

His approach follows a three-phase model:

1. **Accumulation phase (2026–2036):**
   - The first investment property is purchased in 2026 for $639,000.
   - The initial loan is for $570,546 at 88% LVR, including LMI.
   - Loan repayments are structured as P&I to take advantage of slight interest rate reductions.
   - Investment property remains negatively geared, with Adam covering shortfalls from surplus cashflow.
   - The second investment property is purchased in 2031 for $758,364.
   - The new loan structure is $606,691 plus $197,174 in equity from Investment Property 1.
   - At this stage, peak investment debt is reached, with rental income covering most holding costs.

2. **Debt reduction phase (2037–2048):**
   - By 2040, Adam's first property will be positively geared, with rental income covering all expenses.
   - By 2043, his second property will also be positively geared.
   - From this point, surplus rental income is directed to offset accounts.

- By 2048, both investment loans will be completely repaid, leaving Adam debt-free at age 47.

3. **Wealth-building and pre-retirement phase (2049–2060):**

- With no investment debt remaining, Adam shifts his focus to building a strong superannuation balance by directing surplus funds into his retirement accounts.

- Rental income now serves as a fully passive income stream to fund his lifestyle.

- Adam maintains financial flexibility, with options to purchase a third property if desired, though it's not necessary to meet his financial goals.

By paying off his investment loans by 47, Adam secures a strong financial position, allowing him to retire at 60 with a fully self-sustaining property portfolio and a significant superannuation balance.

Projected debt reduction

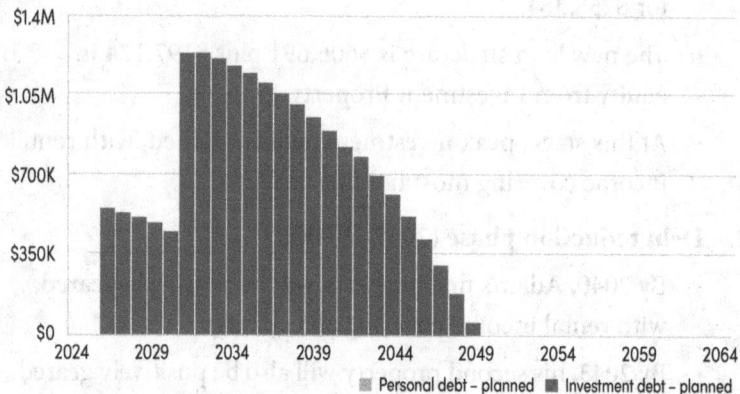

Legend: Personal debt – planned | Investment debt – planned

The passive rental income story

Adam's passive income journey also follows a structured three-phase approach, transitioning from early cashflow deficits to a fully self-sustaining investment portfolio by retirement. The phases include:

1. **Early growth and negative gearing (2026–2040):**
   - Both investment properties are initially negatively geared, meaning rental income does not fully cover holding costs.
   - Out-of-pocket costs are manageable due to tax deductions and salary growth.
   - The first property (purchased in 2026) breaks even around 2040, moving into positive cashflow.
   - The second property (purchased in 2031) follows by 2043.

2. **Break-even and cashflow transition (2041–2048):**
   - By 2043, both investment properties generate surplus cashflow, funding extra loan interest savings.
   - By 2048, all investment loans will be offset, meaning every dollar of rental income is now passive income.
   - Adam then diverts the excess cashflow into superannuation and additional investments.

3. **Fully passive income mode (2049–2060 and beyond):**
   - From 2049 onwards, rental income from both properties is entirely passive, covering all living expenses.
   - By retirement at 60 (2060), Adam is generating $2,000 per week in passive income, fully funding his lifestyle without reliance on employment income.
   - This excludes rent, as he remains a rentvestor, maintaining flexibility in where he lives.

By strategically acquiring and managing two investment properties, Adam secures a self-funded retirement, meeting his ambitious $2,000 per week target. His decision to remain a rentvestor aligns with his lifestyle preferences while leveraging the power of property investment to achieve financial independence.

Projected rental income

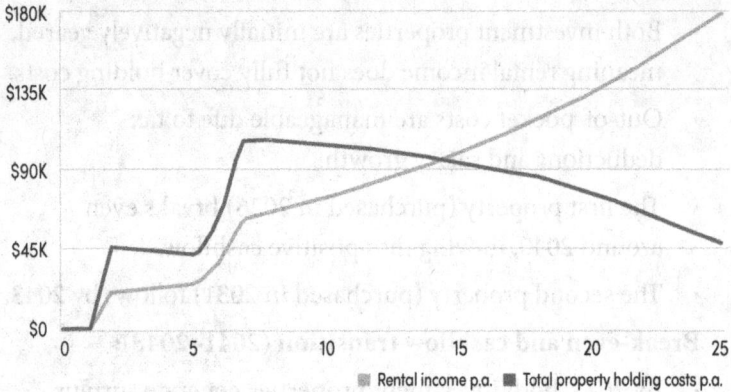

Rental income p.a.   Total property holding costs p.a.

Wealth projection overview

Adam's journey as a rentvestor demonstrates the power of starting early, leveraging financial discipline, and maintaining flexibility. By structuring his portfolio strategically and focusing on high-growth assets first, he has positioned himself for long-term financial success while maintaining the freedom to live and work wherever he chooses.

Key outcomes by retirement at age 60 (2060) include:

- **Fully offset investment portfolio:** Both investment properties are debt-free, ensuring 100% of rental income flows directly to Adam.

- **Strong passive income:** Generating $2,000 per week, excluding property-related expenses, with the property portfolio providing 62% and super providing 38%.
- **Long-term financial flexibility:** By choosing not to overextend himself with a third investment property, Adam remains financially flexible, allowing him to enjoy life while still growing his wealth.

Timeframe financial snapshot

Adam's financial strategy also offers options for early retirement and additional savings. Key points include:

- **Early retirement optionality:** With all debts cleared by 2048, Adam has the option to semi-retire at 55 while continuing to build additional wealth.
- **Superannuation and additional investments:** After clearing his property debt, Adam redirects surplus cash into his superannuation, increasing his long-term retirement savings.

Property portfolio wealth projection model

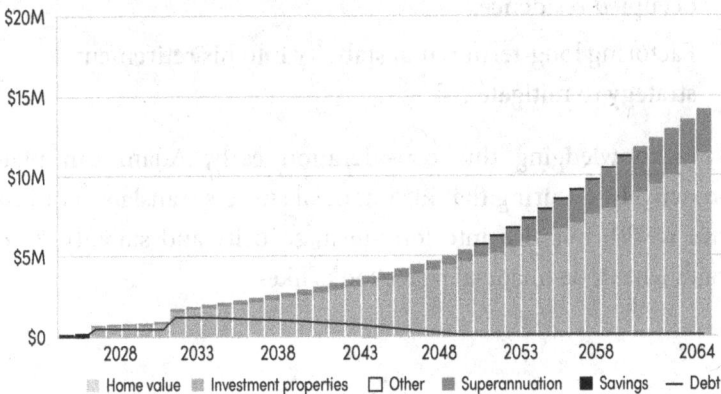

Home value | Investment properties | Other | Superannuation | Savings | — Debt

Adam's financial success stems from a combination of:

- rental income from his debt-free investment properties
- strategic redirection of surplus funds into superannuation, boosting his retirement savings.

Unlike traditional homeownership paths, Adam's rentvesting strategy has enabled him to enter the property market sooner, benefiting from compounding growth. It has also allowed him to retain the flexibility to live in different locations while building wealth and reaching financial security without being locked into a large owner-occupier mortgage.

While Adam's rentvesting strategy successfully meets his passive income goals, one key consideration remains: he does not own his own home in retirement. This creates potential risks that require careful planning.

To address this, Adam may consider:

- Using equity from his investment properties to fund a future home purchase.
- Selling one property in later years to secure an owner-occupied residence.
- Factoring long-term rental stability into his retirement strategy to mitigate risk.

By acknowledging this consideration early, Adam can plan proactively, ensuring that his financial success translates not just into wealth but also into long-term security and stability. And that's what true financial peace looks like.

Wealth projection overview

	Now (2024)	10 years (2034)	20 years (2044)	30 years (2054)	Retirement (2060)
Savings	$75,000	–	–	$26,921	$30,693
Superannuation	$27,000	$174,114	$470,374	$1,691,550	$2,851,975
Total savings and superannuation	$102,000	$174,114	$470,374	$1,718,471	$2,882,667
Investment property	–	$1,948,044	$3,506,258	$6,324,672	$8,501,329
Other investments	–	–	–	–	–
Total investment assets	–	$1,948,044	$3,506,258	$6,324,672	$8,501,329
Personal property	–	–	–	–	–
Total assets	$102,000	$2,122,158	$3,976,632	$8,043,143	$11,383,996
Total debts	–	-$1,177,167	-$613,959	–	–
Net worth	$102,000	$944,992	$3,362,674	$8,043,143	$11,383,996
Nest egg	$102,000	$944,992	$3,362,674	$8,043,143	$11,383,996
Nest egg (present value)	$102,000	$738,226	$2,052,142	$3,834,509	$4,679,889

Part IV – Wrap

Your number, your choice

These seven case studies prove that financial security is within reach for most aspiring Australians – if they commit to trapping surplus money and putting it to work. Because let's be clear: it's a far better alternative than working past retirement age, taking on extra jobs, or grinding harder in later years in an attempt to achieve the same $3,000 per week outcome.

And as we've said throughout the book, your number doesn't have to be $3,000 per week. Your version of financial peace might look different. That's the beauty of a 'lifestyle by design' – you get to define it.

If we were sitting down for a post-planning coffee (metaphorically, since neither of us actually drink it!) with each of these case study clients prior to final sign-off, we'd take a moment to pressure-test their targets, making sure they truly align with what matters most to these people. Do they really want to increase their future spending, or would they rather pull retirement forward and enjoy more of life sooner? Could they tweak the balance between time and money to create a lifestyle that feels right for them?

We hope these case studies have inspired you to see what's possible for anyone who aspires to financial peace – and how others have mapped out their journey. Do they provide a guiding light for your final decision on what to aim for? We certainly hope so (fingers crossed!).

The right number for you could be $3,000 per week – or you may find that true financial freedom would come from less money, but more of what truly matters. Our hope is that these examples inspire you to define what's right for you, so you can spend your precious time pursuing what brings real impact to your life – not what social media's envy culture suggests, but what your heart is truly calling for.

So, as we finish this part of the conversation – coffee in hand ;-) – we'll leave you with this:

What's your number?

It's yours to decide.

PART I

PART II

PART III

PART IV

Your call to action

You've reached the summit. You're now standing at the peak – equipped with everything you need to create financial peace. Let's take a step back and reflect on everything you've learned up to this point.

First up, you've come this far, so clearly, you don't want to get a $10 haircut (or perhaps you want to get one fixed)!

By now, you'll also realise that you can't save your way to retirement – if you want to live a comfortable life, putting your head in the sand and hoping for the best simply won't cut it. You must act on the knowledge you've just learned.

You've discovered the Property Investment Formula – the ABCD of asset selection, borrowing power, cashflow management, and defence. From choosing the right property to structuring your lending, trading surplus money, managing your cashflow, and building a moat of protection around your portfolio, you now have the tools to design your financial future.

Most importantly, you've seen real-life case studies of how aspiring Australians can and have achieved extraordinary results. The common thread? ACTION. They've shown that success doesn't come from standing still – because knowledge without action is like sitting in a rocking chair all day: it keeps you busy, but you're not actually getting anywhere! The key is to start because if you don't, you won't succeed. It really is that simple.

The silent battle

Here's the truth: none of this book is rocket science. It's not brain surgery, nuclear physics or assembling IKEA furniture without instructions! In fact, money is actually quite simple – it's human behaviour that's hard.

But the more knowledge you have, the more you reduce risk, and the better you can overcome the silent battle of behaviour. By reaching the end of this book, you've already started to break the mould and think differently. Keep learning. Keep pushing forward. Keep your eye on the end result. We want you to feel what we have – the indescribable feeling of financial peace.

Join the movement for financial peace

Before you go, we have three final things for you.

Trap more surplus

Take (back) control of your finances by joining a community of savvy property investors at moorr.com.au. It all begins with spending less than you earn, and you'll find simple yet powerful automated systems to trap more surplus and put your money to work. These investors understand the pension isn't their future – and they're doing something about it.

Become an 'insider'

Subscribe to *The Property Couch* podcast. Listen to the first 20 episodes to lock in your foundational learning from this book and

stay up to date weekly with the latest guest interviews, tips, tactics, and strategies. Every episode is
designed to add value and reward you for investing
your most precious commodity – your time.

Pay it forward

Support our movement by sharing this book with a friend or
colleague who could benefit from it. You can also leave a review
on Amazon or wherever you bought this book. It would mean
the world to us, and we promise we read every single one!
#ThePropertyCouchPlaybook.

*

Thank you for letting us be your guide. We hope the knowledge in
this book empowers you to take ACTION, build YOUR lifestyle
by design, and enjoy the financial peace YOU deserve.

There's only one thing left to do: begin.

Over to you.

About the authors

Bryce

LinkedIn: @bryceholdaway
Instagram: @bryceholdaway
X: @bryceholdaway

Bryce Holdaway lives in Torquay, Victoria, with his wife, Andrea, and their two boys, Jack and Sam.

In 2015, Bryce started *The Property Couch* podcast after approaching Ben Kingsley with a simple idea: 'Let's team up and use this "emerging" platform to freely share our knowledge and help as many people as possible'. What started as an experiment quickly grew into Australia's No. 1 property podcast, mentoring thousands of listeners in property, finance, and money management. Today, *The Property Couch* is more than a podcast – it's a movement and a community that has made complex financial concepts simple and accessible to everyday aspiring Australians.

He is also a partner at Empower Wealth, which he joined in 2012, and has played a pivotal role in helping grow it into one of the most trusted and awarded advisory companies in Australia, specialising in helping people achieve financial peace through property investment.

Bryce has an extensive background in television, too, having hosted *Location, Location, Location Australia* and *Relocation, Relocation Australia* on Foxtel's Lifestyle Channel, and *Escape from the City* on the ABC. His expertise also makes him a regular voice in national media, including television, radio, podcasts, and leading publications.

He has co-authored two best-selling books with Ben, *The Armchair Guide to Property Investing* and *Make Money Simple Again*. Together, these books have helped thousands of Australians navigate the complexities of building wealth through property and achieving financial independence.

As a qualified accountant, financial planner, property investment adviser, and buyer's agent, Bryce holds a full real estate licence in multiple states. He led the Empower Wealth buyer's agency team to claim the Real Estate Business Awards 2020 Buyer's Agency of the Year award. His true passion lies in simplifying the complex – breaking down financial jargon so that everyone can understand and enjoy the financial peace they deserve. He's particularly passionate about helping people avoid the pitfalls of conflicted advice from those who exploit complexity for their own gain.

Away from professional life, he practices what he preaches. He and Andrea have built their own multi-million-dollar property portfolio, generating $3,000+ per week in passive income to support their shared love of travel, personal growth, and adventure. Bryce also enjoys water sports with his kids, watching the NBA, and immersing himself in world-class conversations and stories through podcasts and audiobooks. And while he's yet to see his beloved Fremantle Dockers win their first premiership, he's holding out hope that their time will come!

Ben

LinkedIn: @benkingsleyau
X: @benkingsleyAU

Ben Kingsley lives in Melbourne with his wife, Jane, and their two boys, Jack and Harry. In 2007, Ben founded Empower Wealth with a clear dream and belief that everyone has the potential to achieve financial well-being and security. Since then, Ben and a dedicated purpose-focused team have built a nationally recognised and award-winning advisory firm specialising in Finance, Property, and Wealth services. Headquartered in Melbourne with additional select offices across Australia, Empower Wealth supports clients across Australia, including Australians living abroad.

In 2015, Ben teamed up with Bryce Holdaway to launch *The Property Couch* podcast. Since then, it has become Australia's No. 1 podcast in Property, Finance, and Money Management, regularly charting in the top 5 for the investment category and top 10 in business.

At the time of writing, Ben serves as Chair of the not-for-profit Property Investors Council of Australia (PICA), advocating for property investors and educating them to run their small private rental accommodation businesses more effectively. He is the former Chair of the Property Investment Professionals of Australia (PIPA).

Ben holds an Associate Diploma of Business, a Diploma of Finance and Mortgage Broking Management, and is a Qualified Property Investment Adviser (QPIA). He is also a licensed real estate agent across VIC, NSW, QLD, SA, and WA. During his time advising clients directly, Ben was named Property Investment

Advisor of the Year in 2014 and 2015 and was runner-up in 2016. After stepping back from day-to-day client work, Ben led Empower Wealth's property advisory team, which was awarded *Your Investment Property* magazine's inaugural Property Investment Advisory Business of the Year in 2018.

Ben's expertise in property, lending, and personal money management has made him a trusted voice for Australian media. He is frequently featured on national television, print, radio, and podcasts and has authored numerous articles for leading publications.

Ben genuinely believes everyone has the potential to build a better financial story, no matter where they're starting from. Through education and empowerment, he inspires people to take action and create their 'lifestyle by design'.

Outside of work, Ben walks the talk – creating his own property portfolio plan to build a multi-million-dollar investment portfolio that supports his family's lifestyle and provides $3,000+ per week in passive income. When he's not working, you'll find him keeping tabs on politics, business, basketball, fishing, or cheering on his kids' sports teams. And yes, he's a Collingwood footy fan through and through, but don't hold that against him.

Dive deeper into property investing

Additional free resources

We are big on providing you with further knowledge and educational content relating to property, finance, and money management. If you're hungry to learn more in this space, we're very excited for you! Here are some of our other resources.

The Property Couch podcast

To listen to our weekly podcast, *The Property Couch – the Insider's Guide to Property, Finance and Money Management*, please visit **thepropertycouch.com.au**.

Online masterclass

If you prefer a more visual and interactive learning experience beyond what this book offers, check out our FREE Masterclass! It walks you through the essential frameworks and strategies to build a high-performing property portfolio in five easy-to-digest sections. Check it out at **thepropertycouch.com.au/masterclass**.

Free property report

Learn more about the suburb you're planning to buy in. Get our comprehensive property report containing 20+ statistics on the intricacies of the suburb, its community and its properties. Download it for free at **thepropertycouch.com.au/propertyreport**.

Money, property and lifestyle management app

Available on both web and mobile, Moorr automates your money and property management, giving you full control in one powerful platform. Trap, manage, and track your finances with ease – all while living your lifestyle by design. Start spending without guilt and confidently plan for your future today at **moorr.com.au**.

Professional services

If you would like to know more about our wealth advisory, Empower Wealth, or learn about our Property Portfolio Plans designed to guide you on your property journey, please visit **empowerwealth.com.au**.

We hope you find these additional resources helpful! We'd love to hear your feedback on the book – feel free to leave a review on Amazon or wherever you purchased it. It truly means the world to us, and we read every single one! You can also share your journey on social media using **#ThePropertyCouchPlaybook** or connect with us directly at **thepropertycouch.com.au/playbook**.

Moorr

The cloud-based Moorr platform began its journey in 2017 as the MyWealth Portal, a client portal designed to help Empower Wealth staff gather a household's financial details to better advise clients on their personal and financial journeys. Since then, Moorr has become a comprehensive financial management tool, continually evolving to help users manage their money, properties, and personal goals.

In 2018, building on the success of our growing advisory business and the popularity of *The Property Couch* podcast, we launched the MoneySMARTS money management system. This system was initially created for clients but was soon made accessible to the general public, inspired by the success of our best-selling book, *Make Money Simple Again*. Users could now manage their finances using Moorr instead of spreadsheets.

In 2019, we unveiled MoneyFIT, an insight tool answering the question, 'How is my money working compared to my peers?' Users could anonymously compare their household finances with others across key metrics like income, spending, and net worth.

MoneySTRETCH was introduced in October 2021, offering users a powerful cashflow modelling tool to project the impact of different income or expense scenarios on their financial future.

In July 2022, we rebranded to Moorr, reflecting our broader vision. By November, we had launched a mobile app, allowing users to manage their finances on-the-go, and introduced MyGOALS for tracking personal and financial (lifestyle) objectives.

In 2023, we launched several innovative tools, including WealthSPEED, WealthTRACKER, and WealthCLOCK, which provide real-time financial gauges offering a forward-looking view of users' financial journeys. We also introduced MyFINAN-CIALS in November 2023, empowering users to set up tailored financial cards, providing better control over their finances. Paired with Opti, our AI smart assistant, MyFINANCIALS is designed for future open-banking integration, paving the way for automated financial management.

January 2024 saw the introduction of Historical Tracking, allowing users to input historical financial data for a seamless transition to cloud-based personal financial management. In July 2024, we released the Investment Property Cashflow Projection Tool, providing a 12-month forward-looking view of property income, expenses, cashflow, and tax implications, including potential offset benefit calculations.

At the end of 2024, we launched MoneySMARTS 2.0, a major update connecting MoneySMARTS with MyFINANCIALS, supporting multiple bank account setups and offering more flexible rollover options.

Today, Moorr offers over 200 tools, features, and insights, empowering users to save money, increase earnings, save time, manage property investments, achieve personal and financial goals, and ultimately attain financial peace. Our vision includes putting finances on autopilot to simplify money management further.

Moorr is built on four core pillars: Lifestyle (Goals), Money, Property, and Wealth. We're committed to continuously enhancing the platform to help users manage their household finances, properties, and wealth while achieving their personal goals.

Our product roadmap includes exciting new tools such as MyKNOWLEDGE, an educational hub with online learning resources, and additional MyFINANCIALS features including financial transaction tracking, bank feeds, and comparison dashboards for financial time periods. We are also developing MyTIMELINE for organising priorities, MyDOCUMENTS for centralised document management, MyPROPERTIES for comprehensive property investment management and tax tracking, and MyRESEARCH for advanced due diligence tools and property market analysis.

To enhance communication, in the future we are planning to build and launch MyCOMMS for seamless communication with Opti, the AI assistant, and secure access for professional advisers. Opti will also evolve into a personal money coach, helping users budget effectively and maximise savings.

We release updates fortnightly to ensure a frictionless user experience, making Moorr intuitive and highly engaging. As an all-in-one platform, our mission is to empower users to design their lifestyle and achieve financial peace.

You can learn more about Moorr at: **moorr.com.au**.

WHAT LISTENERS SAY ABOUT
THE PROPERTY COUCH PODCAST

A huge thank you 🎧 Leehaaammm

Thank you Ben and Bryce and the team behind the scenes. I've been a listener to the podcast for over two years. I was a consumer spender for over 12 years. Over $80K of debt, not including the interest I've paid. *The Property Couch* was the first podcast I came across and has been the lifeline I needed to get my spending in order. Two years later, no debt left at all and now hopefully buying my first IP by the end of the year. A huge thank you to you guys, without this podcast I would probably still be spending well beyond my means. Also, thank you for changing my mindset around money management.

Can't believe this is free INDIA 2 1 ALPHA

I've been listening to *The Property Couch* for three years, I've read both books and I put all the lessons I learnt into purchasing three investment grade properties. As of 2022 my portfolio has appreciated around 40% across the board and I'm receiving around 4 to 4.5% yield. Now we just sit back and let the location and time do the heavy lifting. Simply the greatest podcast on Australian property investment.

Life Changing Podcast ☆ LoveLexi2

This podcast has literally change the trajectory of my life. The genuine nature of Bryce and Benji (couldn't help myself 😊) is evident. With the plethora of information available today it has become increasingly important to evaluate the credibility of the source. I'll save you the trouble, these guys are the real deal. Simple, practical and authentic information.

Absolute gold ✹✹ bknm Jayne

I wish I had found your podcast years ago (currently up to episode 10) I am absolutely excited about what the future holds for us and our future now I have the information and knowledge. We are currently working with the Empower Wealth Team thanks to your podcast and we are creating a property portfolio plan as a roadmap to our bright future.

So Much Great Advice! Mere Mortals Podcast

Ben and Bryce are spot on with their extensive knowledge but, more importantly, have the ability to communicate it simply and effectively. This podcast really opened my eyes to just how much the ability to make good financial decisions rests on the emotional considerations, not just the numbers.

Start listening ASAP from the start Mick Hampton

I wish I had of known of Ben and Bryce years ago. I feel like I have made every mistake they talk about. I bought in a mining town when I was younger, bought an apartment at GC and built a new investment place (investment stock not investment grade). These guys make a lot of sense and wish I'd had mentors like this when I started out. Do yourself a favour and listen to the first few episodes as this can save you a lot of heartache and money! Great podcast guys, keep up the great work.

Thanks! Ken Montoya

Thanks for pointing out every single mistake that I have made!
I won't do it again.

The best property investment podcast out there! alliejh87

I have been listening to Bryce and Ben for a few years now, (love the footy commentary by the way boys – Go pies!!!!) very early on, and for someone that grew up knowing absolutely nothing from my parents about finances, investment and property, I cannot believe how much I have learnt from this podcast on all things property and property investment. Not long after I started listening to the podcast, I read their books, and we started using the MoneySMARTS system in our household. Just our change of mindset from listening to this amazing podcast is unbelievable. In January 2019, we then went to Empower Wealth to work on a property plan and, fast forward two years, we are well on our journey to building our property investment portfolio to assist us now and through our future. I still listen to each and every episode and thank you Ben and Bryce for your time and knowledge! Would highly recommend, whether you are experienced in property or just starting out I guarantee you that you will learn something! :) Allie :)

Never too late DJW0264

Having made EVERY mistake over the years that Ben and Bryce advise against, I have gained hope from this podcast that in my 50s it is not too late to 'put my ducks in a row' for retirement income. I look forward to the knowledge provided each week and information on how to act on it ...Thankyou :)

Pure gold. Krystlekt

I can't recommend this podcast enough. I wish I'd found this content before I started on my investment journey – but I've binge-listened to the lot for the past three months and I've learnt so much. You guys have changed my focus, my mentality and I'm so grateful I found this!

Invest in Gold! Jacqobe

I first started listening to investment podcasts back in 2018 and it wasn't long before I was listening to *The Property Couch* podcast. Although I started nearly

200 episodes behind, I was hooked from the very first episode and wanted to learn as much as I could to get started on my own investment journey. Since then, my partner and I have purchased our PPR, completed some major renovations and have used the manufactured equity to springboard into an investment property purchase. Needless to say, we would not have known how to do this without listening to the podcast. The insight provided by Ben and Bryce is pure gold and, just like gold, its value is increasing more and more during these uncertain times. So do the right thing, invest your time into listening to their gold!!

Analysis Paralysis PolaBear23
I've been a follower and listener since the beginning and love the content and no-nonsense approach. I've put my famiy's finances in order thanks to your invaluable advice. I now need to take the plunge in investing but there's always a 'what if' thought that hamstrings me. Too many earlier mistakes to work through and put to bed. Investing is just as much about the mind as the money. Love your work. 🙈☺

7-day float is a game changer. Bored listener.
I have spent the last few months binge-listening to your podcast and I feel like my brain is buzzing with all the new info I now have. I just want to thank you for the idea of the 7-day float. We are new in implementing the MoneySMARTS program but we finally have a system which minimises the money loss through unconscious spending, and allows myself and my husband to know exactly where we are day to day – with very little work!! Looking forward to our property journey going forward with your fantastic education. Natalie – PS – Go Sports!!!

Two nice smart guys giving good practical advice. Dses1509
Really informative, no-nonsense and practical advice. The hosts are qualified and well informed about the Australian market, which is useful. The hosts are down-to-earth and make the effort to simplify their advice for the audience, which is good for a property newbie like me! Definitely check out this podcast if you are interested in one day buying a home or building an investment portfolio.

Thank you property couch A++ Alex sssc
I am so very glad that I have tuned into your podcasts before beginning to invest. The tips and tricks you guys have poured into these podcasts are informative and insightful. Property is a huge step for a first time investor. I'd absolutely love to see you guys dedicate a podcast to first time investors/ young people that breaks down some of the jargon/information used in prior podcasts. Keep them coming! Alex Delis

Sooo happy to have found you. Lisawithane

Am LOVING *The Property Couch* podcasts, I stumbled upon the podcast after hearing someone else mention it. You're making my daily commute so entertaining. Thoroughly enjoy listening to you share your knowledge, lots of great guests speakers and a variety of topics. Coincidentally, I'm reading your book at the moment too, so it's all coming together nicely. Love Bryce's many inspirational quotes and Ben dreading the international sign off :) Great content and appreciate your commitment to teaching us 'average joe' investors how to avoid the pitfalls and get ahead in life from people you can trust who are not trying to take my money!!!

If there are 10 stars I would have given 10 Getedmund

Great, easy-to-follow podcast. I would recommend to anyone who is interested in property or is looking to start somewhere. Listening to the podcast can even prevent accidents on the road as I don't get tired anymore when doing long drives while listening to *The Property Couch*.

Gold, gold, gold! VJ David

I recently listened to all podcasts in about three months and I wish I had listened sooner. Ben and Bryce give a plain-English perspective on property investment, which is packed full of gold. Loved the international sign offs but I'm also enjoying the life hacks and 'did you know?' endings. Thank you for making my commute to and from work enjoyable. Keep up the great work!

Gold! Helen_Mark

If only we'd had this information before we started investing! Everything is explained in simply and unpacked to the nth degree. Their philosophies and messages are consistent throughout the podcast journey. I am so pumped to purchase our next property with my eyes open so much wider and a much more investment savvy mindset. Thank you Bryce and Ben!!

Genuine and Unselfish Wealth of Knowledge Keno_D

Ben, Bryce and Ivise, I just want to thank you all for the time you provide in educating all Australian households and the community. Your tireless efforts are definitely noticed within the space (I've been to one of your seminars and it's always a packed house!) You all personally had an impact on directing my family's goals, mindset and property plan to the right path, with the nuggets of gold you all unselfishly give. To anyone who's reading my comments, and is still unsure whether you should be listening to *The Property Couch*, do yourself a favour and start from Episode 1. Once you're up to date, you'll wish they would release one every day. Keep up the great work!

Excellent fun-damentals RobjCooper
Listened since the first podcast – great, solid investment advice, especially steering investors/buyers away from making bad choices. Listening to the fundamentals of what makes an investment-grade house made me rethink a decision in 2015 that would have cost me hundreds of thousands.
Keep up the good work – Rob.

Fantastic content! Courtney NSW
Wish I'd had this kind of advice 10 years ago, but it's been valuable to have listened to over the past six months and will help extremely with my future planning. Thank you for the time and knowledge shared by Ben, Bryce and the team!

Never too late... tuffy56
Hi, if you're planning to be a property investor in the future or getting very close to doing it; it's never too late to get advice. And one of the best sources of that is *The Property Couch*. It's information that's up to date, relevant, interesting and presented in a casual way that's easy to listen to. The podcasts are five stars. Great stuff!

Clarity and insight zwiftkid
Great content. Love regularly going through all the various property topics and it's inspirational to my own career preferences. Keep it up gentlemen.
Carn Freo! 🤜

3 things are certain in life pposter1
Three things are certain in life – DEATH, TAX and *The PROPERTY COUCH* will ultimately improve your mindset, intelligence and beliefs on not only property investment but also money management, goal setting, personal development and economics. A must for any person wanting to get the most out of themselves!

Marriage Saver Sophmaree j
Thanks Bryce and Ben, you literally have saved my marriage. My husband is using your MoneySMARTS system and we have finally turned our finances around and we are nearly ready to purchase our first investment property. He even sold his 'investment car' that definitely wasn't an investment (Yes!!!). Loving the books and the weekly podcast! Life changers!! Thanks so much *The Property Couch* team.